TOMMASINO

Thomas Gainsborough, *Thomas Linley the Younger*, *c.* 1772 (oil on canvas, 75.9 × 63.5 cm, DPG331, by kind permission of Dulwich Picture Gallery, London).

TOMMASINO

The Enigma of the English Mozart

TONY SCOTLAND

SHELF LIVES

2022

Published in 2022 by
Shelf Lives
The Pottery, Baughurst RG26 5SD
https://shelflives.org/

ISBN 978-0-9955503-6-0

Designed in Cycles by Libanus Press, Marlborough
Printed and Bound by TJ Books Limited, Padstow

Contents

For Julian Berkeley

. . . my little countryman, [Thomas] *Linley . . . was at Florence when I arrived there* [in 1770], *and was universally admired. The 'Tommasino', as he is called, and the little Mozart, are talked of all over Italy, as the most promising geniusses* [sic] *of this age.*

CHARLES BURNEY

The Present State of Music in France and Italy: or, The Journal of a Tour through those Countries, undertaken to collect Materials for a General History of Music.

London, 1771, pp. 246–7.

The north front of Grimsthorpe Castle, Lincolnshire, designed by Sir John Vanbrugh in 1725 (engraving by Henry Hulsbergh after a drawing by Colen Campbell).

I

Squall

GRIMSTHORPE CASTLE 5 AUGUST 1778

Tom had finished his two hours' practice, and the sun was streaming into his bedchamber after last night's rain. He moved the music stand back against the wall, and slipped his violin into its green baize bag. Then he raised the sash window and looked out across the park towards the Great Water. The sky was blue, and a warm breeze was drying the leaves on the trees, but he could still smell wet grass and something else in the air, something pungent, like old mushrooms. The swallows, he noticed, were flying low. Perhaps there was a storm on the way. He pulled the bell for a valet. He did not have a servant of his own, preferring always to dress himself, but the duke had provided one for the summer.

Taking off his banyan of soft Chinese silk, and passing it to the young servant, Tom rolled up a pair of finely-woven white knitted stockings over his knees and up to his close-fitting linen under-drawers. Over these he drew on a pair of breeches, leaving the valet to adjust the gusset ties in the back of the waist, and the buttons at the knee. Then he put on a white linen shirt with lace ruffles stitched to the cuffs and neck, and the valet added a starched white stock over the upturned collar of his shirt, securing it with ties at the back. Over the shirt a waistcoat, and over that a frock coat.

Thomas Linley was twenty-two, tall and trim, his skin pale, nose straight, lips not full but well shaped.[1] He was softly good looking, if not as strikingly handsome as his equally famous siblings, but his grey-blue eyes shared with theirs a wistfulness – and a watchful-ness. He was 'extremely engaging' and pleasantly sure of himself.[2] His siblings called him 'Tom' or 'Tommy', and his brother-in-law, Richard Brinsley Sheridan, 'Tam', but to his father he was 'Master', partly out of respect for his musical talent, but mostly to remind him that he was still the lower-case, junior partner in the family music-making business.

They were all Romantics, the Linley children, and most were emotionally all over the place, happy one moment, wretched the next, and never sure why. Friends who knew them well thought they had been pushed too hard, too far and too early by their ambitious father, Thomas Linley senior, composer, singing teacher and musi-cal impresario. None of them had time for anything but music. The eldest, Elizabeth Ann was one of the finest sopranos of the time, and one of the greatest beauties too, but no longer singing now that she was married to the playwright Sheridan, who thought it unladylike; Mary and Maria were singers too; Samuel had been an oboist and was now a midshipman in the Navy; and Tom himself was a violinist and composer, widely recognised as one of the most promising musicians of the age.[3]

They all knew they were special. Once as a small boy, Tom had been asked by a bishop visiting the Linleys in Bath, if he too, like his siblings, was a genius – 'Yes', came the answer, 'we're all geniuses here'. At that time they were all actually children, but now, emotion-ally, they still were. All three had such looks and such presence that gatherings fell silent when they entered, but they were so unspoiled that none of them noticed the effect they produced. Of course it helped that they were extraordinarily talented and successful – the oratorio stars of London, Bath and the cathedral cities. But no one would have guessed that they were all so unsure of themselves, and so unhappy. Like a martinet their father had schooled them, and like a drill sergeant he had pushed them to perform in public at an early age, piling on the engagements and pocketing the earnings (which,

Thomas Gainsborough, *Elizabeth and Mary Linley*, c.1772 (retouched 1785, oil on canvas, 199 × 153.5 cm, DPG320, reproduced by kind permission of Dulwich Picture Gallery, London).

in the case of Elizabeth, when she was still singing, were huge). In common with his other pupils and his colleagues in the concert rooms and theatres, his children were frightened of Mr Linley.

When he was twelve Tom had been sent to Italy to study for three years, and there he picked up many of the foreign ways which young Grand Tourists brought back home so proudly – the foppish clothes, continental manners, Italian opera and more. But he was no 'macaroni': his affectations weren't extreme. As a professional performer, and a celebrity at the Theatre Royal in Drury Lane, he was, it is true, a bit of a showman, but, for all his assurance on stage, he was, like Elizabeth, diffident, even wary, off it.

Thomas had many weaknesses, and clothes, if not the greatest, was one of them. He always took care over his dressing, today more so than ever, though only he knew why. Sitting on a chair beside his four-poster bed, its damask curtains still drawn closed, he raised his feet into the air so the valet could help him into his top-boots, Tom tugging the soft black leather right up to his thighs, then turning down the tops – to free his knees, and reveal the contrasting colour of the cotton lining – while the valet pushed each boot upwards from the sole. Crossing to the dressing glass, Tom brushed back his thick, auburn hair (the pride of all the Linleys), pulling it tight into a single queue at the back, which the valet tied with a ribbon. Then he drew on his wig, adjusted it, and the servant gave it an all-over frosting of white powder, and a squirt of scent. Finally he put on his gold-trimmed cocked hat.* It was the full works today.

Such a profusion of clothes might have seemed excessive in August, yet there was more to come. He told the valet to bring his new greatcoat from the armoire, and heave it on over the frockcoat. Then he checked his reflection, turning to left and right, noting, if not approving, his heavy silhouette.

Downstairs he walked through the arched screen on the ground floor, and entered Vanbrugh's Stone Hall. Waiting for him, beneath the giltwood chandeliers, and in front of the massive chimneypiece, were his third sister, fourteen-year-old Maria, who had been staying with him at the castle all summer, and the Italian tutor, young Oliva-rez.† If Maria was surprised to see him so over-dressed for a summer day she did not say so – unconventional herself, she was used to Tom's waywardness, and anyway she knew that the boots and greatcoat were new, and he had been longing to try them out. Besides, who could stop Tom Linley once his heart was set on something.

Their host, the Duke of Ancaster, who had been ill for some weeks with a 'Complication of Disorders',[4] was still upstairs, resting in

---

* See his portrait by Gainsborough, c. 1771 – perhaps at the same time as his father's second portrait – showing him in a red coat and yellow waistcoat, with powdered wig, and his tricorn, made of beaver-hair felt, reversed and tucked under his left arm, as a mark of his status as a gentleman. For further details of this portrait see Hugh Belsey, *Thomas Gainsborough*, Yale, 2019, pp. 554–5).
† According to contemporary newspaper reports the sister whom Tom took to Grimsthorpe was 'Miss M Linley'. By the rules of address of the time, this indicated his younger unmarried sister, Maria. The elder one, Mary, had assumed the senior designation, 'Miss Linley', when the eldest of the three, Elizabeth, had married Sheridan. Nothing whatever is known about Olivarez (see Chapter X).

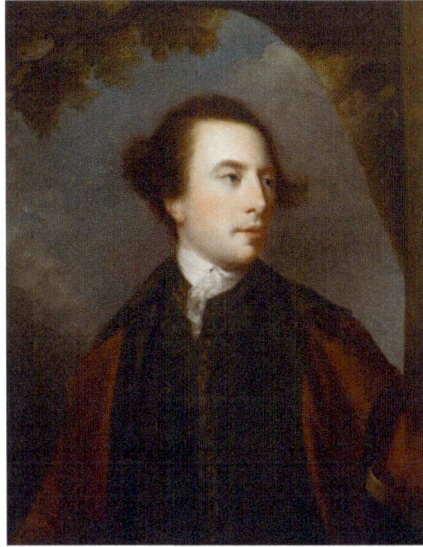

bed, and the duchess rarely left her dressing room before midday. Eager to get on, Tom kissed Maria goodbye, promising to tell her all about everything at dinner. Then he made for the front door, the metal-heels of his boots clattering on the marble floor. With him went the mysterious Olivarez, and behind them, at a respectful distance, a footman carrying a small picnic basket under a white cloth. Cutting across the courtyard, they skirted the fountain basin, passed through the wrought iron gates, and turned left into the park and down the gentle slope to the lake. Although it was half a mile away, they could just see a figure waiting for them on the jetty, beside a sailing boat.

The lake was large, covering about ten acres,[5] but probably no more than four or five feet deep and shaped like a watering can with a long spout. It had been created from a series of canalized fishponds at the beginning of the century. Lancelot 'Capability' Brown, then relatively unknown, had been called in to give his advice in 1741, but in the end the job had gone to a local man, the Lincolnshire civil engineer John Grundy Junior. It was he who built the earth dam, as

The Great Water at Grimsthorpe Castle, Lincolnshire.

high as a house, to impound the ornamental lake known as the Great Water.* Since then the lake had been further extended, and a causeway built across it, disguised as a multi-arched bridge, but it had not been properly maintained, and silt had built up on the clay bed, with hornwort weed clogging parts of the surface.

Thomas and Olivarez waited as the footman stowed the basket in the locker under the foc'sle, then they stepped aboard, arranging themselves aft of the mast, one on either side, for balance. The young boatman, smart in the Ancaster livery, cast off, and sat himself in the stern, trying not to notice Tom's greatcoat on this hot day. He took the tiller and the other two young men paddled the boat forward into deeper water.

Thomas himself probably knew how to handle a sailing boat, and he was a swimmer too, which was not so common then. After all he had not spent two years on the Mediterranean coast just

---

* Most accounts of the park at Grimsthorpe suggest that Capability Brown himself carried out the construction of the lake, in about 1741, or at least extended it later, but the garden historian Jane Brown argues that Grundy created the lake, and that Capability Brown, on his return to Grimsthorpe at the peak of his career in 1771, did no more than design a sham bridge to cross the lake (*Lancelot 'Capability' Brown – The Omnipotent Magician 1716–1783*, Pimlico, 2012, pp. 36–7 and 269–70). The *Heritage Gateway* website carries a report on Grimsthorpe Castle gardens and park which states that Brown extended the lake in 1770–1, and that Grundy and the duke's estate workers made a causeway, the Red Bridge, which crosses it. The historic landscape consultant Steffie Shields suggests that the third duke may have consulted Brown in about 1776 about undertaking further work at Grimsthorpe to create a magnificent piece of water to match Brown's masterpiece at Blenheim ('"Mr Brown Engineer": Lancelot Brown's Early Work at Grimsthorpe Park and Stowe', *Garden History*, vol. xxxiv, no. 2, Winter 2006, p. 186). See also A.W. Skempton and others (Eds.), 'Grundy, John, Jr.', *A Biographical Dictionary of Civil Engineers in Great Britain and Ireland*, Tom Telford, 2002, vol. i, 1500–1830, p. 279).

playing the violin – and it was not the first time this summer that he had ventured out in one of Grimsthorpe's pleasure boats for some rowing, fishing or sailing.[6] But the duke, who knew how impetuous he was, had insisted that the boatman should take them out today.

As the boat headed into the breeze, Tom hauled up the sail and made fast the halyard, while the boatman pulled the tiller over to catch the wind. Once the canvas was full, they gradually picked up momentum, but just as they reached the middle of the lake, the sky darkened, rain started to fall, and the wind got up, whipping itself, without warning, into a squall.

Suddenly destabilized, the boat crashed into a gybe and the boom swung over, hitting Tom and Olivarez before they had a chance to avoid it. The weight of all three men was now on the leeward side, so the boat heeled over and water flooded in over the gunwales. With no built-in buoyancy, she soon began to sink down through the shallow water into the mud.

'However', reported the *General Evening Post*, in a dramatic account copied by other newspapers around the country, for Tom was famous, and his hosts were national figures, 'they all hung by the mast and rigging for some time, till Mr Linley said he found it was in vain to wait for assistance, and therefore, though he had his boots and great coat on, he was determined to swim to shore, for which purpose he quitted his hold, but had not swam [sic] above a hundred yards before he sunk [sic].'[7]

The Duchess of Ancaster was watching as it happened, from her dressing-room window on the first floor of the west wing of the castle. Hardly believing her eyes, she sent her maid to summon help. The fastest of the household's forty male servants[8] raced down to the lake, and launched another of the pleasure boats to rescue the stranded young men.

It was not long before Olivarez and the boatman were rowed safely ashore, but it was nearly three-quarters of an hour before Tom's body was found – under water, stuck in mud – and, though

Thomas Hudson, *Mary, Duchess of Ancaster*, 1757, in costume for a Masquerade at Ranelagh (oil on canvas, 277 cm × 176 cm, reproduced by kind permission of Baroness Willoughby de Eresby, Grimsthorpe Castle).

every attempt was made to revive him, it was soon clear he must be dead.

The local paper broke the news the very next day. Tom was identified as a 'Musician to His Grace', no name given, and, by implication, he was blamed for jumping into the water 'to save himself'. The account ignored the long delay in finding the body, presumably in the interests of protecting the duke from any suggestion of negligence, and it invented 'an aged father and mother' left destitute by Tom's death. In fact both Thomas and Mary Linley, not yet fifty, were alive and well in London, managing the Theatre Royal, Drury Lane, which they and their son-in-law Sheridan had recently bought from the actor-manager David Garrick.[9]

Six days later the *London Evening Post* ran a longer version of events, which, it claimed, might be 'depended upon as the melancholy particulars of the death of the late Mr Linley junior'. In this apparently definitive scenario Tom was said to have 'made a small party to go a fishing', with 'Mr Olivarez, an Italian master' and a boatman.

When they were some time upon the lake, a strong gust of wind rose; upon which, not considering the very great attention of managing a sail in a small boat, they hoisted up one, which in a little time overset the boat, by which all the three were thrown into the lake.

According to the *Post*'s account, the boatman swam over to Tom, who 'generously declined' his assistance, sending him instead to Olivarez, whose need was greater. The boatman did as he was told, 'and in a little time shoved the young gentleman [Olivarez] to the bank side', where they both hauled themselves up on to dry land. When they had got their breath back, they looked around for Tom, and, failing to find him, assumed he had already reached land on the other side of the lake, and made for the house to change his clothes. But when they themselves returned to the house and found no sign of him there, they began to worry. 'Taking down with them two or three of the servants, they returned to the side of the lake, and after some search hauled him up'.[10]

The *Public Advertiser* added further grim details, revealing that when at last the body was retrieved, 'every possible Method (according to Mr. Hawes's Plan) [was] used for his Recovery'.[11] Dr William Hawes was an eminent physician who had founded the Royal Humane Society four years earlier, to promote the new technique of resuscitation. It was his firm belief that a drowned body could be brought back to life if treated correctly, and with specialist equipment. If, as the *Advertiser* claimed, the Hawes method was followed to the letter at Grimsthorpe that day, Tom's body would have been stripped and held upside down, to remove any water that had gathered inside, then carried back to the house and up to his chamber. There he would have been wrapped in a blanket, laid out on a sheet and gently rubbed with flannel cloths sprinkled with spirit.

The next stage of the Hawes Plan involved inserting a pipe in the rectum, and blowing tobacco smoke into the intestines through the bowels, ideally with a fumigator, but, failing that, with bellows. At the same time the belly was to be gently pressed upwards with the hand. Dr Hawes warned that it might take an hour or more for the blood to start circulating again, but, his published instructions urged, 'do not become discouraged if it takes longer'.[12]

The relevant equipment for this mediaeval procedure was probably available at Grimsthorpe, for the duke, as Lord Lieutenant of his county, and Lord Great Chamberlain of England, would have been expected to show a lead in the protection of life. Besides he

Joseph de Gardane,
Dr Hawes's technique for restoring life to a victim of drowning (engraving Wellcome Collection, London).

was known to be open to new scientific ideas, such as electric shock therapy, which he had used to treat his convulsive daughter Mary (who had died, despite it, aged only thirteen).* But it seems unlikely that the full extent of Dr Hawes's Plan would have been applied to Tom, if only because it must have been clear from the moment he was found that, after forty full minutes under water, there was little chance of life returning.

The press speculated that the drowning occurred when Tom 'stuck in the mud near the bank side and from thence was not able to disengage himself'.[13] Possibly he tried to stand as he swam into shallower water, hoping to walk ashore, but the sucking clay must have drawn him down under the weight of his heavy clothes and boots. He would then have suffocated as his head sank below the surface. The Bath paper was not alone in using the opportunity to issue a public warning:

---

* The treatment was recommended by the American polymath Benjamin Franklin for a condition that reduced Lady Mary Bertie to 'a most Miserable condition with spasms and convulsions' that shut her jaw and deprived her of speech and swallowing (letter from Sir John Pringle to Benjamin Franklin [March 1767], with annotations by the American Philo-sophical Society and Yale University at https://founders.archives.gov/documents/Franklin/01-14-02-0049

Persons who go into the river, etc. to bathe, should by no means venture where the bottom is muddy; as, besides the natural tendency of the body to sink in from its weight, there is a great attraction in the mud, perhaps from the want of air, which often renders it impossible to escape, and totally destroys the natural buoyance [sic] of the water; and when the body once sinks in the mud, it never rises again.'[14]

The duke had heard the commotion as the servants carried the body upstairs, and demanded to know what was going on. The duchess, though distraught herself, tried to spare him the details, for Tom Linley had been one of his special favourites and she was afraid it might be too much for him in his weakened state.

As well as being a prodigy, Tom was softly attractive, gentle and playful, and these qualities had enchanted the musical duke ever since he saw him dance a hornpipe for the royal family on stage at Covent Garden, at the age of eleven. It was probably he who financed Tom's three years of study in Italy, and ever since the boy's return, the duke had helped to promote his progress as soloist and composer.

The duchess couldn't keep the news from her husband, and on learning of his protégé's death, the duke had another of his bilious attacks and was now in a state of collapse, his own survival hanging in the balance.

With their only son away in America, fighting Washington's revolutionaries (and conducting scandalous affairs with the ladies of New York), the duchess took charge.[15] A strong and practical woman, she first of all sent a messenger to ride to London at speed, to call two of the most eminent doctors of the day, the physician Sir Richard Jebb and the surgeon William Bromfield, to attend the duke in what looked like his last illness.[16] She then dispatched a footman to summon the Steward and the Parson to discuss arrangements for Tom's funeral (and to be ready for the duke's too), and instructed the housekeeper and head housemaid to begin the laying-out of Tom's body.

Maria had found out from Olivarez all that had happened on the lake, and later in Tom's chamber, as the servants carried out their grisly assault on her brother's lifeless body. Determined to protect him from further indignities she tried to enter his room to supervise the laying out, but the women locked the door, while they washed and stoppered the body, straightening the limbs and closing the eyes (with a penny on each, in case they opened and brought a second death).

When all was done they wrapped the corpse in a winding sheet, ready for removal to the parish church at Edenham, where it was to spend a few days lying in the cool of the Ancasters' vault, deep in the crypt, while a lead coffin was constructed and the funeral planned.

Now there was the question of how to convey the news to Tom's family in London. Maria wanted to go straightaway, with her maid as chaperone, and a sturdy footman joining them as protector. It was a long journey – 110 miles straight down the Great North Road. In the stage coach it would take two days, with an overnight stop at an inn. To save time it was decided they should take the duke's private road-coach, a light, fast carriage drawn by four horses. But Maria was in no state to travel immediately, so she was put to bed with a sleeping draught, and called early the next morning.

If they could make an average speed of 10 mph, and stop for nothing but changing the horses, they might be there by midnight. But on the way, buffeted by the steel-sprung carriage and the uneven road, spattered with mud, exhausted and overcome with grief, Maria became sicker and weaker with each mile. By the time they reached London she had lost consciousness, so they went straight to the duke's town house, Ancaster House in Berkeley Square, where, the newspapers reported the next day, Maria now lay dangerously ill.[17]

A messenger rode over to the Linleys in Norfolk Street to break the news of Tom's death and Maria's collapse. The father's grief, one paper wrote, was such that 'no language can express'[18] – one of his singing pupils recalled that even years later that 'tears of mental agony rolled down his cheeks' and on to the keys of the harpsichord as he accompanied her[19] – and Elizabeth was said to be 'inconsolable'.[20]

For Elizabeth the shock was compounded by concern for her husband, Richard Sheridan, who had recently had a serious accident. Riding an unruly mare to their country cottage near Ealing, he had been thrown and kicked violently on the head,[21] and for a few days his life was in danger. But he soon recovered – as indeed he had bounced back from all the other dramas of his young life.

On 10 August, five days after the Grimsthorpe tragedy, Mr Linley, though not, it seems, Mrs Linley or any other members of the family, took the coach to Lincolnshire for the funeral.[22] On arrival at the castle, finding the house in turmoil, for the duke was sinking fast, Linley continued on to Edenham village, and sat in the church, awaiting the arrival of the funeral procession from the castle.*

After the Committal, heartbroken and exhausted, he travelled back to the castle with the duchess, excused himself from the dinner table and went straight to bed, leaving the duchess to tend her mortally sick husband. In the early hours of the following morning, 12 August, the duke died, aged sixty-four. The papers blamed Tom:

It is thought that the unfortunate Accident of Mr Linley's being drowned at Grimsthorpe the Week before so far affected the Duke as to accelerate his Death, as he was then pretty well. ... His Lordship is succeeded in Title and Estate by his only Son the Marquess of Lindsey, now in America.[23]

Mr Linley slipped quietly back to London as discreetly as he could after breakfast, while the duchess set about organising a

---

* An Ancaster family tradition claims that Tom Linley was buried in the family vault, but a memorial plaque inside St Michael's Church, Edenham, confirms that he lies buried in the churchyard, even though there is no contemporary record, on paper or stone, confirming this.

second funeral, and dispatching a letter by express to her son in New York. Robert, who was only five months younger than Tom, now became fourth Duke of Ancaster and hereditary Lord Great Chamberlain of England, and his mother needed him home to take up his new responsibilities.*

It cannot have been easy for Linley first reading the harrowing details of his son's death and now finding that this was thought to have hastened the duke's death. For weeks the story occupied the London papers – and the provincial papers which picked up the crumbs and fed them on to the rest of the country – and few stopped to consider the character of the life that had been lost. But one London paper found room for four lines of obituary on the 11th:

Mr Linley was about twenty two Years of Age, a most accomplished Performer on the Violin, and of a very promising Genius and Talents as a Composer; of the most sweet and amiable Disposition; and an irreproachable Conduct in Life; and there is no Doubt that his Loss will be felt and regretted [as] *much by the Public, as it is sincerely and deeply lamented by his Relations and Friends.* [24]

---

* Robert Bertie, Marquess of Lindsey, had joined the 7th Regiment of Foot as a cornet in British-held New York the previous year. In March 1778 he was promoted to captain as ADC to General Sir Henry Clinton, C-in-C, North America, and by mid-August he was at sea aboard HMS Isis, limping back to New York after fighting a battle with a French warship (*Derby Mercury*, 16 and 21 October 1778). It was not till the end of September that he found the letter informing him of his father's death, whereupon he immediately set sail for home. He arrived at Grimsthorpe on 10 December, when 'an ox was roasted whole, and plenty of liquor given to the populace' (*The Date Book for Lincoln and Neighbourhood, from the Earliest Time to the Present ...*, Lincoln, 1866, p. 195). Robert the 4th duke lived but seven more months, dying at Ancaster House, Berkeley Square, on 8 July 1779, of 'scarlet fever, contracted by drinking and rioting' (Horace Walpole, letter to Sir Horace Mann, 7 July 1779, *Horace Walpole's Correspondence*, Yale Edition). Robert never married, but left by his mistress a daughter, Susan, who later married his fellow officer from the American campaign, General Banastre Tarleton. The dukedom passed to his father's cousin, Brownlow Bertie, but when he died in 1809, without a male heir, the title became extinct.

This must have been some small consolation for Linley as he returned home to London, and to his work at the Theatre Royal, Drury Lane, where Tom had been leader of the orchestra and popular soloist. But there was no time to indulge his grief, for he was immediately caught up in preparations for a new production at the theatre – a musical entertainment called *The Camp*, satirising the government's attempts to organise home defences in anticipation of an invasion, following France's declaration of war in June. Sheridan was the author, assisted by General John Burgoyne, a controversial figure in the American War and a minor playwright himself, and the actor, David Garrick; and Linley was writing the music.

While all this was going on, and Maria had recovered her strength in the care of Ancaster House and had been brought home to Norfolk Street, but the memory of the tragedy at Grimsthorpe still haunted her. One day she wandered off alone to the fields in front of Lord Leicester's house half a mile away. Sitting on the stubble in what is now Leicester Square, she composed a poem lamenting Tom's death. It speaks of Tom's genius which 'Charm'd ev'ry ear, and every breast inspir'd', of the 'magic sweetness' of his voice, and of 'the soft melting strains' of his music which 'Heal ev'ry pain, and lull the mind to rest'.[25]

Simultaneously her elder sister Elizabeth published, anonymously, her own, more ambitious, lament, after the manner of 'Lycidas', Milton's elegy for a young friend who drowned when his ship sank.[26] Five years later, missing Tom still, she wrote a third lament, addressed to his violin:

Sweet instrument of him for whom I mourn,
Tuneful companion of my Lycid's hours,
How liest thou now, neglected and forlorn,
What skilful hand shall now call forth thy pow'rs!

Ah! None like his can reach those liquid notes,
So soft, so sweet, so eloquently clear,
To live beyond the touch, and gently float
In dying modulations on the ear.

She hopes the violin will remain for ever 'Unstrung, untun'd, forgotten', for without Tom, it is worthless; with him it lived, with him it must die.[27] Till she herself died in 1792 the violin probably remained with her as a treasured reminder of her beloved brother; thereafter it may have gone to her younger brother Ozias, then a minor canon at Norwich Cathedral and later Junior Fellow and Organist at Dulwich College. One of the first of the modern Linley biographers, Clementina Black, speculates that it took its place with 'the many musical instruments of different kinds' that used to hang on Ozias Linley's walls at Dulwich.

Not long after *The Camp* opened in October, there was a new crisis in the Linley family. Tom's younger brother, Samuel, who had given up a musical career to join the Navy earlier in the year, fell ill aboard his ship, HMS *Thunderer*, and was put ashore at Portsmouth and sent back to London for some home nursing.

Thomas Gainsborough, *Samuel Linley*, 1778, (oil on canvas, 75.8 × 63.5 cm, DPG302, reproduced by kind permission of Dulwich Picture Gallery, London).

One of Mrs Linley's servants in the wardrobe department at the theatre, fourteen-year-old Emma Lyon, was given the task of looking after him, and the pretty young couple fell in love (for Emma was so exceptionally beautiful that she later became one of the most famous courtesans of the age). But as soon as Samuel was better his ship recalled him to duty. Towards the end of November he became feverish again, and the ship's doctor diagnosed cholera, so he was sent back to the family in London. Emma was put in charge again, and, at sight of her, Samuel rallied, but not for long, and in the first week in December he died, still only nineteen.[*]

The funeral took place on 6 December. Emma attended, but was too heartbroken to return to the Linleys', and they never saw her again.[†]

The loss of a second son – actually a fifth, for as well as Tom and Samuel, Linley had already lost George, Thurston and William – and the premature loss in the following fourteen years of three daughters – Elizabeth (Sheridan), Mary (Tickell) and Maria – were blows from which he never fully recovered, though he lived on till 1795. But the death that affected him most deeply was Tom's, as a contemporary account confirms:

The unhappy father's grief at this afflicting termination of all his long-cherished hopes of a favourite son, produced a brain fever, from which he ultimately recovered, but was never restored again to the health and happiness he had till then enjoyed. His son had

---

[*] It is ironic that if Samuel had survived he would have lived for no more than two years, because his ship, the *Thunderer*, went down with all hands off the coast of Jamaica in 1780 when the Great Hurricane of the West Indies tore into the Caribbean islands, killing more than 20,000 people.

[†] Instead she wandered alone into the streets of Covent Garden, where she was found a few nights later by the notorious Mrs O'Kelly, 'Abbess' of a grand brothel in King's Place, and trained up as a *fille de joie*. Sold to Sir Harry Fetherstonhaugh – 'a witless playboy' – she was passed on to Charles Greville, who passed her on to his uncle, Sir William Hamilton of Naples, who married her and shared her with Admiral Lord Nelson. The Linleys never saw her again (Henry Angelo, *Reminiscences ...*, vol. ii, 1904, pp. 182–183).

been the pride of his existence, the partner of his studies; his name had mingled with the father's in a united reputation; he was the 'admired of all observers of his growing genius'; and these were bereavements which an affectionate father did not, and which indeed he could not, cease to mourn to the last hour of his life.[28]

If Mrs Linley seems strangely absent from these domestic references, it is because in all the accounts of the family she emerges more as housekeeper than mother. She and her husband were devoted and mutually dependent, but Mrs Linley seems to have had little time for tender feelings towards her children. Admittedly there were twelve of them in all, and she would have been stretched to provide and care for even those who survived, but her instincts seem to have been more mercenary than motherly. She liked nothing better than scrimping and saving as she and Linley had been forced to do at the start of their marriage. She continued to let rooms in the family's house in Bath long after it was necessary, and there's a story that as wardrobe mistress at the Theatre Royal, Drury Lane, she used to trim off pieces of material from the costumes of the singers in order to cover a footstool, or a cushion at home.[29] It was probably because of the mother's concern with household and business affairs and the father's driving musical ambitions for their talented children that the siblings were so emotionally damaged.

Samuel's death, though tragic in one so young, so talented and so fine looking, was entirely natural: he simply caught a dangerous and highly infectious disease which was common in the Royal Navy. But Tom's death is shrouded in mystery. Like the poet Thomas Chatterton who died in the same decade aged only seventeen, his death captured in a romantic painting by Henry Wallis, Tom has become a symbol of doomed artistic genius. At the very least his family must have wondered why he was wearing a greatcoat and riding boots for a summer sail. What lay behind it?

One theory is suicide, precipitated by unrequited love, but Tom had never been associated with anything approaching love interest, apart from a brief but intense friendship with Mozart when both were young adolescents. Another theory – put forward by the painter Ozias Humphry, who was virtually a member of the Linley family – is that he died 'from an attack of a kind of paralysis', brought on by his father's having trained him too severely and sent him to perform too early and too often.[30] This was the reason later given for the early deaths of Tom's three singing sisters – this, and the family's history of TB and 'brain fever'.

A modern, fictional, account claims that Tom was murdered – by the duke's wild son, Robert (though he was still then in America), on the grounds that Tom had had the impertinence to allow himself to be seduced by Robert's mother, the duchess.[31] Mary Ancaster, Mistress of the Robes to Queen Charlotte, was then forty-eight but still a celebrated beauty and much given to gambling, routs, masquerades and other extravagances – not always with her husband. For Peregrine, the duke, may have sired their six children, but he was responsible for two illegitimate children by other women, who included the notorious Mesdames Baddeley and Armistead, both acquaintances of Tom, through his work as leader of the orchestra at the Theatre Royal, Drury Lane, and there were more lurid stories too.

What really happened that day at Grimsthorpe, and the story behind it, seems to have been deliberately hushed up at the time, and has remained a mystery ever since. The Ancasters, no strangers to scandal themselves, were anxious to avoid any attention which might embarrass the court, for the duke was Hereditary Lord Great Chamberlain, a Lord of the Bedchamber and Master of the Horse to the King, and the duchess was a Lady of the Bedchamber and Mistress of the Robes to the Queen. And the Linleys were no less keen to keep their heads down, following all the publicity surrounding the elopement of Elizabeth with Richard Brinsley Sheridan, his famous duels with his rival for her hand, and his re-telling of the story in the play *The Rivals* and the comic opera *The Duenna* (for which Tom wrote most of the music).

Thomas's father was now a major force in British music, and the last thing he wanted was an exposé of Tom's private life. Whether for this reason, or because he was simply stunned into inaction by the loss of his favourite son, all Tom's papers and much of his music have disappeared over the passing years. There are no surviving letters, beyond one from Mozart, when both he and Tom were children, and only a handful of autograph scores. Of Tom's twenty violin concertos and seven violin sonatas only one of each has come down to us today,[*] along with parts of copied scores for the comic operas, *The Duenna* and *The Cady of Bagdad*, incidental music for *The Tempest*, three cantatas, two anthems and *A Lyric Ode on the Fairies, Aerial Beings and Witches of Shakespeare*. None of this music was published in his lifetime. After his father's death in 1795 his mother published a collection of catches, songs and glees by father and son, without identifying who wrote what.

Did the drowning happen as the papers reported, or was there a cover-up? Perhaps the accident wasn't an accident at all, but the consequence of a secret that everyone preferred to forget.

---

[*] The three-movement *Sonata in A Major* violin and continuo by Thomas Linley junior is available on CD in a recording made in 1991 by Elizabeth Wallfisch and the Locatelli Trio on Hyperion CDA66583, and the three-movement *Concerto in F Major* for violin and orchestra was recorded in 1996 by Elizabeth Wallfisch and the Parley of Instruments conducted by Peter Holman on Hyperion CDH55260, and in 2010 by Mirjam Contzen and the Bayerische Kammerphilharmonie conducted by Reinhard Goebel on Oehms Classics OC 753. The MSS of both, in the hand of the singer and copyist Joseph Gaudry, are preserved in the Royal Music Collection at the British Library (R. M. 21.h.10)

II

Prodigy

BATH AND LONDON 1756-63

In the year that marked the birth of Mozart and the publication of his father Leopold's famous violin treatise, the Linleys of Bath had a son, a musical prodigy who was destined to be one of Britain's finest violinists and most promising composers – and a special friend of Mozart. Thomas Linley junior – known to his friends as Tom and to history as the English Mozart, was born on 7 May 1756, in a house in Abbey Green, Bath, once a walled and gated courtyard to the abbey, and still today a quiet and characterful corner of the ancient city.

Thomas Linley senior was the son of a humble carpenter in Wells, who prospered with the growth of Bath and bought a fine house in the Lansdown Road in about 1743.* He was set to follow his father into the building trade, but his life changed when he heard the organist of Bath Abbey, Thomas Chilcot, playing, and when Chilcot heard Linley singing he was so impressed by the voice that he persuaded him to study music.[32] Starting as errand boy, then organ pumper, Linley was soon formally apprenticed to Chilcot, learning to play the organ and the violin and to sing, and studying the rudiments of composition. On completing his seven years, he

---

* 9 or 10 Fountain Buildings, just south of Belmont (Wright, 'Ozias Humphry …', *Index of Bath Artists*, Victoria Art Gallery, Bath).

Thomas Gainsborough, *Thomas Linley the Elder*, c.1770 (oil on canvas, 76.5 × 63.5, DPG140, reproduced by kind permission of Dulwich Picture Gallery, London).

went to London to study with the Italian composer Pietro Domenico Paradies, who polished his understanding of harmony, improvisation and voice production.[33] Back in Bath, now hugely fashionable under the presiding genius of Beau Nash, he found constant work at the Pump Room, the Assembly Rooms and the Theatre Royal, as a bass soloist, continuo player and violinist, and at home he began to build a practice as a singing teacher.

In 1752, aged nineteen, Linley married Mary Johnson, who was said to be as musically accomplished as himself, but, bearing twelve children in fifteen years, she soon found herself a full-time mother and housekeeper, carrying out what her lodger, the painter Ozias Humphry, called 'the more useful and amiable offices of domestic concerns and the cares of her children'.[34] Some of those who knew her in the early days, especially young Humphry who was rather smitten, said she was beautiful and had a sweet singing voice. Later in her long life contemporaries remarked on her strong character, and her vulgar and penny-pinching ways. The Linley biographer, Clementina Black, went further, painting her as mean, bad-tempered and even violent, and the Bath historian Reginald Wright noted that 'She took a domineering and exasperating part in the affairs of her family throughout her long life'.[35] And this is what she looks like in her portrait by James Lonsdale at the end of her life: a thoroughly disagreeable old woman.[36]*

James Lonsdale, *Mrs Thomas Linley*, *c*.1815–20 (oil on canvas, 76.5 × 63.5 cm, DPG 456, reproduced by kind permission of Dulwich Picture Gallery, London).

As a singing teacher, Linley had few opportunities to prove his worth till his own three eldest children – Elizabeth, Tom and Mary – were old enough to perform in public, and the moment they were and did he won a reputation which brought him all the teaching he needed. Since his children were not only unusually talented but beautiful too, he soon built up a considerable fortune from their fees, which he continued to enjoy till they were of age, when he started to earn his own fees as composer and music director.

Linley was a task-master –'Unremitting in his zeal and energy … for success at all costs'[37] – and he looks it in the portrait Gainsborough painted in about 1771.[38] Handsome though he undoubtedly was – tall and dark, with the finely-cut brows and mouth which Tom and Elizabeth inherited – he was also 'cold, shrewd and calculating'.[39] Writing in her diary in 1773, Fanny Burney, described him as 'a very sour, ill-bred, severe, and selfish man',[40] and a quaking teenage pupil called him 'dark, stern, gigantic'.[41]

These were Tom's parents, both devoted to the children in their own way, but both cold and hard, the father 'a strict disciplinarian', driven by musical ambitions, the mother ratty and parsimonious.[42]

* The Lonsdale portrait is now in the Dulwich Picture Gallery, and the Humphry portrait in the Victoria Art Gallery, Bath.

Thomas Gainsborough, *Self-portrait, c.* 1758–59 (oil on canvas, 76.2 × 63.5, National Portrait Gallery, London).

When Tom was three, in the year that Handel died, the painter Thomas Gainsborough moved to Bath, with his wife, their two daughters and his viola da gamba and Shudi harpsichord – for he was passionately fond of music and musicians. (His friend, the organist and composer William Jackson of Exeter, recalled that Gainsborough was so convinced that the secret of music lay in the instrument that he bought Felice Giardini's violin, Carl Friedrich Abel's viola da gamba, Johann Christian Fischer's oboe, a harper's harp and a German professor's theorbo. Though he had 'the ear, taste, and genius [of a musician]', Jackson wrote, 'he never had application enough to learn his notes', yet 'there were times when music seemed to be Gainsborough's employment and painting his diversion'.)[43]

Gainsborough lived first in a large house in Abbey Green, only minutes from the Linleys', and became intimate with the family – so much so that he used to offer 'hints and instruction on the education of little Tom'.[44] He painted at least seven portraits of the family between 1759 and 1787, starting with the handsome father in about 1760.* Gainsborough, who had two daughters but no boys, was fascinated by the charms of the Linley children, and about six years

---

* The identity of this portrait, once in the possession of the Tickell family and now believed to be in a private collection in Bath, has been disputed. Ellis Waterhouse, in his *Gainsborough* (London, Spring Books, 1966, p. 79), claims it is Thomas Linley junior, painted in 1777/8, but Susan Sloman, in the Catalogue of the exhibition *Pickpocketing the Rich – Portrait Painting in Bath 1720–1800*, at the Holburne Museum of Art, Bath, 2002, argues convincingly that it is an early portrait of Thomas Linley senior, probably dating from Gainsborough's first years in Bath, and Hugh Belsey, in his definitive *catalogue raisonné, Thomas Gainsborough* (Yale, 2019), pp. 552–553), is in no doubt that the subject is Linley senior, painted in about 1760.

later he attempted to adopt 'a little boy of singular beauty'.* In 1766 he moved uphill to The Circus, the Palladian ring of houses newly built by John Wood the elder, and remained there till he left for London in 1774.

Nor was Gainsborough the only painter of the Linleys' acquaintance. In 1760 Ozias Humphry, then a student of eighteen, moved in to their house as a lodger. He was fascinated by the whole family and seems to have brought out the best in Mrs Linley, who used to sing

Gilbert Stuart, *Ozias Humphry*, 1784 (oil on canvas, 69.9 × 59.1 cm, The Wadsworth Atheneum Museum of Art, Hartford, Connecticut).

while she did the housework so that he would sometimes call her into his rooms to entertain him while he painted. Little Elizabeth observed his taste for music, and when her mother was not looking, she too would creep in, perch herself on a stool at the foot of his easel and sing songs from such popular operas of the day as Thomas Arne's *Thomas and Sally* and *Love in a Village*, and William Boyce's *The Chaplet*. Elizabeth was 'a rising bud of matchless beauty', Humphry said.[45] She had such an angelic face that her father used to post her at the door of the Pump Room with a little basket of benefit-tickets to rustle up an audience for his concerts.[46]

Humphry dined with the family and noted that their habits

---

* It happened after he had moved to London, and was walking in Richmond woods when he came across the little boy, Jack Hill. Gainsborough took him home, had him washed and dressed, 'and was so impressed by his appearance that he offered [the boy's mother] to take entire charge of him from that time forth', but she said she could not part with him because he was too valuable as a beggar.(William Thomas Whitley, *Thomas Gainsborough*, 1915, p. 232; W. B. Boulton, *Thomas Gainsborough: His Life, Work, Friends and Sitters'*, Methuen, 1905, p. 279). Nevertheless the boy was installed in Gainsborough's house in Pall Mall, where he sat for several pictures, and became a great favourite of the ladies. It is said he was still there when Gainsborough died and that Mrs Gainsborough later got him into the Blue Coat School in Westminster (Sir Walter Armstrong, *Gainsborough & his place in English art*, 1898, p. 159).

were 'frugal, their meals short and temperate' so that they could get back to music, which was their chief preoccupation. Sometimes, when visitors came, they lingered at the dinner table, to sing catches and glees in harmony.[47] The young painter's fondness for them all was returned, and when a seventh child arrived in 1765 the parents named him Ozias after their favourite lodger.

Thomas, the second son, began singing and dancing almost as soon as he could walk, and 'gave such early, and strong passion for Music' that his father decided 'to fix him in that Profession', using the boy's natural aptitude and his interest in his sister Elizabeth's music lessons as a way of introducing him to the musical notes and their relative values, so that he was soon able to read a simple score. When he was five and already playing the violin and the harpsichord, he began to study the theory and practice of music seriously, along with his home schooling in reading, writing and arithmetic, and it was probably the following year that his father handed him over to the violin virtuoso David Richards, leader of the orchestra at Linley's Bath concerts. In an eccentric dictionary of musical biography published anonymously in Bath in 1780, in which the subjects are given redacted names, this 'RICH.:DS' is described, 'in lieu of flattery', as 'a regularly rude, rugged, rough rasper'.[48] But this must have been intended as a joke because Richards was very highly regarded and later became leader of the orchestra at the Theatre Royal, Drury Lane.

At all events Tom made rapid progress with the Rasper, assisted by occasional classes with such visiting maestros as the composer and violinist Felice Giardini, the composer Johann Christian Bach ('the London Bach') and the composer and gamba player Carl Friedrich Abel, three of the great European musicians who occasionally drew the *beau monde* to the concert rooms of Bath.

Mr Linley was so pleased with his prodigiously gifted son that he allowed him to make his first public appearance as a violinist on 17 November 1762, at David Richards' benefit concert in Mr Wiltshire's assembly rooms in Bath, even though he was only six years old.[49]

The following summer Mr Linley himself had a benefit concert – at Mr Loggan's Rooms at the Hot Wells in Bristol. He was bass soloist, David Richards was leader of the orchestra, and Richards' little pupil Tom, now seven, was not only treble soloist but allowed to play a violin concerto too.[50]

Linley soon realised that Tom needed coaching at a higher level still, so he asked William Boyce, Master of the King's Musick – probably a Freemason like himself, and a regular visitor to Bath – if he would take the boy as apprentice.

Mason Chamberlin (attrib.), *William Boyce*, 1765–1770 (oil on canvas, 75 cm × 62 cm, Royal College of Music, London).

Dr Boyce was 'so captivated by the Child's Genius, and disposition,' that he agreed to teach him for five years, and to provide basic tutoring in the standard subjects of Latin and Greek.[51] Furthermore Linley decided to sit in on the music lessons too. So after the concert season in Bath in July 1763, and every summer thereafter till 1768, father and son took the coach up to London to stay with Boyce at his house in Kensington Gore, so they could study counterpoint and composition together.[52] This may have pushed Tom harder than was normal for a boy of seven, for it is likely that after Boyce's lessons were over, Mr Linley insisted on giving more of his own afterwards, so that Tom saw little of life beyond Dr Boyce's four walls. While consolidating the foundations of the soundest possible musical training, this cannot have left Tom's personality unscarred.

It wasn't all graft, though, for Boyce was a kind man, and Linley no monster, and on Sundays they would walk the two miles east to the Chapel Royal in St James' Palace, to hear Dr Boyce playing the organ and the boys singing the Communion service at eight, or Morning Prayer at ten, in the Tudor chapel. There were ten boys with unbroken voices in the choir at any one time – six juniors (or

Richard Buckner, *A Boy Chorister of the Chapel Royal, c.* 1873 (oil on panel, 45.1 cm × 29.2 cm, Victoria & Albert Museum, London).

'fags') and four seniors – and they were supplemented in chapel by the tenor and basses of the Gentlemen from Westminster Abbey, and the other official musicians and musical assistants who included a lutenist, viol player, bell ringer and organ blower.[53] The Children of the Chapel, as the boys were officially known, were taught, clothed, and boarded by the Master of the Children, the organist and composer James Nares.

Thomas was fascinated by these disciplined boys, and no less by their striking uniform of scarlet coat embroidered with gold braid, matching breeches and white lace ruff and tabs (though they always wore white surplices in chapel). Talking to one of the 'fags' after the service one morning, he was interested to learn, and had reason not to forget, that they sometimes sang the minor soprano roles in Handel's oratorios at Drury Lane.[54]

Tom generally did not return to Bath till the winter – though sometimes he stayed on for Christmas and lingered to February – but his father had to go back much sooner, to plan his concert seasons and resume his teaching.

At the end of their second year with Boyce, they may have seen, possibly even met, the Mozarts who were in London on a grand family tour designed to introduce the two gifted children – Wolfgang and Maria Anna ('Nannerl') – to the courts of western Europe, to make contacts which might lead to appointments and engagements, and to raise money from public concerts.

As Boyce was composer to the King, he would probably have been invited to the Mozarts' concert on 5 June 1764, celebrating the birthday of George III, and would surely have taken Tom and his father, so they could see and hear 'the celebrated and astonishing Master Mozart, a Child of Seven Years of Age [actually eight and a half], justly esteemed the most extraordinary Prodigy, and most amazing Genius, that has appeared in any Age'.[55] And if they were not there on that occasion, they may have paid their five shillings each a little later, to hear Mozart playing his own compositions on the organ and harpsichord in the Rotunda at Ranelagh Gardens, in aid of the Surrey Lying-in Hospital.[56] Goethe had seen Mozart in

Louis Carrogis Carmontelle,
The Mozart Family on Tour, c. 1763
(watercolour, 19.5 cm × 12.5 cm,
Musée Condé, Chantilly).

Frankfurt the year before and always remembered his first sight of 'the little fellow … with his powdered wig and his sword'.[57]

Mozart celebrated his ninth birthday in the January following, and is thought to have been taken, as a present, to see J. C. Bach's new opera, *Adriano in Siria*, at the King's Theatre, Haymarket. The London Bach, as he was known, had had a profound influence on him ever since he arrived in London in the spring of 1764 – and he may even have had lessons from him the previous autumn when he was quietly composing in Chelsea, while his father, Leopold, was recovering from a condition known as 'a quinsy' – an abscess behind the tonsils. As friends of both Bach and of Giusto Fernando Tenducci, the castrato who created the title role of Adriano, the Linleys would not have wanted to miss the premiere, if they were in town then.

One thing Dr Boyce could not do for Tom, deaf as he was, overweight too and given to gout, was teach dancing, which Tom had always loved, so the boy was sent to Drury Lane to study under the Irish master Robert Aldridge. Principal dancer at the Theatre Royal, and a violinist himself, Aldridge was well known for the ballets he created for the intervals of the popular operas (whose airs Elizabeth and Mrs Linley were always singing at home in Bath). An audience favourite was *Irish Lilt*, which he put together from a selection of Irish airs learned when he was working at the Smock Alley Theatre in Dublin. Then there was the *Bog of Allan*, and a whimsical piece called the *Fingallian Rant*. But the dance that Tom liked best was a fast hornpipe which Aldridge learned from a hornpipe master in Drogheda. Tom picked it up so well that when Aldridge had a benefit concert at the New Theatre in Bristol, in September 1766 he put the boy on stage to dance it.[58]

Probably it was his success in the Bristol concert, together with Aldridge's enthusiastic support, that led to a starring role at Covent Garden the following year, when Tom was still only ten. The King had made it known that he wanted to give his little son and heir, George, Prince of Wales, his first taste of the theatre, and he hoped that Covent Garden might stage some suitable entertainment for this royal child of four and a half. On 29 January 1767 the curtain went up on Thomas Hull's masque, *The Fairy Favour*, inspired by *A Midsummer Night's Dream*, with music by J. C. Bach, music master to the Queen, and a cast of children. Tom was given the role of Titania's malicious fairy, Puck, in which he was able to show off all his talents – dancing the hornpipe, singing, playing the violin, and, in a new string to his bow, an unusual one in a small boy, that of comedian, with a line in jaded foppishness. He proved it in his very first song:

> *Quick, and light as the air,*
> *In and out, here and there,*
> *Have I tript, till I'm weary to death;*
> *Lend, lend me your hand,*
> *For I hardly can stand —*
> *Lack-a-day! I am quite out of breath.*

The show ran for eight performances, and Tom – or, rather, his father – was paid £20.[59] There is no record of how much his sister Elizabeth was paid for her singing part, but within five years she would be earning hundreds of pounds for a single performance. Of Tom's performance, one newspaper wrote that 'Not enough can be said of the little gentleman that play'd the part of Puck; his singing, playing on the violin, and dancing the hornpipe, are all beyond expectation, and discover extraordinary abilities in one, who must be considered a child.'[60]

The royal family must have liked it too, because a fortnight later Tom was commanded to give a violin solo at Covent Garden, in the presence of the King and Queen and other members of the royal family.[61] It's likely that the Duke and Duchess of Ancaster attended too, in their court capacities, and if they had not already come across Tom, this could have been the occasion when they marked him out for special favours.

A year later the young Prince of Wales, now five and a half, and his younger brother, Prince Frederick, Duke of York, aged four and a half, made their very first public visit beyond the confines of the palace, and it was to Ancaster House in Berkeley Square that they chose to go. 'There was different Entertainments of Musick', reported the newspapers, 'and an elegant Supper, provided for them' by the duke and duchess, and they stayed till nine.[62] It is hard to believe that the little boys wouldn't have wanted to see Puck again, and that Tom wasn't called on to give a reprise of his hornpipe.

By now Mr Linley had taken over the management of the old (lower) Assembly Rooms in Bath, where he had been harpsichordist since 1755, and had moved his growing family to a rented house with eleven rooms, in Orchard Street, around the corner from the Theatre Royal (now the Masonic Hall).* This was not only larger but grander, with an Ionic doorway, an elaborate staircase of oak and mahogany and decorated plaster cornices.[63]

At a benefit concert for the Linleys in Bath on 7 May 1767, Tom's eleventh birthday, he himself played a violin solo and Elizabeth sang, possibly with their sister Mary, and maybe Samuel played his oboe too. The presence of these talented children, so pretty and

---

* The house was actually in what is now Old Orchard Street, at the point where it becomes Pierrepont Place.

charming, must have had their usual beneficial effect on the takings, for Linley posted a notice in the local paper a week later, thanking the public for 'the great Honour and Encouragement his Children received'. He promised, 'by every Effort in his Power', to promote their continued improvement, in order to merit future favour.[64]

But not everyone approved of his methods of promoting his talented children's continued improvement. One Bath lady attending his weekly concerts that spring reported that although 'Linley's daughter [Elizabeth]… has a sweet voice … he makes her sing *too much* and *too hard* songs , for she is very young'.[65] She was certainly young, not yet thirteen, but Tom was only eleven, Mary nine and Samuel seven, all of them were being pushed too hard, and the cracks would show later.

In the winter of that year, when Tom was on leave from Dr Boyce in London, he played a solo at a concert in Gyde's Rooms in Bath, and Elizabeth sang in a concert, which included a musical setting of Milton's *Lycidas*. Ever since she had been able to sing, Elizabeth had shown a talent for writing too, and in particular for poetry. She was greatly impressed and affected by this elegy of Milton's, in memory of his beloved young friend, Edward King, who died when his ship went down, and she must have stored it away in the back of her mind, though she cannot have known that when next she returned to it she would be using it as the model for her own lines in memory of her beloved Tom, drowned too.

Ten days after *Lycidas* – on 21 May 1768 – the Linleys put on a performance of Handel's *Acis and Galatea* at the Theatre Royal as a benefit for Elizabeth, and Tom played a solo.[66]

He had now completed his apprenticeship with Boyce, who reported that he had made 'astonishing Progress' with his composition studies. His father was as pleased with the boy's dedication to his studies, as he was with his results: he was developing as a musician just as he himself had done under Chilcot and Paradies.[67] Now it was time to find him a master to do for his violin playing what

Boyce had done for his composition. There were plenty of virtuosi in London and Bath at the time – Giardini, Wilhelm Cramer, Giuseppe Agus, François-Hippolyte Barthélemon, and only last year Gaetano Pugnani had taken over the music at the King's Theatre, Haymarket.

Pugnani had been a pupil of Giuseppe Tartini, perhaps the greatest violinist of the eighteenth century, and Tartini happened to be one of Tom's favourite composers. He also happened to run one of the most famous violin schools in Italy, the *Scuola delle Nazioni* in Padua, which offered musical and violin training, modelled on the human voice – on the resonance and articulation of speech. But it also offered a network of relationships not only with the European musical world, but also with the literary, diplomatic, scientific and political world of the time. Furthermore the Master was known to maintain relations with his student's benefactors and to draw his students into his social circle even after they had left.[68] Tom loved Tartini's violin music, and was eager to study with him, but the old man had recently suffered a stroke and his school was closing down.

From his old composition teacher, Paradies, still working in London, Linley could have discovered that one of Tartini's most famous graduates, Pietro Nardini, was running a school in Livorno, the seaport and naval base on the Tuscan coast with such strong English connections that it had its own English name, Leghorn, still sometimes used today. This would be ideal for Tom, who would be able to adjust more gently into Italian life through the English merchant colony settled there. Furthermore Paradies could have told him he knew a boy studying there, Joseph Agus, now nineteen, the English son of his friend Giuseppe Agus, the Italian violinist and composer well known for the ballet music he was writing for the Italian opera in London.

Giovanni Battista Cecchi (attrib.), *Pietro Nardini*, 1782 (Bibliothèque nationale de France, Paris).

It would not have been difficult, given these contacts, for Linley to write to Nardini directly, to propose his son for consideration as an apprentice, to forward references from Boyce, and to draw up an agreement. But how was he to pay for it all – the fees, the travel, the board and lodging for three years? He had reasonable hopes that the exceptional gifts of his eldest four children would soon bring handsome returns, and their income would be his till they came of age – even if he cannot have known that within six years the earnings of Elizabeth alone would 'support the whole household in affluence'.[69] But at this early stage in his life he was still struggling to support a growing family of six surviving children, all under twelve, with three more yet to come, and there was no money to spare. So who was the benefactor?

According to an entry in an early nineteenth-century dictionary of music,[70] the Duke of Ancaster took Tom under his wing at an early age, and it seems likely that it was he who underwrote the Italian project, although the Linley scholar Dr Rebecca Gribble has found no supporting evidence of any payment or any letter in her examination of the Ancaster papers.[71]

There is sound evidence of the approximate date when he left England, for on 11 May 1768, four days after Tom's twelfth birthday, Gainsborough recorded that he was painting 'a large Picture of Tommy Linley & his sister', adding that 'The Boy is bound for Italy the first opportunity'.[72]

The picture (see Frontispiece) is a charming study of the children as 'A Beggar Boy and Girl', wearing peasant clothes in rustic surroundings. A puckish Tom, with thick auburn hair and large, bright eyes, looks – a little warily – at the viewer, and leans his head towards the safety of his sister's shoulder. Elizabeth, aged thirteen and a half – going on twenty – gazes sadly into the distance over his head. Knowing he'll soon be far away for three years, she's already missing him.

Thomas said goodbye to his family in Bath in late May, with Elizabeth probably supervising his packing and making sure he remembered to include the set of six violin sonatas he had recently completed at Dr Boyce's.[73] Perhaps, as an experienced European traveller, Agus senior advised her to remove the buttons from Tom's shirts and coats, to prevent their being torn off by the violent jolting of coach travel.[74]

At twelve, Tom could not have travelled to Italy on his own, and must have been accompanied by an adult tutor or guardian. Young noblemen on the Grand Tour were usually accompanied by a clergyman or schoolmaster, known as a 'governor', 'cicerone', or 'bear-leader', someone who knew the ropes, had done the Tour himself, could negotiate fees, speak the languages, protect and guide his young charge on the journey, show him the sights, tell him the history, and keep him, more or less, on the straight and narrow. It was never the father, for one of the objects of the Grand Tour was to give the son his head, free of the constraints of home. In Tom's case, travelling not as an aristocrat for fun but as a musician for study, it might have been his father, if his father had not been committed to concert engagements in Bath and the West Country, and busy managing the diaries of the two eldest girls – for Mary, now ten, was already singing in public with Elizabeth. In the absence of any evidence, it seems likely that Mr Linley would have nominated one of his Italian musical friends. His old teacher Paradies is a possible candidate, but he had concert dates fixed in London during this period, so possibly it was Agus senior, a man in his mid-forties, who was recruited for the job. He must have been wondering how his son was getting on at Nardini's school so far away, and would have welcomed the opportunity to visit him – especially at someone else's expense.

Thomas was well used to the company of older men, after years of study with his father, then with Richards and Boyce, and would have been glad to be travelling with someone who was not only a professional violinist, with whom he could talk music, but an Italian, who could tell him something of Italy, of Nardini, of Livorno, perhaps even given him some Italian lessons along the way.

III

Nardini's Disciple

LEGHORN 1768–70

On a necessarily tight budget, Agus – if indeed it was he who played the role of bear-leader – would have steered Tom down the cheapest and most direct route to Italy, southeast through France, anticipating Dr Burney's musical journey two years later.[75] But first they had to make their way from London, along the Old Kent Road to New Cross, braving the footpads and highwaymen on Shooter's Hill and Gad's Hill, then on via Rochester, Medway and Canterbury to Dover.[76] From Dover they would have crossed the Channel by packet boat to Calais – hoping for better luck than the Mozarts, who had made 'a heavy contribution in vomiting' when sailing in the opposite direction in the spring of 1764.[77]

Once on French soil, they probably picked up a four-wheeled post coach for Paris via Lille, and travelled on, with overnight stops, to Lyons, Geneva and Lanslebourg in the Savoie. There they would have crossed the Alps by the Mont Cenis Pass, probably on mules, which cost less than the marginally faster and more comfortable sedan chairs .The *milordi* usually chose to cross by chair, leaving mules to carry their baggage, their servants and sometimes even their coaches. and, at the end of the Pass they came to what Burney, on his journey, called a 'terrific and fatiguing' descent down into the Piedmont, hanging on to 'a kind of field stool fastened to 2 poles' carried by two men.[78] If, as Ozias Humphry reported on his trip in

1773, the carriers 'walked with too swinging a footstep', it must have felt like being at sea – over a pass of 190 miles which took them six days to cross.[79] In Novalese their bags were opened and searched by Sardinian Customs,[80] before they hired a coach to Turin and on to Genoa, then down the Mediterranean coast, via Pisa, to the port of Livorno, taking care to tip the ostlers and postilions generously along the way, for they would have been forewarned that, when these men did their duty, they were very 'necessary beings' indeed.[81]

In all they had to cover a thousand miles, a distance which took a letter from Horace Walpole at Strawberry Hill a month to reach his friend Sir Horace Mann in Florence, and Burney three months of Grand Touring. But, with fewer and much shorter stops than Burney, and making, say, twenty miles a day on the rough roads, Tom and his guide could have covered the same ground in two months. So they may have arrived on the Tuscan coast by the end of July, but would have needed a week to recover, for it was a dangerous and extremely uncomfortable journey, being bumped about in spring-less carriages, in all weathers, with overnight stops in unheated inns, fleas in their beds, nothing much to eat. The Mozarts knew all about it: 'Imagine', wrote Leopold after a journey from Florence to Rome in 1770, 'a largely uncultivated country and the most appalling inns, filth everywhere, nothing to eat except – if we were lucky – the occasional meal of eggs and broccoli'.[82]

Agus will have done the journey more than once before, so he knew the main ports of call en route, but it was the sea that told them they were nearly there. Each was in his corner, half sleeping, half waking when about twelve miles out of Pisa they passed into a current of salt air, which braced them as effectively as it did the horses, breaking into a trot as they sensed the journey's end.[83]

Once arrived at the northern city gate of Livorno, Agus was able to direct the coachman to the palazzo where Nardini ran his little school. He shared it with an Englishman, a musical merchant called Hempson, but nothing more is known of their establishment –

how many pupils and teachers – or of Nardini and Hempson themselves – whether married, whether fathers – or anything about their daily lives. The little we do know comes from English travellers such as Charles Burney and Hester Piozzi.

The visitors arrived in the middle of a drought, with fever raging in the city, and the people carefully avoiding fruit, and gargling with 'flour of brimstone'.*[84] But Nardini was safe, and gave them a warm welcome.[85] A seasoned traveller himself, who knew the toll it took, he gave his guests their first decent meal in weeks, then sent Tom early to bed – probably sharing a room with Agus junior, so that Tom could talk in his own tongue till he had learned Italian, and get to know something of the older boy – while the two older men sat and talked – about Agus junior and Tom, about the journey, violins, music in London, friends in common.

Ever soft-hearted, as his violin music itself conveys, Nardini could not fail to have been drawn to his new English pupil, charming, bright-eyed and only twelve – exactly the age he himself was when he travelled north to Padua to begin his studies with Tartini 34 years earlier.

As soon as Tom was up the next morning, Nardini took him for a walk around the small city that was to be his home for the best part of two years. Enclosed by fortified walls with five gates, Livorno sat on a tongue of land jutting into the sea, with the Navy based in the harbour, protected by a dangerous entrance, and the foothills of the Appenines rising behind. Otherwise there was not much to see beyond some canals, one very long straight street and one very large wide square, and a stately palace for the governor. The city was designed during the Italian Renaissance as a sort of Utopia, and was still ruled from Florence by the Grand Duchy of Tuscany.

If it never quite became Utopia, it soon became the most important port in the Mediterranean, as European trade with the Ottomans

---

* A solution of powdered sulphur and water, then thought to cure diphtheria.

declined and trade with the New World increased – a crossroads between cultures, religions, and goods.

Trade was what it thrived on, and trade was what it smelled of, as Tom cannot fail to have noticed as he strolled along the mole and quays – just as the American writer James Fenimore Cooper did half a century later:

> ... *we feasted our eyes on the different picturesque rigs and peculiar barks of this poetical sea. Long years had gone by since I had seen the felucca, the polacre, the xebec and the speronara, and all the other quaint-looking craft of the Mediterranean ... The fragrance of the bales of merchandize, of the piles of oranges, of even their juice, saturated as it was with salt, to say nothing of the high seasoning of occasional breathings of tar and pitch, to me were pregnant with 'odours of delight'.*[86]

But beyond the sea, the ships, the smells and a cemetery for the Protestant dead – perhaps the only one in Italy at that time[87] – Fenimore Cooper found little to interest him: in fact he dismissed it as 'vulgar and mean'.[88]

As a free port, Livorno's commerce was mostly in the hands of foreigners, who had been forced to leave their native lands because of persecution, and now gave the place an extraordinary ethnic diversity. If Jews played a central role in the coral and diamond markets, forging important trading partnerships in North Africa and London, British merchants, or factors as they were known, managed the business of Livorno. It may have been the only city in Italy where English was understood by most people, but one Grand Tourist, noting that it had 'no considerable libraries, nor any academies of Wits,' dismissed Livorno as good for nothing but 'letters of exchange and traffick'.[89]

Dr Johnson's Bluestocking friend, the much-travelled Hester Piozzi, visited Livorno at about this time and described the city as 'a magic lanthorn exhibiting a prodigious variety of different, and not uninteresting figures':

> ... *a Levantine Jew, dressed in long robes, a sort of odd turban, and immense beard* ... *a Tuscan* contadinella [countrywoman] *with the little straw hat, nosegay and jewels* ... *an Armenian Christian, with long hair, long gown, long beard, all black as a raven, who calls upon an old grey Franciscan friar for a walk; while a Greek woman* ... *throws a vast white veil all over her person, lest she should undergo the disgrace of being seen* ... *a broad Dutch sailor, a dry-starched puritan, an old French officer* ... '

Richly colourful they might all be, and prosperous certainly, but Mrs Piozzi thought them a feeble breed, with 'a tender frame and an unhealthy look, occasioned possibly by the stagnant waters'.[90]

Livorno's chief manufacture was coral, but it traded in silk, the plaited straw hats known as Leghorn bonnets, fruit, wine, marble, hemp and anchovies. For the last few decades it had been a favourite and profitable haunt of British expatriates – among them the merchant and shipowner Thomas Earle, who dealt in coffee, wine, hides, marble and sugar and shipped back home paintings, sculptures and artefacts bought by the Grand Tourists. He was also a major slave trader. At one point Earle shared his house with his clerk, William Hempson, a great lover of music, but Hempson eventually went into business on his own, and must have flourished for he had a substantial house in both Livorno, and later in Florence too, both of which became home to Nardini and his pupils.[91]

Hempson may have been a son of the soprano Celeste Gismondi, who sang in Handel's company at the Queen's Theatre in London in the early 1730s, and was known to have married a Mr Hempson. William Hempson played the recorder, and put on concerts at home.[92] This recorder greatly interested Dr Burney, who heard it in Florence later, and doubtless would have fascinated Tom too, because Hempson played it in a most peculiar way, 'blowing it through a spunge [sic]', attached like a beehive cap over the mouth-piece, probably to absorb the moisture from his breath, and so to improve the quality of the sound.[93]

Along with the unfamiliarity of the sights and smells, the climate, and the language, Tom had to adjust to a new diet, which began with a Tuscan breakfast of salted meats and cheese, accompanied by bread and wine – no hot tea, coffee or chocolate, because it was generally thought that hot food and drinks ruined the teeth of young people and weakened their temperament.[94] And he may have been advised to avoid tossing his salad in too much oil, because it was believed that 'relaxing food in a hot Country often occasions rupture'.[95] The Mediterranean climate was a peril for English consti-tutions too, and Tom was careful not to go from the blazing sunshine into the sudden cool of 'a Church or lower Appartment of a Palace when he was hot, many having lost their lives by this indiscre-tion'. Nor was he to attempt to 'walk out on foot in the day time in the great heats which often occasioned Violent and fatal Fevers'. But, with no money, he will not have needed the words drummed into every Grand Tourist: '… when the Italians ask any sum for any Purchase … if you offer them a third only, you will [still] be cheated'.[96]

In due course, as custom required, Tom was presented to the English Proconsul, the Rev. Andrew Burnaby, who was also Chaplain to the English mission (with the King's arms over the door) – and, with the British Envoy in Florence, Sir Horace Mann, an undercover monitor of the activities of the Young Pretender, Charles Edward Stuart, and his Jacobite court then living in exile in Rome.[97]

On the last day of that first month in Livorno, the French Consul, Pierre-Jean de Bertellet, invited Hempson and his friends to his house for a *conversazione*, at which Nardini played.[98] It was the first time Tom had heard his master actually giving a concert, and he was glad of the chance to study the famous 'magic bow', which was said to produce sounds closer to the human voice than to a violin – sounds so passionate and affecting that even Nardini himself shed tears that ran down his cheeks and to his instrument.[99] Slow, sad movements were the master's speciality – and soon became Tom's too. Whether the music was *triste* or *cantabile* (singing), the bass line moving in quavers provided a perfect platform on which to show off a floridly emotional solo line.[100] In Bath three years later Tom was praised by the violinist Thomas Shaw for a bowing trick he had picked up from Nardini: 'a Management of lengthening out a Single Note in a Slow Movement, which is as difficult as serviceable, and pleasing in a leader'.[101] But both master and pupil were equally at home in another characteristic of the Italian violin school, bravura fluency in fast movements.

A few months into his studies with Nardini, Tom wrote a seventh violin sonata,[102] inspired as much by his master's playing as by the music of Luigi Boccherini, the cellist in the *Quartetto Toscano* (arguably the first professional string quartet), which Nardini had recently founded in Livorno.[103] According to the conductor Peter Holman, who has studied the only surviving sonata, in A Major, and the one surviving concerto, in F Major, both works show that Tom must have had 'a phenomenal technique', with the violin part 'playing most of the time at the extreme upper register of the instrument'. It is clear, he writes, that Linley had 'mastered the graceful *galant* style of J. C. Bach'. The three-movement sonata has a final movement a 'rondeau', which imitates hunting horns, in 'a delightful display of youthful high spirits', and the concerto, also in three movements, has 'an impassioned slow movement ... in the Scotch style fashionable at the time', and a finale with hints of distant bagpipes'.[104]*

There is no way of telling what sort of violin Tom played, but it is a fair guess that Nardini will have taken him to the workshops of the Livorno violin-maker Antonio Gragnani, who was, that very

---

* For links to recordings and manuscript sources see footnote on p. 30.

year, completing an instrument constructed on the Amati model: full-sized, but with slightly reduced proportions, so that it perfectly suited a player with smaller hands – a player like Tom. And he would have been fascinated to learn that the material used for the black inlay around the edge of the front of the instrument was not stained wood but whale bone.*

That autumn of 1768 there was a week of grand celebrations in Florence for the installation of Sir Horace Mann, the British Envoy Extraordinary, as a Knight of the Bath. Officially this was carried out in London by the King, with Sir Horace's nephew (the cricketing Horatio Mann) standing proxy, but in Florence the Grand Duke of Tuscany, Pietro Leopoldo I, did the honours. The ceremony itself was on 21 October, with a grand ball the following night; a magnificent dinner at Lord Tylney's on the Sunday; a performance of Handel's St Cecilia's Day ode, *Alexander's Feast*, at Lord Cowper's on the Monday; and the next day a concert given by a visiting Grand Tourist, the Welsh landowner and patron of the arts, Sir Watkin Williams-Wynn.[105] Duke Pietro Leopoldo loved music and employed a court of virtuosi, and it is inconceivable that Nardini, one of the greatest violinists in Italy at the time, would have been excluded. The distance from Livorno to Florence was about sixty miles and it

Pompeo Batoni, *Grand Duke Pietro Leopoldo I* (left) *with his brother, the Emperor Joseph II*, 1769 (oil on canvas, 173 cm × 122 cm, Kunsthistorisches Museum, Vienna).

---

* This instrument, still bearing its original manuscript label dated 1768, was acquired for $160,000 by the Musical Instrument Bank of the Canada Council for the Arts in 2017. See also John Dilworth, 'Antonio Gragnani', at Brompton's Fine & Rare Instruments online.

would have taken a day and a half by coach, but Nardini would have known it was more than worth the discomfort, not just for the fun of the thing but for his future prospects.

In the summer of Tom's second year in Livorno, Nardini had a letter from Padua telling him that his beloved old master Tartini, now 77, was mortally ill, and on 3 June he set out on the long journey, two hundred miles northeast, if not yet to say goodbye, certainly to comfort him.[106] Tom would have wanted to go too, and Nardini might well have been tempted to show off his favourite pupil, but, given the circumstances, he would have thought better of it. In the event Tartini lingered on till 26 February the following year, when he died after gangrene spread up his leg from one of his feet.[107]

By that time Nardini had long since returned to Livorno, where, that same month, February 1770, he took part in the magnificent wedding of a rich Sephardic merchant, Jacob Aghib, and his cousin, Anna. The celebrations lasted a week and involved concerts and banquets in the Palazzo Aghib, the pictures and furniture in its great salons illuminated by silver and crystal chandeliers. And in the Duomo, Nardini took part in a performance of a wedding cantata specially composed for the occasion by the *maestro di cappella*, Orazio Mei. On the last day of the celebrations the Aghibs held a musical *accademia*, for which the Grand Duke lent the musicians and singers from his court in Florence. And the week ended with a ball, 'all the more pleasurable as liqueurs, fruit pre-serves, and sorbets were served all night long ...'.[108]

This may have marked Nardini's farewell to his native city, for in March he and Tom and the other pupils, together with their music and violins moved inland to a richer artistic milieu and a new life.

V

Spring Awakening

FLORENCE 1770–71

Florence was a nexus – not just the capital of Tuscany, but the birthplace of the Renaissance, and a centre of European culture, trade and finance ever since. Now that the Medici dynasty had died out, the city was under the control of the Austrian Empress, Maria Theresa, and ruled by her son, the enlightened and reforming Grand Duke Pietro Leopoldo I.

This Leopoldo was a generous friend of the arts, subsidising the theatres, and employing musicians and singers. In addition to the virtuosi soloists attached to his court, he also supported an orchestra, choir, and a *maestro di cappella* for the performance of sacred music in the court chapel (the Chiesa di Santa Felicità), the Duomo and other city churches. A firm believer in the educational power of music, he offered further patronage to musicians as tutors to his thirteen children, though at this point in his life he was still only five years married and a father of only four.[109]

Pietro Nardini had long wanted to enter the Grand Duke's service, to join two friends from Livorno, the French composer Charles-Antoine Campion (Carl' Antonio Campioni), once a pupil of Tartini, and now *maestro di cappella* to the ducal court, and the French flautist Nicholas Dôthel (Niccolò Dothel), who had been recruited for the duke's band. In the summer of 1769 he had written asking for a post.[110] Pietro Leopoldo must have been delighted, for

Nardini was the one virtuoso his band was lacking, and on 14 July he was formally appointed court violinist. His highly-paid job required him to play as a soloist, with the orchestra and with chamber groups, and under his leadership Florentine music rose to fame throughout Europe.[111]

But he may not have moved to Florence till the early spring of 1770. By then his friend and landlord, the recorder-playing Mr Hempson, had set up in business on his own and acquired a palazzo in Florence. It must have been large because he invited Nardini and the little school to move in with him, as they had in Livorno.[112]

Almost immediately the newcomers found themselves caught up in an exciting whirl of activity, for music mattered above all in this refined and civilised city, and the arrival of Maestro Nardini – favourite pupil of the great Tartini – with his own favourite pupil, Linley the prodigy, caused a great stir.

Detail, 'Sir Horace Mann', from Johann Zoffany, *The Tribuna of the Uffizi*, 1772–78 (oil on canvas, Windsor Castle).

Once Tom had presented himself to Sir Horace Mann, possibly with an introduction from the Duke of Ancaster, and Mann had presented him to the court, the city was his. Mann was the kingpin of Florentine life, he knew everyone, went everywhere and kept open house for the English at the Palazzo Manetti, where he held 'a great assembly ... once a week (to which everybody comes)'.[113] On these occasions, all the apartments on the ground-floor were lit up with candelabra, 'and the garden was a little epitome of Vauxhall', which might have reminded Tom of London and outings to the Gardens with Dr Boyce.[114]

The visiting Grand Tourists fell over themselves in praise of Mann's charm, his kindness, his generosity – nothing was too much trouble for him when it came to showing off Florence (where he had lived for thirty-three years), and entertaining the young *milordi*. Burney called him 'a very handsome old man ... his countenance full of grace, intelligence and dignity'.[115]

But Mann was nothing if not eccentric, and Tom must have been taken aback by his affected ways. For a start he was a chronic hypochondriac, often in bed with gout. The young Lord Winchilsea, who was fond of him, said he had never seen 'so fiddle faddle a man ... he thinks of nothing Else but his health ...'[116] But his foibles went beyond health, and it is a tribute to the warm regard in which he was held that all his oddities were accepted, in an Italian spirit of tolerance. The young Lord Fitzwilliam admired him nonetheless:

> *Sir Horace is the most finical man in the world: if you speak a little loud, he can't bear it, it hurts his nerves, he dies – and he v-m-ts if you eat your petite patee before your soup; take him as he is, without the least notice, he is a perfect character for the stage. He has been so long out of England, that he has lost the manliness of an Englishman, and has borrowed the effeminacy of Italy. But with all his little airs, he is a good kind man , and is very civil.[117]*

Sir Horace Mann was a polished and effective diplomat with powerful contacts, who did a bit of dealing in paintings and antiquities to defray the costs of his lavish entertaining, but he was not actively interested in politics, music or science, and his private circle was conspicuously effete. It included John, Earl Tylney, who had fled from England after being 'detected in the consummation of an amour after the manner of Tiberius with two of his servants at the same time'.[118] Known to be both rich and generous, Tylney was described by a fellow Englishman as 'an unhappy man who could not resist the temptations & instigations of a passion, contrary to reason, & at which nature shudders'.[119] Another notable member of the Mann circle was the portrait painter and caricaturist, Thomas Patch, who had a soft spot for youths, and had recently been

Thomas Patch, *British Gentlemen at Sir Horace Mann's, Florence*, 1763–65, showing Lord Tylney, seated left, in red, and (probably) Sir Horace Mann, seated far right (oil on canvas, Yale Center for British Art, Paul Mellon Collection, USA/Bridgeman Images).

banished from Rome for a sexual indiscretion, probably with his boy servant, who had subsequently 'died of the pox'.[120] Patch's activities were so widely known that a fellow painter felt it necessary to warn a prospective Grand Tourist that 'A certain Mr Patch at Florence is a ---', the noun too awful to utter.[121]

Similar rumours, though with no surviving evidence, surrounded another of the long-term English expatriates in Florence, George Nassau, 3rd Earl Cowper. Aged thirty-two and, as yet, unmarried, he was one of the richest men in Europe and a major patron of artists, poets, scientists and musicians. Not only did he amass a magnificent art collection, but he also maintained his own orchestra, led by Salvador Pazzaglia, and played a significant role in bringing Handel's operas and oratorios to Florence.[122] After his death in 1789, *The World* newspaper accused him of 'having led a wicked and profligate course of life ... [in] ... the practice and use of the most criminal and unmanly vices and debaucheries ...'. The family sued for libel, claiming the article brought them into 'great scandal, infamy and contempt'. The judge agreed, on the curious grounds that the libel 'tended to a breach of the peace', but at a re-trial, the Lord Chief Justice reversed the original judge's decision, on a technicality, and, so, to some extent, the mud has stuck.[123]

If Italy itself was sometimes seen as 'the mother and nurse

Johann Zoffany, *George Nassau, 3rd Earl Cowper*, after 1772 (oil on canvas, 51 cm × 41.5 cm, private collection/Bridgeman Images).

of sodomy' at this time, Florence in particular had held a special reputation as 'a sodomitical hotbed' since the time of Dante.[124] Erotic relationships between men and boys were an accepted feature of life in Renaissance Florence, and their continued tacit acceptance five hundred years later dangled a carrot for certain Grand Tourists of the Enlightenment. At home these men were constrained by the law and censorious public opinion, but in liberal Florence it was 'Gather ye rosebuds while ye may'.[125] The last but one Grand Duke, Gian Gastone de' Medici, was so given to rosebuds that he abandoned his (admittedly sour) wife,* and spent the last eight years of his life lying in bed in the Pitti Palace, served, in every possible way, by an entourage of handsome peasant boys (the 'Ruspanti'), who were encouraged to call him, not *Altezza Real* (Your Royal Highness),

---

* The Grand Duke claimed that his wife, the Duchess of Saxe-Lauenburg, spent her time in the stables talking to the horses, but she claimed he was 'absolutely impotent' (G. F. Young, *The Medici: Volume II*, London, John Murray, 1920, p. 474, and Paul Strathern, *The Medici: Godfathers of the Renaissance*, London, Vintage, 2003, p. 404.

but *Altezza Realona* (Fat Queen).[126] These boys and their pimp, the duke's valet and majordomo, Giuliano Dami, ran the court and charged visitors for admission: not that many would have relished a visit, for the duke's bedchamber was far from fragrant.

The present duke, Pietro Leopoldo I, was a different kettle of fish, but what did Tom make of life at this exotic court? He was thirteen and probably looking for friends of his own age – something entirely new in a life which had been spent under the strict rule of, successively, a controlling father and two middle-aged masters. Presumably, like any other child at puberty, he was also becoming sexually aware. It is interesting to speculate on the influence of his fellow student at the Nardini school, Joseph Agus, who, now twenty-one, was nothing if not sexually aware, judging by his arrest in London seven years hence on a charge of raping his eleven-year-old god-daughter. But not a whiff of any kind of indiscretion attaches to Agus before that time.

For a charming, artistic child like Tom, a thousand miles from home, Florence could have spelt danger: we would certainly think so today. But his single-minded preoccupation with music, combined with Nardini's fatherly protectiveness, and the social skills he himself had developed as a prodigy, probably kept him safe from predatory old birds. Certainly there is no record of his having been involved with Lords Cowper and Tylney in any but an occasional musical capacity, and with Patch none at all – more's the pity, for a portrait of Tom Linley away from home might have revealed much, particularly through Patch's wickedly observant eye.

If Mann's concert parties, *conversazioni* and *accademie* were Tom's introduction to Florentine social life, they were not the only assemblies he attended. The improvising poet, violinist and celebrated free spirit, Maria Maddalena Morelli-Fernandez, was At Home in the via della Forca every evening, and the more intellectual English used to gather there. Under the name of Corilla Olimpica, Signora Morelli was a member of the *Accademia dell'Arcadia*, the literary academy which promoted the virtues of classical pastoral poetry.* At forty-three, she still had a string of lovers, who included the Grand Duke himself, then only twenty-three, and Don Luigi Gonzaga, Prince of Castiglione,[127] and she was known to be 'an affectionate admirer' of Nardini, as well as one of his violin pupils.[128]

It was probably at one of Corilla's parties in the winter of 1769/70 that Tom first learned that Mozart and his

Corilla Olimpica, 1740 (engraving after Francesco Bartolozzi).

father were now in Italy, and heading for Florence. They had set off from Salzburg just before Christmas, and reached Milan on 23 January, where Wolfgang was commissioned to write the opera, *Mitridate, re di Ponto*. From Milan they travelled on to Bologna, and their next stop was Florence. Whether Tom ever did meet Mozart on that first London tour in 1764/5, when he was studying with Boyce, he will certainly have heard all about him, and he may have known that his own name was now being linked with Mozart's.

The two boys were to have played at a splendid concert at Lord Cowper's house at Fiesole, the Villa Palmieri, on 30 March, the very day the Mozarts arrived in Florence. But Wolfgang caught a cold on the wet and windy journey over the Appenine Mountains from Bologna, and when they reached their inn, *l'Aquila Nera* (the Black Eagle), near the Duomo,† he was put to bed with 'tea and violet juice',

---

* Nardini was also a member of the *Accademia dell'Arcadia* (under the name of Terpandro Lacedemone), and in 1778 he played a part in the campaign to have Corilla crowned as poet laureate in Rome, in a re-enactment of the ceremony in which Petrarch had been crowned with a laurel wreath four centuries earlier.

† The *albergo Aquila Nera* was in the Palazzo del Bembo, later Palazzo Bezzuoli-Martelli, which still stands in via dei Cerretani, on the corner of Piazza dell'Olio. The Mozarts seem to have had a fondness for Black Eagle Inns, which they patronised in Liège (1763), Olmütz (1767), Innsbruck (1772), and Munich (1777 and 1790).

to help him sweat it out in his lofty chamber four floors up.[129] Dr Burney stayed there five months later and said the ceilings were so high he felt he was *nel mondo della luna* (up in the world of the moon).[130]

Thomas will have been bitterly disappointed to have missed meeting Wolfgang on this occasion, but he was promised there would be another opportunity, and meanwhile his consolation was that he was the only soloist with the famous castratos Tommaso Guarducci and Carlo Niccolini. The *Gazzetta toscana* reported that 'Mr. Linley, a youth of great merit, played a concerto on the violin,' observing that he was the English boy who was often noted for bringing credit to his master Nardini.[131]

On the 31st Mozart was still ill in bed, but the next day he was up again, and after Mass in the Court Chapel, and an audience with the Grand Duke, he and his father went to the Tintori Theatre, to play for the *Accademia degli Ingegnosi* with Nardini, the violinist and composer Giovanni Piantanida – and Tom.[132] What a quintet of violins: three virtuosos, including Leopold Mozart, and two prodigies.

The boys cannot have failed to recognise their similarities. Both played the violin and composed, both were the same height and the same build, both were nice looking, both were the same age (Tom nearly fourteen, Mozart just fourteen), both were as childlike in behaviour as adult in intellect. They were bright and observant, full of fun, well aware of their prestige as prodigies and not a little cocky. Furthermore Tom was English, and Wolfgang loved the English: '… *ich ein ErzEngelländer bin*' (I am an out-and-out Englishman), he once told his father.[133]

There was no time for more that night, as the boys and their protectors had to get home to their beds, but more was to come. The very next day the entire court, 150 Florentine nobles, assembled at the Villa del Poggio Imperiale, the Grand Duke's country house in Arcetri, south of Florence, for a musical workshop in the presence of the Infanta Maria Luisa of Spain. Nardini was invited too, and

Tom is unlikely to have let his master go without him, particularly now that he had established such a personal stake. They were all there to witness Maestro Mozart put through his paces.

First of all the boy was invited to play some of his own

Giuseppe Zocchi, *La Real Villa detta il Poggio Imperiale*, 1744 (etching, 33.3 cm × 50.5 cm, Metropolitan Museum of Art, New York).

compositions on the harpsichord and the violin, then the Court gave him some scores to read at sight, and some verses to turn into improvised arias on the spur of the moment. But the *pièce de résistance* came when the director of music at the court, the Marchese Eugenio di Ligniville, himself a composer, and an acknowledged expert in counterpoint, presented the boy with a series of difficult musical themes, and challenged him to improvise fugues upon them. The Court reeled in amazement as Wolfgang, seated at the harpsichord, spontaneously, and apparently effortlessly, worked them all out, and played them off, 'as easily', his proud father reported, 'as one eats a piece of bread'. Nardini, 'that excellent violinist' accompanied him.[134] Afterwards the Grand Duke's steward handed Wolfgang a fee of twenty-five gold zecchini, which today would be worth about £4,000.[135]

The *Gazzetta toscana* noted that 'Sig. Volfgang Motzhart [*sic*], the excellent Player of the harpsichord at present in the service of His Highness the Bishop of Salzburg, had the honour of performing last Monday before the Court, where he received all the applause due to his ability ... The most learned Professors cannot do otherwise than admire this boy ..' And the *Gazzetta di Mantova* described him as 'a musical miracle ... a Corilla to eclipse poets'.

Corilla herself was there, saw and heard it all, her antennae picking up every nuance. Recognising the boys' interest in one another, she invited them both, with Leopold Mozart and Nardini, to a *conversazione* at her house the next night. Her hunch was right: the two boys fell into one another's arms, like old friends – and raced off to the music room to play. The physical and musical similarities that drew them to one another were obvious, but as the evening wore on, they discovered they had so much else in common too. Both had been trundled around the concert circuits by authoritarian fathers, both adored their older sisters, both were impetuous, loved dancing and had strongly affectionate natures. They may not then have noticed other likenesses, which ran deeper, but probably brought them instinctively together: both were emotionally insecure and immature, essentially lonely, possibly narcissistic.[136]

Leopold was enchanted by their rapport. Reporting to his wife that 'the little Englishman' was 'a most charming boy' who '<u>plays wonderfully well</u>', he said they 'performed one after the other throughout the whole evening, constantly embracing each other'.[137] Wolfgang – or 'Wolferl' as he may have invited his new friend 'Tommaso' to call him – played some of his own pieces, and Tom some of his, including the violin sonata he had written in Livorno the previous year. Perhaps he even showed Mozart a sketch of his *Violin Concerto in F* (though it was not completed till a year or two later), because its tenderly pleading 'Adagio' is very like a section of the 'Rondeau' of the *Violin Concerto No 3 in G* (K 216) which Mozart wrote in Salzburg in September 1775, having perhaps kept it in his mind for five years.

And it's a fair guess that they discovered they shared much the same musical tastes too, not just in the lighter, clearer textures and stricter rules of the Classical period, replacing the ornate tunefulness of the baroque, but in violin playing too – the sweet and expressive tone of Tartini, his perfect intonation and bowing, and discreet use of vibrato: Tom had learned these characteristics through Nardini, and Wolfgang through his father.

All that music and all that hugging may have brought home to the father how profoundly these two gifted boys, old beyond their years, yet children still, must have been longing for friends of their own age; perhaps Tom felt this even more acutely than Wolfgang. But Leopold was more concerned with looking after Wolfgang, keeping him fit for his concerts, getting his music ready, and the day-to-day details of their headlong rush through the courts of Italy. He was also a bit worried about the wear and tear on his clothes. When they got back to their inn after Corilla's evening, he wrote to his wife, asking her to send him two camisole sleeves from his grey woollen suit so that he could use the material to mend his breeches which were wearing thin.[138]

Not content with a night of music in the via della Forca, Tom went round to see the Mozarts at the Black Eagle the next day, having sent a servant ahead with his violin, and the two boys made music all afternoon. Sometimes they played duets for two violins, sometimes Tom played solo sonatas with Wolfgang accompanying at a keyboard, and sometimes they stopped to talk about their lives and hopes, getting to know one another as young friends do when they first meet.[139]

It was the same thing the next day, the 5th April, when the Mozarts and Tom were invited to spend the day with the family of Giuseppe Maria Gavard des Pivets, administrator of the Grand Duke's finances. Only their playing was now so confident that

Anon., *Two Young Musicians said to be Wolfgang Mozart and Thomas Linley junior, with the Family of Gavard des Pivets*, Florence, April 1770 (130 cm × 160 cm, private collection).

Leopold was moved to tell his wife that they played 'not like boys, but like masters!'[140] The Gavards' son, slightly younger than Tom and Wolfgang, sang treble with them, and a large oil painting has survived which is believed by some to show all three performing, while M. and Mme. Gavard preside with proud half-smiles.[141]

It is not known who painted this picture or when, but if indeed it does record this occasion, it must have been commissioned by the Gavards after the event, as a memento. It shows, from left to right, Gavard *mère*, seated and clutching in her left hand the blue-green ribbons of a pink embroidered bag; her son, standing singing from a sheet of music in his left hand, while holding a scroll of music in his right; Gavard *père* standing at the rear of the group, his left hand gesturing towards wife and son; Wolfgang, sitting at what looks more like a spinet than a clavichord, his head turned away from the music in front of him, so that we can see his face; and Tom, on the right, playing what looks more like a viola than a violin, while reading from a sheet of music which stands on the lid of the spinet. The picture is carefully and prettily painted, presumably from the Gavards' memory of the scene. The painter must have been a musician, because the sheet music is accurately written out. The boys' faces are well done too, but all three look older than their years, and it must be said that Tom and Wolfgang bear little resemblance to their other portraits of the period (but then Mozart never looks the same twice in his). Tom is wearing a moss-green frockcoat with large buttons, and Wolfgang is in a beige coat and breeches with a white ruff folded over the coat's collar. All three boys are wearing their own hair brushed back over the head and powdered white.*

Thomas needed no painting to keep the memory of that week alive. The friendship, the music-making, the conversation with his new friend meant so much that he would never forget it for the

---

* The identification of the sitters has recently been questioned by certain historians, on the basis of iconographic and clothing arguments. Nevertheless the painting was sold for 22,500 EUR by Christies in 2019, and is now in a private collection in Paris.

rest of his life. When the little party came to an end, he could hardly bear to say goodbye, so he didn't – he walked with the Mozarts back through the city to the Black Eagle. Once there, as Leopold later wrote to his wife, 'Little Tommaso … wept bitter tears, because we were leaving on the following day.'[142] The Mozarts had hoped to stay longer, and Leopold wrote back to Salzburg to say he wished his wife might see Florence one day, for she would agree that 'one should live and die here'.[143] (Everyone felt like this about Florence – and Tom would have agreed with Hester Piozzi's verdict, that Florence was 'homeish and Bath-like'.)[144] But the Mozarts very much wanted to reach Rome in time for the Holy Week ceremonies at the Vatican, and needed to leave the next day.[145]

Instead of going home to Hempson's palazzo that night, Tom went to see Corilla Olimpica, whose house was just around the corner. He knew she would understand, so he poured out all his feelings at finding his first real friend, and then, as suddenly, losing him. The romantic Corilla was moved to compose a poem expressing the passion of his feelings. Perhaps she asked Tom to play an adagio on his violin, while she worked, for her Improvisations always seem to have involved musical inspiration. When the poem had formed itself in her mind, she wrote it down for him, telling him she had conceived it as a Farewell – 'Per la partenza del Sgr. Amadeo Wolfgango Mozart da Fiorenze' (On the departure of Sgr Amadeus Wolfgang Mozart from Florence).* She suggested he should take it home, copy it out in his own hand, in Italian, sign it at the bottom and deliver it in person to Wolfgang before he left for Rome in the morning.[146]

With the poem folded in his pocket, Tom walked home to Hempson's, picking his way over the broad paving stones in the narrow, dark, old streets. In his chamber he did as Corilla had

---

* Corilla may have put the Christian names in the wrong order, but at least she knew that Mozart had moved on from his full baptismal name, Joannes Chrysostomus Wolfgangus Theophilus Mozart.

Thomas Linley's Sonnet *On the Departure of Mozart from Florence*, 6 April 1770 (Cliff Eisen, et al., *In Mozart's Words*, Letter 175 <http://letters.mozartways.com>).

instructed, proudly copying out the loving phrases, then tossing and turning for the rest of the night.

After breakfast on Friday the 6th he took the poem around to the Black Eagle. Arriving at nine, he found that Wolfgang and his father were still having their breakfast, because they had decided to postpone their departure till midday. 'With many embraces', he presented the poem and watched as his friend read it aloud through his tears:[147]

Since Fate has divided us,
I can follow you only in my thoughts,
All joy and laughter replaced by melancholy;
But in the midst of sadness a hope we'll meet again.

That sweet harmony of Paradise
Which released my feelings in an ecstasy of love
Still resounds in my heart, and all at once
Transports me to Heaven for a vision of Truth.

Oh happy day! Oh lucky moment
In which, astonished, I saw and heard you –
And became a lover of your powers.

May the Gods decree that from your heart
I never shall fall: I will love you constantly,
And follow you always.

> *In token of my sincere esteem*
> *and affection*
> *Tommaso Linley.*

It was very much in Corilla's flowery style, and, even if the words weren't quite Tom's, the feelings were his. Besides the Italian language was as effusive as Italians themselves, and struck a chord with both these sensitive boys, who responded to its music and its warmth – and doubtless cried some more. Wolfang kept the letter with him till they reached Rome a few weeks later, when his father sent it home for safekeeping.* While the servants packed the bags, and Leopold went around their rooms checking that nothing was left behind, the

---

* Letter Leopold Mozart to Anna Maria Mozart, 21 April 1770. Mozart scholars claim that the enclosed poem (now in the Bibliotheca Mozartiana in Salzburg with the letter itself) is a copy in the hand of Leopold Mozart, but the manuscript published online looks more like Tom's hand.

boys talked and played and made promises. Then Leopold presented Tom with two engravings as a memento. One may have been of a watercolour portrait by Louis Carrogis Carmontelle showing Wolfgang, then aged seven, playing a square piano, with his father playing the violin and his sister Nannerl singing (see the picture on p. 39). The Mozarts were especially fond of this picture, and used to give prints of it to friends and patrons on their tours.[148] The other picture was perhaps one of Leopold's collection of engravings of sights they had seen on their journey.

By twelve the four-seater open carriage was loaded up – some of the Mozarts' luggage strapped to the back, the rest, with the instruments, on and under the two spare seats. Leopold paid the Black Eagle's bill, then said goodbye to Tom, and the boys embraced. As the two horses set off, Tom didn't stand waving, he ran alongside the carriage, talking to Wolfgang through the quarter-lights. And on he continued to trot beside them, all the way across the Arno by the Ponte Vecchio, down to the Palazzo Pitti, along the edge of the Giardino di Boboli, till they reached the great Porta Romana, the southernmost gate in the old city walls. There the boys finally parted, embracing for the last time, with more goodbyes and tears, as Leopold paid the gate fee and the Custom House officers searched the Mozarts' bags, warning that there would be further searches on their entry into the Pope's territories.[149]

At last the coachman flicked his whip at the horses' shoulders and the carriage moved off, picking up the road south, via the Villa del Poggio Imperiale, where the boys had played earlier in the week, and on down through the hills of vines and olives to Rome, two hundred miles and five days away. Tom could no longer keep up with the carriage as it gathered speed, and waved instead, till it was out of sight, then he turned back through the great gates into the city, and slowly, sadly, retraced his footsteps towards the Black Eagle, the scene of such happy times.

Leopold was deeply moved by the English boy's devotion, and

must have thought about it all the way to Rome, because three days after their arrival, and after all their well-recorded Easter experiences in St Peter's and the Sistine Chapel, it was still on his mind, and he wrote home to tell his wife all about it, wishing that she had been with him to see for herself the boys' affection for one another.[150]

What must have touched him so acutely was the intensity of the friendship, the emotional charge it had generated in barely five days. This was more than friendship. For the first time in his life Tom had found a friend as like him as both of them were unlike all others. They played, thought, dressed, looked and laughed alike – they even wrote their lower-case d's identically, as Greek deltas, with a backward flick of the tail. Their souls were knit. Yet no sooner found than lost.

It is interesting – but perhaps irrelevant, for the boys are unlikely to have viewed their friendship in such a sophisticated light – that when he was eleven Wolfgang wrote a Latin opera for the students of the Benedictine university in Salzburg.* *Apollo et Hyacinthus* tells of the love of the sun god for a beautiful boy whom he accidentally kills when they are sporting in the woods. Mozart set if for two boys in the chapel choir, a treble of twelve for Hyacinth, and an alto of the same age for his lover.

As the coach and horses tore Wolfgang from him on that April day in 1770, Tom must have felt something of the same loss as Apollo, suddenly abandoned after such closeness, and the promise it seemed to hold for the future. Therapists today call this kind of emotional shock 'abrupt amputation of affection' and treat its effects as 'profound psychic trauma'. Often it leaves lasting psychological damage; perhaps it did in Tom's case.[151]

Back in the Piazza del Duomo, tired after the long walk to and

* The librettist of the opera was a teacher at the university, Dom Rufinus Widl, who recognised the homoerotic essence of Ovid's re-telling of the myth, and carefully added a princess, Hyacinth's sister Melia, for Apollo to fall in love with, after the tragic death of his boy lover. Mozart set the part of Melia for a fifteen-year-old treble (*en travesti*). The opera is said to have been a great success, but never performed again in Mozart's lifetime.

Letter from Leopold Mozart to his wife, Anna Maria, Florence 3 April 1770 (Cliff Eisen, et al., In *Mozart's Words*, Letter 177 <http://letters.mozartways.com>).

from the Porta Romana, the boy looked across at the Black Eagle in the Palazzo del Bembo, empty and meaningless now, then turned with a heavy heart into the via della Forca and rang the bell at No. 2. A servant showed him into a room that already felt like home – and Corilla Olimpica, knowing what had happened, probably took him into her arms, offering *consolazioni materne*, as only an Italian can. Walking him back home later, she would have spoken to Nardini about him, and both would probably have agreed that the best medicine for a wounded heart was work. So, as the spring turned to summer, Tom buried himself in his violin lessons, his composing, his performing.

At the beginning of June, a month after his fourteenth birthday, he gave a concert in the oratory of Santo Spirito in Pistoia, under *trompe l'oeil* frescoes newly painted on the ceiling by Mauro Tesi and Vincenzo Meucci. His old friend, the *Gazzetta toscana*, reported that 'the well-known Sig. Linley Inglese' received the greatest applause for a bravura performance.[152] Later in the summer, Nardini and the court flautist Niccolò Dôthel, with Tom in tow, gave a concert in the garden of the Marchese Santini, the Luccan Ambassador at the Grand Ducal Court: the *Gazzetta* called it 'a sumptuous academy of sound and singing'.[153] And the very next day, to celebrate the Feast of St. Philip Benizi, Tom and the castrato Giovanni Manzuoli sang in an eight-part Mass by the Tuscan composer Pasquale Soffi, on the loggia of the Servite Basilica of the Santissima Annunziata in Florence. Manzuoli, now at the end of his career, his soprano having dropped to contralto, later sang a motet 'in his usual sweet manner', and Tom performed a violin concerto 'with great delicacy'.[154]

Joshua Reynolds, *Charles Burney*, *c.* 1781 (oil on canvas, Muzeo internationale, Bologna/ Bridgeman Images).

Then in September, just as Tom was nearing the end of his studies in Italy, he made a new friend, rather older than Mozart, not a brother this time but a father figure, the music historian and composer, Charles Burney (newly raised to the degree of doctor) who was on his Grand Tour of Italy, collecting materials for a projected history of music. He had recently arrived in

Florence, from Bologna, and, like the Mozarts, he was staying at the Black Eagle. If Burney had not already met Tom two years earlier, in London – at Boyce's, or the Chapel Royal – he had certainly met his father when Mr Linley was a boy of fourteen, a year older than Tom now, serving as Chilcot's apprentice in Bath.[155] He knew of Elizabeth's reputation as a rising star of English choral music, and he was well aware of Tom's reputation too, as he recorded in his notebook:

> ... my little countryman, Linley, who had been two years under Signor Nardini, was at Florence when I arrived there, and was universally admired. The 'Tommasino', as he is called, and the little Mozart, are talked of all over Italy, as the most promising geniusses of this age.[156]

The two Englishmen, one forty-six, the other a child, took to one another instantly and threw themselves into a feast of Florentine music for a full week, starting on the 9th when 'little Linley came to see me after dinner'. Despite a downpour earlier in the day which flooded the city streets, they rode out to a farm belonging to the Grand Duke, where they took the air. Afterwards they went to the *Bottegone* coffee house near the Duomo and probably had 'a dish of music and chocolate', over which, in Burney's phrase, they might have 'set their horses very well together', meaning they found they had much in common, and were able to set the world to rights.[157]

The next day, after exploring the Laurentian Medici Library, where the ancient books were chained to desks, Dr Burney went to a great *accademia* at Mr Hempson's where their host played his recorder, in his own eccentric way – and Nardini and 'his little scholar Linley' played solos and concertos. Nardini's tone was 'even and sweet; not very loud, but clear and certain' with a great deal of expression in the slow movements, a habit caught from Tartini. In short, he was 'the completest player on the violin in all Italy'. Corilla, 'the famous *improvvisatrice*' was there too and Burney and she 'had a good deal of chat'.[158]

On the 11th Burney inspected some Gregorian Chant manuscripts at the Magliabecchi Library in the morning, and after visiting Sir Horace Mann ('who was in bed with the gout and Lord Tilney with him'), he went on to a private *accademia*, 'where the best thing I heard was little Linley'.[159]

Wednesday saw him at Hempson's for breakfast with Nardini and Linley. 'The former played an old solo of Tartini delightfully ... [and] the little man played a great many of Nardini's things'. At night there was a grand *accademia* in the house of Signor Domenico Baldigiani: 'Nardini led, and played a solo admirably, little Linley played a concerto very well – Mr Hempson one on the flute ... and some *misses* played and sang vilely.' The *improvvisatrice* was there too and sang a *scena* from an opera by Gaetano Latilla, with recitative and aria accompanied by Nardini and Tom, 'in which the music was charming – full of expression and new passages'.[160] But Burney longed to see Corilla's wonderful talent of composing and speaking verses extempore upon any given subject.[161]

On the night of the 13th his wishes were to have been met at a party in her own house, but it didn't go according to plan:

> *There was Nardini, the little Linley ... and 2 or 3 more of her* [Corilla's] *particular friends and we begun* [sic] *to be very comfortable and she in a very good disposition to satisfy my great curiosity concerning the manner of pronouncing and accompanying poems 'al l'improvistà', when behold! A heap of disagreeable people came in and spoilt all – there was nothing but politicks going forward, and every other subject but music and poetry'...* [He tried to guide the talk back to music by asking when eunuchs were first used as singers. This] *'was discussed a long time, but to no useful purpose ... [and] I was obliged to come away from hence without my errand.'*[162]*

---

* Burney may never have heard one of Corilla's extempore performances, but an English visitor who did, a year or two later, likened her to the Pythian Prophetess, recalling that

At some point in the next three days, according to a modern Italian version of his *Musical Journey in Italy*, Burney at last saw the *improvvisatrice* at work, and observed with great interest that she performed while holding her violin 'in her lap, thus resembling the 10th Muse [Sappho]'. In addition to 'her extraordinary talent for improvising verses on any subject', he noted that she was capable of playing the *tutti* part of an orchestral score on her violin, and that she sang 'with great expression and skill'. Sometimes, there were trios at Corilla's house, with Nardini in the main part, Corilla in the second, and Burney himself accompanying them on the viola.[163]

Sunday the 16th was Burney's last day, and after doing the rounds of all his new friends to say goodbye, he found himself again at Corilla's in the evening, where there was music and a great deal of company but no further improvising. It was probably there that he took his leave of his new young friend Tom. Summing up his impression of Florentine music before he pressed on to Rome, Burney was harsh in his criticism. He said that with the exception of Nardini, Campioni and Dôtel in the Duke's band, and the castratos Manzuoli and Giacomo Veroli, who were 'singing birds of passage', music was worse served in the Tuscan capital than in any other great town in Italy.[164]

Perhaps this disagreeable parting shot put him in a bad mood because, when he went back to the Black Eagle, he had a row with the waiter and a row with the postilion, both of whom seemed to be in league to fleece him, he believed, and at the Porta Romana he had further rows with the coachman and Custom House officers, before finally setting out for Rome on the 17th.[165]

Thomas was on his own again, and missing his indefatigable companion, when a letter arrived which brought back memories of

---

her manner was rather cold as she began singing 'her unpremeditated strains with great variety of thought and elegance of language', accompanied by two violins. But gradually she became more animated, her voice rising, her eyes sparkling, and the rapidity and beauty of her expressions and ideas seemed supernatural'. (John Moore, quoting a friend, in *A View of Society and Manners in Italy* ...vol iii, 1786, pp. 21–22.)

an even dearer, more special friend. The letter was addressed to him care of the Gavard des Pivets family. He had never seen the hand before, but he knew immediately whose it was. It was dated Bologna, 10 September 1770, and as he gently broke the seal, he saw that the writer was indeed Wolfgang Mozart, trapped in Bologna after visiting Rome, where he had been invested with a papal knighthood of the Order of the Golden Spur, and before travelling up to Milan, where he was due to rehearse his opera, *Mitridate*.

'My dear Friend', it began – all in Italian, 'Here is a letter at last! Indeed I am very late in replying to your charming letter addressed to me at Naples, which, however, I only received two months after you had written it.' Wolfgang then went on to explain that he and his father had hoped to travel from Bologna to Milan via Florence, 'and thus to surprise you, arriving unexpectedly…'. But one of the horses of their two-seater carriage had stumbled on the road to Bologna, and his father had gashed his leg rather badly, so he had had to stay in bed for three weeks. As a result they had missed the good weather necessary for the journey over the mountains to Florence, and would now have to travel to Milan via Parma instead:

> *I assure you that this accident has annoyed us very much. I would do everything in my power to have the pleasure of embracing my dear friend, and my father and I would very much like to see Sigr. Gavard again, together with his dearest and most courteous family, to say nothing of Signora Corinna [Corilla] and Sigr. Nardini, and then to return to Bologna. This we would do indeed, if we had the slightest hope of recovering even the costs of our journey…*

Referring to Tom's last letter, Wolfgang remembered that Tom said he had lost both the engravings they had given him in Florence, so his father, who wanted to give Tom a present, had bought some replacements, and would send them on to Florence if Tom would supply a safe address. And the letter ended:

Keep me in your friendship and believe that my
affection for you will endure for ever.
  Bologna, 10th September, 1770.
  Your most devoted servant and loving friend,
  Amadeo Wolfgango Mozart *

There was a P.S. from Leopold Mozart:

Please be so gracious as to give our compliments to all our friends,
both ladies and gentlemen.
  Leopoldo Mozart.

Thomas will have been deeply touched by the tone of the letter, but bitterly disappointed by its news, for it now looked as though they might not meet again before the Mozarts returned to Salzburg, and perhaps never, because Tom was due back in England in six months. He took his friend's loving words to heart, and kept the precious letter as one of his most treasured possessions for the rest of his life.

It is a curious and lamentable fact that not a single letter from Tom, and only this one letter to him, has survived to the present day. Yet it is inconceivable that his parents and his siblings didn't write during his three years in Italy, or that he didn't write to them. In Florence there was plenty going on to write home about – and in Bath the very springs would soon be boiling with drama – Linley drama.

---

* The whereabouts of the original of this letter are unknown. According to Edward Holmes in his *Life of Mozart* (1845) it was then in the possession of Tom's brother, the Rev Ozias Linley, of Dulwich College, who told him that Tom 'esteemed this document, in the handwriting of the composer of *Don Giovanni*, beyond all price'. At one point in the early 19th century it was owned by the Duchess of Gloucester who gave it back to the Linleys. By 1898 it was in the hands of the Novello family, who allowed Giulio Piccini Jarro to publish the text in his *l'Origine della maschera di Stentorello*, from which this translation was taken by Emily Anderson (Trans. and Ed.), in her *The Letters of Mozart and His Family*, Macmillan, 1989, pp. 160–61. In the twentieth century the original autograph was rediscovered, and sold in Marburg in 1975. It is now in a private collection.

V

The Maid of Bath

Two years had passed since Tom left home for Italy, much had happened and much more was yet to happen. The Duke of Grafton had resigned as Prime Minister of a Whig administration, and Lord North had replaced him with his 'Ministry of the King's Friends'; the invention of the 'Spinning Jenny' had given a fillip to the Industrial Revolution, and the Boston Massacre had pushed America closer to war; Captain Cook discovered Botany Bay; Gainsborough painted *The Blue Boy* – and in Oxford, undergraduates rioted for a glimpse of Tom's beautiful sister, Elizabeth.

The Linleys were still living in Bath, still running the music there, but word had spread about Elizabeth's voice, her grace and beauty, and invitations were pouring in for performances further afield. On 19 March 1770 she sang in Handel's oratorio *Messiah* 'before a very crouded Audience' in the Holywell Music Room in Oxford. The man from the *Public Advertiser* joined her fans:

> *Miss Linley, from Bath* [is] *a young Lady of whose rising Merit the World may justly form the most pleasing Expectations. In the Air, 'I know that my Redeemer liveth', it was impossible which to admire most, the inimitable Sweetness of her Voice, or the enchanting Simplicity of her Manner of Singing: Add to these the Elegance of her Form and the Beauty of her Features, it is no*

Wonder that she made a deep Impression on the Hearts of many
young Academics, who endeavoured by their unanimous Applause
to testify their Approbation ... [166]

On Monday 14 May, in the same venue, Elizabeth sang Dr Burney's anthem, *I will love Thee, O Lord, my strength*, for soprano, chorus and orchestra, which he had written as his MusD exercise at Oxford on 22 June 1769. It did not go well, but neither Elizabeth nor Burney was to blame. The papers reported that Elizabeth's singing and looks so inflamed the undergraduates that it produced a sort of contagious delirium that led to a riot. But there was another problem too: the Italian work forming the second part, Pergolesi's *Stabat Mater*. Objecting to this 'Monkish Rime', the undergraduates drove the performers off the stage in a hail of loud hisses and catcalls – '"Oratorios for ever!", they cried, with catcalls, groans and screams, "No Italian music. No Popery!"' – and a riot ensued, with some students trying to rip out the benches. After the Room had been cleared and an hour had passed, Elizabeth and the other performers rallied, and launched into the Pergolesi. A Junior Fellow of Queen's College who witnessed it all, wrote to a friend afterwards implying that the riot was as much in favour of the delicious Elizabeth as it was an expression of disapproval of the Latin cantata.[167]

It is not known whether Burney was present – and if he was, what he may have reported to Elizabeth about his adventures in Florence with Tom. But it is known that he adored 'that most charming and accomplished of female beings ... and regarded her as an angel in correctness and form, conversation and voice, indeed I cd neither look at her nor listen to her divine breathings but with extatic [sic] rapture.'[168]

Back in the same Oxford venue in July Elizabeth took part in Handel's oratorio *Judas Maccabaeus*, and the *Bath Chronicle* reported that 'Miss Linley, a young lady from Bath, whose general excellence in every accomplishment which can adorn and render amiable the female character, and whose particular talent, as a singer, justify the most extravagant description.'[169]

And at the end of July she made an appearance at the Three Choirs Festival in Worcester, singing Handel, Purcell and Boyce with the castrato Tenducci (a friend from earlier Bath days), and a band led by the virtuoso Felice Giardini (both old acquaintances of Tom's from his Bath days). After performing *Messiah* in the cathedral on the Friday morning, she and Tenducci gave a concert of their favourite songs in the College Hall, and Elizabeth was hailed as the most accomplished singer that this country has ever produced. 'Having a sweet and powerful voice, with very superior musical talents, she acquired such favour with the public, that she gave popularity to any performance in which she took a principal part.'[170]

Later that year Elizabeth was singing *I know that my Redeemeth Liveth* in Salisbury Cathedral when a bullfinch, mistaking her 'for a feathered Chorister of the Woods', perched on the Gallery above her, 'and accompanied her with the musical warblings of its little Throat'. But it flew away when 'a lubberly, senseless Fellow that played on the Bassoon … took Aim with his Instrument, as with a Gun.'[171]

And in November she was in Oxford again singing in Handel's *l'Allegro ed il Penseroso* (the third part, *il Moderato*, was usually omitted by the Georgians) 'to a very crouded and brilliant Audience' in the Music Room. The *Public Advertiser* reported that 'The excellence of Miss Linley's Merit was display'd through every Part with inimitable Grace and Elegance, particularly in the Air, "Sweet Bird that Shun'st the Noise of Folly" (which may have reminded Elizabeth of the bullfinch episode in Salisbury), and in two Italian Songs from the Opera *Orione* by Mr Bach'.[172]

The legend was laid, and everyone wanted a piece of Elizabeth Linley. George Colman, the manager of the Theatre Royal, Covent Garden, begged her father to allow her to join his company, but Linley refused: he would never stoop so low as to sell her as an actress, he said. Nevertheless he took advantage of Colman's enthusiasm and buttoned up a deal for 71 oratorios for 200 guineas with one clear benefit performance, all proceeds to Linley.[173]

Years later Burney's daughter tried to explain the Elizabeth Linley phenomenon. She sang, she said, 'with a sweetness and pathos of voice and expression that, joined to the beauty of her nearly celestial face, almost maddened, with admiring enthusiasm, not only the susceptible young students, then in the first glow of the dominion of the passions, but even the gravest and most profound among the learned professors of the University ...'[174]

In another autograph fragment of memoir, written after Elizabeth's death, Burney himself went further. Arguing that Elizabeth's beauty alone could never have accounted for her extraordinary success, he pointed out that her voice had 'a native Sweetness & true Intonation'. And in explaining why, he reveals something of the teaching that produced her brother Tom's musicianship:

> By being Educated from her Infancy by her Father, a Master of
> great experience & established Reputation ... Music was become
> a Language wch she read with as much facility as her Mother
> Tongue. And she had so long studied the Oratorios of Handel & so
> frequently sung the best songs in them that she seemed to execute
> them with more propriety of Expression than any one has ever
> done before ... There was something so pure, chaste & judicious
> in her manner of Executing them that joined to her articulate
> and correct pronunciation of the Words, seraphic Looks, and
> truly natural and Pathetic Expression ...[175]

There was also a psychic intimacy about her performance, so that all those in the audience felt she was singing to and for them individually.[176] Elizabeth Linley, 'queen-bird of the Nightingales of Bath', was a celebrity, the Jenny Lind of the day.[177] She was not only the finest, most beautiful and most exciting singer in England, but a cult figure, and the dramatic unfolding of her love life in the early 1770s simply spread the word.

Her trouble, as one biographer has written, was men: 'Her good looks were her undoing ... [and] ... she was often frightened and puzzled by the effect she had'.[178] Her particular admirers included the counter-tenor and composer Thomas Norris; a hot-headed Oxford undergraduate called Nathaniel Brassey Halhead; a married rogue by name of 'Captain' Thomas Mathews; and the two sons of the Irish actor and theatre manager, Thomas Sheridan. But there was another, more pressing suitor than all the others because he was so rich, and because Mr Linley put his heart and soul into the match: Walter Long of South Wraxall, an elderly but honourable bachelor with vast acres in Wiltshire, and an income of ten thousand a year.

Things began to get difficult at the end of 1770 when the Linleys, coming up in the world, largely thanks to Elizabeth's earnings, left Orchard Street and moved into a grand new house in The Crescent (now Royal Crescent). 'Captain' Mathews became a regular visitor, charming the parents but alarming the sixteen-year-old Elizabeth

The Royal Crescent, Bath (engraving after a drawing by T. H. Shepherd, in John Britton, *Bath and Bristol*, 1829).

with his sexual advances. She felt she could not report the details to her father, in case he called Mathews to account and worse trouble ensued, so the harassment increased.

Then the Sheridans, newly moved to Bath, started paying visits to the Linleys, cautiously because they considered mere musicians were socially inferior. But there had to be contact between the two families because Mrs Sheridan was taking singing lessons from Mr Linley, and Thomas Sheridan, the father, was coaching Elizabeth for his 'Attic Entertainments', a conflation of songs (including Purcell's *Ode to Cecilia*, sung by Elizabeth), concertos, and recitations (including Dryden's *A Song for St Cecilia's Day*) declaimed by Sheridan. The purpose of the Entertainments was to restore the ancient art of public speaking, but the critics were unimpressed, and the series petered out.[179]

The consequence of the meetings in The Crescent was that Charles Sheridan, the younger son, fell in love with Elizabeth, until he realised that his passion would probably bring him more pain than happiness. So he found himself a post in the British Embassy in Sweden, unaware that he was leaving his elder brother, Richard, to fill the gap. Neither Richard nor Elizabeth admitted their feelings, but Elizabeth knew she had found the one.

Mr Linley, 'from motives of ambition, avarice, or low prudence', was determined the marriage to Long should go ahead, regardless of his daughter's feelings.[180] Settlements were drawn up, jewels presented, a wedding date fixed. But Elizabeth was equally determined not to marry old Long, and she wrote to tell him that she could not go ahead with the match because of her attachment to another. Long decently accepted her refusal, took responsibility for breaking the engagement, settled £3000 on her in compensation (nearly a quarter of a million pounds at today's valuations), and begged her to keep the jewels. Only after this did Elizabeth tell her father that she had unilaterally turned Long down. She was tired of being dragged around theatres, churches and concert halls, being 'caressed and applauded'. She hated the publicity of her profession. 'If she married at all,' Elizabeth told her father, 'she would marry only to be *free*'.[181]

Lurking in Bath that winter of 1770/71 was a scurrilous actor, wit and playwright called Samuel Foote, the one-legged manager of the Theatre Royal, Haymarket. He picked up the gossip from the wagging tongues of Bath, and decided the story of Elizabeth Linley and her suitors would make a good play. Working quickly he finished it in a few months, and it opened in the summer of 1771. *The Maid Of Bath* satirised everyone in the story, from Elizabeth herself (Kitty Linnet) and her mother, to Long (Solomon Flint) and Mathews (Major Rackett). It was hardly great literature, but it was funny and naughty, and audiences loved it. Long and Mr Linley and Elizabeth herself threatened legal action, but no action was ever brought to court. In any case Elizabeth had little to worry about on her account since Foote had portrayed her as the blameless victim,

Jean-François Gilles Colson, *Samuel Foote*, 1769 (oil on canvas, 55.9 × 45.7 cm, National Portrait Gallery, London).

as pure and dignified as the figure she cut with the public. 'Seeing her sweet, pathetic face and hearing her sweet, pathetic voice,' Clementina Black wrote, the public could believe no ill of her.[182]

News of the play set the cat among the pigeons in Bath. Even if Elizabeth's parents refused to acknowledge the shenanigans under their very roof, Richard Sheridan sensed what was going on, and when Elizabeth confirmed it, Mathews, formerly Richard's inseparable companion, became his sworn enemy. There was an element here of the pot calling the kettle black, for Richard himself, though fascinating and brilliant, was to become, but later, no less of a womanizer and no less harassing, threatening, vindictive, dishonourable and even violent. Elizabeth, who was terrified of amorous entanglements, was grateful for Richard's protection, and trusted his integrity, and in March 1772 she told him she was desperate to escape from all the sordid publicity, and had conceived a daring plan.

VI

Partenza

On his own in his last year in Italy, with neither Mozart nor Burney as company, Tom knuckled down to work with Nardini again, studying technical exercises in bowing, tuning and intonation. According to the young Bohemian composer Adalbert Gyrowetz, who heard Nardini playing a decade later, 'purity and sureness of tone … [and] well controlled, firm command of the bow' were the cardinal virtues of his playing, and these were the qualities that Tom wanted to acquire.[183] Nardini was also giving the boy plenty of ensemble practice with the other students in his school, and with professionals in the Grand Duke's band.

Thomas could not have been a student in Florence at a more propitious time than those early years of the reign of Pietro Leopoldo, who was actively reforming the city's church music, through Campioni (his *maestro di cappella*), his instrumentalists and singers.[184] But an even more important aspect of the Grand Duke's musical influence, which was to give Tom a uniquely significant grounding for his future role in London, was the remarkable series of performances of the operas and oratorios of Handel which flourished under his protection.

There was quite a machine at work here. The British Resident, Sir Horace Mann, acquired the music of the works from his friend at home in England, Horace Walpole, asking for '12 *oratorii* of Hendal [*sic*], with their scores, that is all the parts', and promising to send in exchange 'all the pretty airs I can get'.[185] Lord Cowper then paid for the productions at his Villa Palmieri and in the Florentine *accademie*, lending his own band directed by Salvador Pazzaglia. And finally the Grand Duke provided further musicians and singers from his court band, and the prestige of his patronage.

The American musicologist John A. Rice has written that *Alexander's Feast, Messiah, Acis and Galatea* and possibly *Judas Maccabaeus* all received what seem to have been their first performances outside the British Isles in Florence between 1768 and 1772.[186] Tom may have played in some of these performances, and would certainly have attended rehearsals, for this was to be his bread and butter as a professional musician in Bath and London.[187]

Just before he left Florence, he was involved in a Mass which was probably his musical farewell to Italy. It happened on 30 August 1771 when the Grand Duke marshalled all his musicians for a performance of Campioni's *Mass for the Feast of St Rosa of Lima*, in the thirteenth-century Dominican convent of San Domenico nel Maglio (now the School of Military Health) in Florence. Campioni himself conducted, and Nardini led the large orchestra, dividing the violins to left and right of the nave. On one side all the violins were his students, on the other side they were all virtuosi led by Giovanni Felice Mosell. The band ran to more than forty players, and included the cellist Francesco Piantanida, with twenty-four of the court's finest singers, among them the castrato Giacomo Veroli, who added extempore cadenzas to the 'Gloria' and the 'Credo' of the Mass. According to the *Gazzetta toscana*, a large audience of foreigners, nobility, and people was much moved, in particular by the violin concerto which Nardini played between the Epistle and the Gospel, 'with every imaginable delicacy and insurpassable perfection.'[188]

After the performance, a grateful Pietro Leopoldo rewarded Campioni with a gold snuffbox filled with zecchini, 'as a token of gratitude from His Royal Munificence'.[189] Campioni was renowned for his interest in old music – he possessed one of the most complete collections of the madrigals of the sixteenth and seventeenth centuries – and his love spread not only to his employer, the Grand Duke, but to young Tom too, who would never forget. No wonder his father, waiting impatiently at home in Bath, was convinced that the boy would soon shake up the musical world.

Packing his violin, his music, his books and not forgetting the presents he had bought for his family, Tom called on Mann, to make his formal farewell, and on his special friends, Nardini, the Hempsons, Corilla Olimpica and the Gavard des Pivets family, all of whom had made his eighteen months in Florence so happy and so fruitful. He also took his leave of his fellow student Joseph Agus, who was to follow him to London in 1773, when the two picked up their friendship.*

There is some suggestion that Tom may have returned to England by ship from Livorno, to avoid having to fight his way back overland on his own, but, however he travelled, he arrived back in Bath in time for the start of the season in October 1771, and was immediately thrust into the limelight as leader of the orchestra at his father's Wednesday evening subscription concerts in the newly-completed Upper Assembly Rooms. These had been opened with a *ridotto*† on 30 September, and were soon regarded as 'the most noble and elegant of any [Assembly Rooms] in the kingdom'.[190]

But what did his family make of the prodigal back from three years away in Italy? Tom had been a timorous boy of twelve when he left, now he was a polished young man of fifteen. What were the visible effects of three years' exposure to Italian culture, weather, language, behaviour, away from parental control? The Scottish philosopher Adam Smith was later to claim that Grand Tourists came home 'more conceited, more unprincipled, more dissipated,

---

* See footnote on p. 106.

† a public entertainment with music and dancing, sometimes in masquerade.

and more incapable of serious application' than they were before they left.[191] Very possibly, but Tom was not a Grand Tourist, he was a student. As a musician, he had perfected his violin technique, giving it a *finezza* that would bring him fame in London, he had learned the art of playing in both chamber ensembles and orchestras, and deepened his knowledge and understanding of the orchestral and choral repertoire. As a young man he had grown as strong in mind, managing on his own for three vital years of puberty, as he was in body, after all that healthy Mediterranean food and sunshine.

But he may not have been aware of how Italian he had become. Though his early upbringing in a household ruled by his masterful father had given him the habits of reticence, inhibition, even secretiveness, he was by nature graceful, artistic and an actor. All his instincts would have responded to the theatricality of Italian behaviour, and the warmth of its feelings. In no time he would have picked up the music of the speech and the sheer performance of Italian social interaction, with its waving hands and arms, its kinetic facial expressions, its exuberance, excess and passion. If not by now as affected as Horace Mann, he would certainly have been kissing and hugging to the manner born. His sisters would have loved it, but his father and mother might have winced at such unEnglish behaviour, for effeteness was considered dangerously close to effeminacy, and effeminacy, as far as the Georgian gentleman was concerned, spelled a crime of the blackest dye. This was the period of the camp excesses of the returning Grand Tourists, and in particular the grotesque extremes of the macaronis – with their little 'fascinator' hats perched high on powdered wigs, faces powdered and rouged, ruffled lace at the wrist, and tight little suits of pastel silk – and polite society associated such behaviour with 'corruption, weakness, cowardice, luxury, immorality and the unbridled play of the passions'.[192]

For all his '*Bacco!*'s, '*Caro!*'s and '*Che bello!*'s, Tom will have been welcomed home with open arms. Only one thing would have prevented his family killing the fatted calf, and that was his sister Elizabeth – and the continuing drama of her love life. The whole world talked of nothing else, as Tom discovered when he stopped at a bookseller's while waiting for the coach to Bath, and saw 'Miss Linley ... in the fashionable Dress of the Year' on the cover of Newbery's *Ladies Pocket-Book*, with a description inside of the New Assembly-Rooms at Bath, and 'a Genuine account of the amour of W. L. Esq, and the celebrated *Maid of Bath*'.

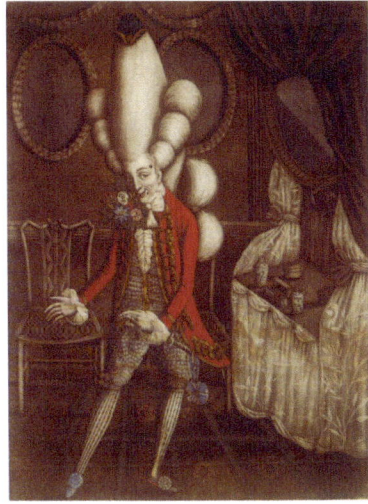

Philip Dawe, *The Macaroni, A Real Character at the Late Masquerade*, 1773 (mezzotint published by John Bowles, London, 3 July 1773).

VII

Elopement and Duels

Elizabeth was tired of being the centre of gossip, tired of Captain Mathews' predatory attentions, of men ogling her every time she appeared on a concert platform, of the stress of performing all over England, of her father's constant demands, and she wanted an escape. Ever since *The Maid of Bath* had opened in the summer of 1771, she had resolved to leave Bath and to run away to France till she came of age four years hence. There she would be safe from the 'infamy' of her pursuer, who had threatened 'to ruin her reputation and carry her off by force'.[193]

For a while she told no one, but she had time to think while sitting for a new portrait by Gainsborough in early March 1772 (see p.13). Actually she wasn't sitting but standing, for a joint picture in a sylvan setting, with her sister Maria. Elizabeth is shown in a blue dress, looking wistfully away to the left; Maria, in a brown dress, sits, bright-eyed and smiling, with a score in her lap, looking directly at the viewer. It must have been at this time that Elizabeth made up her mind to consult two new friends of her own age.

With Sheridan senior back in Ireland after the failure of his Attic Entertainments in London, the Sheridan and Linley families had been mixing more easily. Elizabeth had grown fond of the two daughters, Alicia and Elizabeth (Betsy), and she now told them about her plan. They all realised that she would need a man to

Left: John Hoppner, *Richard Brinsley Sheridan* (Photo © Christie's Images / Bridgeman Images). Right: Thomas Gainsborough, *Mrs Richard Brinsley Sheridan*, *c*. 1775 (oil on canvas, The George W. Elkins Collection, 1924, Philadelphia Museum of Art)

accompany her. Richard Sheridan had recently confessed to his sisters, but not yet to Elizabeth, that he was in love with her, so they encouraged him to offer his assistance in conducting her across the Channel and placing her in a convent in Picardy, where she would be safe from all danger. (One of the sisters had spent time there herself and offered to write a letter of introduction.)[194]

It is not known whether Elizabeth confided the details to Tom, but, given the closeness of brother and sister, and the fact that he himself was probably sitting for Gainsborough at this same time,* which would have given them a chance to talk confidentially away from home, it seems unlikely she did not – particularly as Tom was to play a small part in the plan.

On the morning of Wednesday 18 March Elizabeth refused to get out of bed, complaining, as usual in those stressful months of 1772, of headaches and breathlessness – early signs, though no one recognised them, of the onset of tuberculosis. She was due in Bristol that evening for a rehearsal of Handel's oratorio *Judas Maccabaeus* in the King Street Theatre, with her father, sister Maria and Tom (billed in advanced notices as 'Master Linley (15) ... musical prodigy ... first violin in the orchestra').[195] She had managed to stay calm till now, but her mother had had a miscarriage the day before, and suddenly

---

* For the portrait in the red coat with a cocked hat under his left arm (see dustjacket cover), now in Dulwich Picture Gallery.

it all became too much for her. Fearing that she 'should go distracted', she would not leave her room.[196] Tom, in faithful support, pointed out to their father that they could probably manage without her on this occasion, as it was primarily an orchestral rehearsal, and, if needed, Maria could cover. So he and the rest of the family set off without her.

Once they had gone, Richard Sheridan came round to The Crescent with two sedan chairs and four chairman. After seating Elizabeth in one, and putting her trunk in the other, he left a letter on the hall table addressed to Elizabeth's father. In it he explained that, at Elizabeth's own urgent request, he was removing her from Bath in order to escape the offensive advances of Captain Mathews. Then he escorted the two chairs to a carriage that was waiting on the London road, with horses, postilions and the wife of one of Sheridan's servants, who had been paid to serve as chaperone.[197] Sheridan helped Elizabeth up into the carriage beside the chaperone, and climbed in opposite. Once they were all settled the carriage set off through the night, bound for London a hundred miles away.

Around the corner in The Circus, Gainsborough knew what had happened, and why – and he believed that Tom's father was partly to blame:

> Miss Linley has walk'd off sure enough with young Sheridan; but He is not at the bottom of the mischief... M---ws is the scoundrel, supposed (and with much reason) to have undone the poor Girl – it vexes me much ... because I was just finishing her Picture for the Exhibition. I feel for poor Linley [senior] much. Though in my opinion he did not quite take care enough.[198]

The chaise with the runaways reached London early on the 19th, and, with money borrowed from a friend there, they made their way down to Dover, before a rough crossing to Dunkirk. Elizabeth had never been to sea before and was very sick, but Richard looked after her so tenderly that she began to realise that he might return the feelings she felt for him. At Calais, in a tavern, Richard confessed that he had loved her for months, and pointed out that he could not go ahead with the convent plan, even if that is what she still wanted, because it would be assumed in England that they had eloped, so she would never be able to return home as anything but his wife. Would she therefore marry him? Why, yes, she would. An amenable cleric was found in a nearby village – a Catholic priest who often conducted such irregular ceremonies, no questions asked – and by 15 April they were married.[199] But as they were both minors, and both Protestants, it is unlikely that the ceremony carried any legal weight.

The pair then took a coach to Lille, where Richard arranged for Elizabeth to stay in the guest rooms of a convent, while he put up in an hotel. Almost immediately Elizabeth fell ill again, suffering from fainting fits, and an English doctor (probably guessing the tuberculosis which was to take Elizabeth and her two younger sisters while still in their thirties), prescribed rest, warmth and the expert care of his own wife in their house.

Meanwhile two things had happened at home. The English papers announced that 'the eldest Miss Linley of Bath, justly celebrated and admired for her Musical Abilities, [has] set off with Mr Sheridan, jun. on a Matrimonial Expedition to Scotland'.[200] And a fortnight later Mathews placed a threatening notice in the Bath paper accusing Richard Sheridan of being 'an infamous liar and a treacherous scoundrel', and warning that if he dared to repeat his 'many malevolent Incendiaries' he could depend on receiving the proper reward for his villainy.[201]

Throughout it all the Linleys' concert life went on. Five days after the Handel in Bristol, Tom was engaged to play in Metastasio's serenata *Endimione* at the newly-restored Little Theatre in the Haymarket – with Abel on the gamba, Fischer playing oboe and Wendling flute. The singers included Cecilia Grassi, otherwise Mrs J. C. Bach, with whom the boy violinist was pleased to use his

Italian again.[202] The following week Tom was leading his father's orchestra in performances of *Acis and Galatea*, *Judas Maccabaeus* and *Messiah* at the New Assembly Rooms in Bath, and between the acts of each oratorio Tom played a violin concerto and his father played an organ concerto.[203] As fast as Tom's engagements multiplied, so his reputation grew, though he was still not yet sixteen. The *Bristol Journal* noted that with his 'graceful Manner of bowing' and 'Polish of Tone and Manner', he was a 'most pleasing Musician'.[204]

With Elizabeth gone, and Richard's letter explaining the reasons, it gradually dawned on Linley what his daughter had been going through, and he began to see Mathews not as a family friend but as his daughter's persecutor. At first he seems to have made no immediate attempt to find Elizabeth, nor did he or his wife express any concern about her. They accepted that Richard had removed her for her own safety, and that he would bring her back in due course. But as the days passed, and news filtered through that they were in France, Linley at last resolved to fetch her back.

He arrived in Lille on 24 April, and found Richard, who warned him that Elizabeth was ill and weak and close to breakdown, so he was to proceed with gentleness and kindness. There was no mention of the 'marriage'. Aware at last of his own share of the blame, Linley fell in line, but, ever the businessman, he told his daughter that he wanted her home as soon as possible to fulfil her engagements. Realising that she now had something of an upper hand, Elizabeth struck a bargain. She would agree to return, if her father agreed to reduce her workload, and to allow her to refuse any concert she did not like, whatever the reason. Furthermore she made him promise that once she had carried out all the engagements he had made in her name, she should be allowed to return to France and enter a convent at any time if she so wished.

Linley, Elizabeth and Richard arrived back in England on 29 April. Breaking their journey home at a tavern in London, father and daughter went to sleep, exhausted after the sea voyage, the coach ride up from Dover and the weeks of high drama, while Richard crept out into the night to find Mathews.

At an address revealed by a mutual friend, a place called Crutched Friars near Tower Hill, he located the man who had once been his inseparable companion, and was now his bitter foe. In an all-night confrontation that verged on farce – Richard brandishing his pistols, Mathews in his nightshirt, the door between them locked and the key lost – Richard forced his adversary to agree to publish a retraction of his public insult, though he himself had still not actually seen it. After a lot of talking through the door, like Pyramus and Thisbe through the wall, but rather less amiably, Mathews finally gave his word, and Richard returned to the tavern at seven in the morning.

On 6 May he and Linley and Elizabeth made their way back to Bath, father and daughter travelling down in one post chaise, Richard in another, determined to keep the marriage a secret.[205] In Bath, as Linley and Elizabeth headed for home in The Crescent, Richard turned towards the offices of the *Bath Chronicle*, where he was shown Mathews' notice of six weeks earlier, and saw, for the first time, how gravely insulting it was. He now realised that the second notice which Mathews had promised to publish would be meaningless, in the light of this first one. Daggers were drawn, battle was on.

On Tom's sixteenth birthday the *Bath Chronicle* carried Mathews' apology. Richard did not wait to read it. Instead he took the coach back to London to call Mathews to account, by the laws of honour. As the challenged party, Mathews had the right to choose the weapons, and decided on swords. Where to stage the encounter was a knottier problem. Strictly speaking duelling was illegal, and neither party wanted to risk arrest (even though the courts generally took a lenient view of these gentlemanly affairs of honour). Richard proposed Hyde Park, where the combatants' seconds could keep an eye out for observers, but Mathews thought it was too public, and opted for a tavern in Covent Garden. Then he changed his mind and decided that the park was preferable after all, before changing his mind again and returning to the tavern. There the duel was eventually fought, in a private room, illuminated by candelabra held aloft by the duellists' seconds.

After a thrust and a parry or two, Mathews was disarmed, and begged for his life. Richard asked for his sword, Mathews reluctantly handed it over – then snapped it in two, demanding that Mathews should fight on, or publish a full apology. Mathews agreed, but, by the same laws of honour, his surrender was deemed ungentlemanly, and he was forced 'to fly to the mountains of Wales to forget his infamy among strangers'. News spreads far and fast, and 'shunned like the pestilence', he felt obliged to challenge Sheridan to a second duel.[206]

Elizabeth had shrieked and fainted in advance of the duel, but she was calmer when she learned that Richard was safe, and her tormentor out of the way.[207] The Linleys continued their concert life, with no respite for Elizabeth, despite the agreement made with her father in Lille. On 2 June there was *Acis and Galatea* in Bristol, and for four nights the following week they were in Chester for a feast of further Handel in the Cathedral. According to the local paper 'the amazing Powers of the two Miss Linleys [Elizabeth and her younger sister Mary] conspired to render the Entertainment as great and excellent as ... ever was produced from the human voice'. On one of the middle nights in Chester there was a concert in the Exchange Hall, where , 'amongst other capital Pieces, Mr Linley, jun. distinguished himself as one of the greatest Masters on the Violin which this Nation has produced'.[208]

But there was more than music in Chester. During their three days in the city Elizabeth and Mary attended their very first Masquerade – dressed as a Spanish Lady and a Shepherdess. In a secret letter to Richard, who was still lying low after the duel, Elizabeth said she hated it, and despised the impudent looks of the men. There was 'such a scene of confusion and fright' that she fainted, only coming to when someone started pulling her by the legs, 'as you would a dead horse', and she gave him 'a hearty kick'. The whole thing, she said, was 'a nonsensical puppet show', and she was as bored by it as she would have been by a long sermon.[209] There is no mention of Tom in any of the sources, yet it seems unlikely that he wouldn't have wanted to dress up and join the fun, as he must have done many times in theatrical Florence. But perhaps his father whisked him away.

Then on 25 June they were all in Cambridge for Handel's *Samson*, before a crowded audience in Great St. Mary's Church, at which 'the two Miss Linley's were received with universal applause'.[210] But what the newspapers did not record is that Elizabeth was taken ill during the performance, fainted and had to be carried out, which, as she wrote to Richard, 'raised no small bustle among the Cantabs'. It seems that the undergraduates were as averse to some of the music planned for later in the week as the Oxford under-graduates had been in 1770, and 'a very great riot' was expected. Again, nothing about that in the papers.[211]

Elizabeth's letters to Richard, or 'Horatio' as she had called him ever since his 'heroic rescue' of her, had to be kept secret because both sets of parents were 'very industrious in keeping them sepa-rate'.[212] Elizabeth was on such a tight rein that she could not go anywhere without her father or mother; in particular the Sheridans' house was strictly out of bounds.[213]

Unknown to Elizabeth, who was singing in Oxford, Richard was busy planning the details of his second duel with Mathews. The two men met on the top of King's Down above Bristol, at dawn on 1 July. Both were drunk, and agreed that neither of their seconds was to interfere under any circumstances: this fight was a life struggle, and one of them was to die. Richard had the choice of weapons this time, and went for swords, having been trained in the art by the fore-most fencing master in the land, Domenico Angelo. Mathews, all too conscious of his failure with swords last time, called for pistols but Richard refused. The fight started 'with 'intense animosity and frantic violence', as Richard rushed on Mathews and both men fell to the ground, breaking their swords as they did so. Rolling down a slope they hacked at each other with bits of broken sword. Mathews' jagged fragment was longer and sharper and holding it over Richard he offered him his life if he would surrender. Richard refused: 'No, by God, I won't', he said, whereupon Mathews stabbed him through the ear and neck. It was soon clear that Richard was dangerously hurt, with three or four other wounds in his face, chest and ribs, so Mathews left him for dead and fled the scene in a waiting chaise and four horses.

The seconds carried Richard to another waiting chaise, and drove to a nearby coaching inn, where two surgeons examined him, and pronounced his condition to be very serious. But the inn was so noisy and hot that his sisters, who had been summoned from Bath, insisted on taking him home. When they arrived, he was not only still conscious but reading reports of the duel in the papers: he was hoping to find out whether he was dead or alive, he told them.[214] The general opinion was that he would never recover, but within a fortnight the Bath paper was able to report that he was out of danger.[215]

The news of the duel spread fast. The *Bath Chronicle* carried a report the morning after it happened, and copies made their way to Oxford, where earlier in the night of the dawn duel, entirely unaware of what was about to happen on King's Down, Elizabeth, Mary, Tom and their father were taking part in a performance of *Samson* in the Sheldonian Theatre, for the benefit of the Radcliffe Infirmary. Mr Linley made sure the news was kept from Elizabeth and her siblings, who had another engagement that night and would not have been able to honour it if they knew that Richard's life was ebbing away. It was a concert of religious music, again in the Sheldonian, in which 'the two celebrated Miss Linleys were deservedly admired … and Mr Linley, jun. … gave the greatest satisfaction'.[216] A friend of Richard was there and described the atmosphere:

As her [Elizabeth's] *ignorance of the duel and its consequences were known to every person* [but her]*... her beauty, joined to the effect of her truly enchanting powers, could not fail of exciting a degree of sympathy in youthful and susceptible minds when they thought of the heavy calamity that hung over her.*[217]

It was not till she got home to Bath that Elizabeth learned about the duel and Richard's injuries, whereupon she blurted out that he was her husband, and collapsed in a faint. When she came to, she demanded to be taken to his bedside so she could nurse him, but, as she expected, neither Linley nor Sheridan senior would allow it. Both fathers were violently against the match – Sheridan because he thought Elizabeth socially inferior, Linley because Richard had no money, no job and no prospects. So the lovers were now kept more rigorously separated than ever. But Elizabeth managed to get messages to him through his sisters, and to one of these he replied. In acknowledgement she wrote back, 'Oh! My Horatio, I did not know till now how much I loved you'. If he had died, she told him, she would have dressed herself as a man and challenged Mathews herself.[218]

Elizabeth was now all but locked up at home, when she wasn't singing, and all communications were forbidden. As soon as Richard was on his feet again, he was sent to the seclusion of Epping Forest to read law, in preparation for a new life as a student at Middle Temple. Making up for wasted years at Harrow he threw himself into his studies – and dreamed of Elizabeth. She wrote to him throughout the summer and into the autumn, letter after smuggled letter, at first full of love, then full of bewilderment, and finally recriminations, because Richard answered none of them.

Meanwhile nothing stopped the Linleys' music-making. In August Tom was playing a solo in Chelsea, and on 2 September a violin concerto at a fireworks concert organised by the composer Stephen Storace in Marylebone Gardens for the King's birthday – a spectacular event involving not just 'the greatest Variety of Fire-works ever displayed at once' but also a dramatic simulation of the eruption of Mount Etna, complete with flowing lava.[219] That same night Elizabeth, Mary and their father were in Winchester per-forming *Messiah* before a grand audience including the Duke of Chandos.[220] For three days the following week the sisters and their father, but without Tom, gave more Handel at the Three Choirs Festival in Gloucester. And in November Tom led his father's orches-tra at a concert of vocal and instrumental music, with his sisters, in the New Assembly Rooms in Bath.[221]

All this activity, far and wide, was grist to the publicity mill. In September 1772 the *London Magazine, or Gentleman's Monthly Intelligencer* came out with 'an exact Likeness, neatly engraved ... of the celebrated Miss Linley, the Maid of Bath, together with anecdotes', re-telling her life story, and its culmination in the broken engagement, the elopement and the duels. The 'exact likeness' showed a shrewish young woman with tight lips, staring eyes and a long neck – a deliberately unbecoming engraving designed to reinforce the message of the issue's editorial, 'an Original Essay on What the Fair Sex are, and what they will be'. Addressing his 'dear, dear country-women', the writer of this satirical piece says he loves them all, but, with their 'wanton and lascivious airs', their dissipa-tion, drinking, bullying, romping and scolding, 'they are departing too much from the *feminine* character' and approaching 'too near the *masculine* gender.' And he goes on:

> *I warn posterity not to be surprised, if these viragos should in the reign of George the Fourth throw away the cap, the top-knot, and the tippet, and clip the petticoat close to the knee.*[222]

Long a hot ticket in the concert rooms, Elizabeth was now a hot potato too. Whether she intended it or not, her stubborn refusal to bend to her father's will was seen as unfeminine. It was even thought she had taken up the cause of women's rights, and joined the all-female, radical literary group, the Bluestocking Society.[*]

Notwithstanding the cultural politics now enveloping Elizabeth, no less a figure than the great Garrick, who had long admired her, tried to book her for the coming opera season at the Theatre Royal, Drury Lane. In the autumn of 1772 he wrote to her father to open negotiations, but Linley refused, on the grounds that his daughter was not, and never would be, a common actress, and anyway he needed to keep her under his close and personal supervision.[223] Linley agreed with an earlier Bishop of London, Edmund Gibson, who had objected when Handel wanted to use boys from the Chapel Royal in a staged performance of *Esther*: opera houses, he argued, were immoral places, unfit for ladies, boys and sacred works. Ever since then Handel's oratorios had always been performed with the singers standing respectably stationary on stage – not moving about in the acting mode which Richard Sheridan later condemned in a colourful rant to Linley, conjuring up a vision of scarlet women wantonly displaying the contours of their bodies in a 'Vortex of Temptation and Contagious Vice'.[224]

Over the winter everything changed for the Linleys, when the composer John Christopher Smith, who had been Handel's secretary and amanuensis, and the blind composer and organist John Stanley, invited Mr Linley to join a triumvirate to revive the Lenten oratorios at Drury Lane. Under the terms of the contract Linley, as music director, Elizabeth and Mary as soprano soloists, and Tom as leader of the orchestra and star violin soloist, were to share between them no less a sum than £600 for the six-week season – nearly £50,000 at today's values. Now things looked different. Drury Lane might be an opera house, but the Linleys would be taking part in oratorios, and in the oratorio season there was 'no Action on the Stage'.

---

[*] In 1778 Elizabeth Linley was depicted with a lyre in the centre of a group of 'Nine Muses in the Temple of Apollo', painted by Richard Samuel, now in the National Portrait Gallery.

Under this brilliant arrangement, Linley was able to take his three oldest children up to London, to continue to keep a careful eye on all of them, and to pocket the entire purse, since Elizabeth, Tom and Mary were still under age. The Duchess of Portland put it around that 'the oratorios are to be much the fashion as Miss Linleys are to perform',[225] and Dr Burney's daughter, Fanny, reported that 'The whole Town seems distracted about her ... Miss Linley Alone engrosses all Eyes, Ears, Hearts'.[226] The Drury Lane Theatre was besieged for *Judas Maccabaeus* on 26 February (with Tom playing a concerto by Geminiani) and again for *Acis and Galatea* on 5 March (Thomas, concerto by Nardini);* on 17 and 19 March, more performances of *Judas Maccabeus* (in the presence of the King and Queen, with the Duke and Duchess of Ancaster); *Alexander's Feast* on the 15th; and *Samson* on the 26th (again in the presence of the King and Queen and the Ancasters).

Not everyone approved of the Linleys' monopolising the oratorio season with so much Handel. A correspondent to the *Morning Chronicle* pointed out that there was much more rewarding music to be found at the Haymarket and Covent Garden, where, for example Samuel Arnold's oratorio *The Prodigal Son* was receiving 'lavish and just applause'. Would the Drury Lane audiences have gone to hear Mr Handel's 'tiresome and insipid' pieces if it weren't for the Linleys, who never offered anything new?[227]

As it happened the Linleys' repertoire was about to bring itself up to date, with the emergence in April of the first of a series of choral works by Master Tom. Ever since returning to England, and more frequently since his arrival in London for the oratorio season, he had been taking further composition lessons with his old teacher,

---

* At about this time Tom sent money to Livorno for some of Nardini's violin sonatas (Rebecca Gribble, *Musicians within the Social Hierarchies of Eighteenth-Century England: The Case of Thomas Linley Junior*, doctoral thesis, University of Southampton, 2015, p. 31, quoting an autograph letter from Nardini to Thomas Linley, Firenze, 1773, now in the James Marshall and Marie–Louise Osborn Collection, Beinecke Rare Books and Music Library, Yale University).

Boyce, and re-visiting the Chapel Royal, where he conceived the idea of writing the boys' voices into his new works.

Perhaps through Boyce, who was still Master of the King's Musick, Tom had made a firm friend of the King, who heard him playing a concerto of his own in one of the intervals of the command performance of *Samson*. And at the end of the oratorio, at the invitation of the director, John Stanley, Tom played a set of variations on Michael Arne's song *Highland Laddie*, which is said to have 'remov'd the cloud that over-spread' the King's face and restored 'his wanted [*sic*] chearfulness.'* The newspapers commended Stanley for introducing a tune so calculated 'to elevate his patron's drooping spirits', adding that though Stanley was blind he could 'see into business of this sort as well as any man in the kingdom'.[228] They might have added that it was pretty extraordinary that Stanley could conduct at all without being able to see either the score or the players.

But Tom seems to have alienated the *Westminster Magazine* whose acid critic, 'J. H.', complained that 'The musick Young Linley plays is generally wretched stuff'. Why didn't he follow the lead of the oboist Johann Christian Fischer, 'who takes care never to play us but something that has real musick in it; that commands the attention and captivates the heart.'[229] 'J. H.' may have taken against Tom's habit of playing his own violin concertos in oratorio intervals. He had begun composing these on his return from Italy, and by 1775 he would have written no fewer than twenty, to add to his seven violin sonatas.[230] 'J. H.' was to return to the attack, and more personally, but what really interested Tom now was choral music.

One way or another the famous Linleys were leeching audiences from rival oratorio seasons at Covent Garden and the Haymarket (where Joseph Agus, 'scholar of Signor Nardini', fresh from Florence,

---

* Two years later Tom harmonised the same song for use in his score for Sheridan's comic opera, *The Duenna*.

made his London debut on 26 February, and was now on the staff as a soloist).[231]*As one magazine reported, 'The *Ton* of the public [the fashionable elite], in respect to frequenting oratorios this year is with Drury-lane, on account of the extraordinary merit of the Linley family.'[232] And another made no bones about the reason why:

> *Miss Linley, the syren of Bath ... who is greatly indebted to Nature for the* <u>éclat</u> *with which she is followed, and not a little to the fortuitous concurrences of remarkable incidents in her life, has drawn crowded houses incessantly; and this success has been insured by the constant attendance of his majesty and the royal family at this theatre.*[233]

The King couldn't get enough of Elizabeth Linley. According to Horace Walpole, he 'ogles her as much as he dares to do in so holy place as an oratorio',[234] and at the end of March the King commanded two additional performances of *Messiah* at Drury Lane, which he and the Queen attended with the Duke and Duchess of Ancaster. *Town & Country* reported that the applause Elizabeth received was without precedent, and 'Her taste and judgement could only be surpassed by her voice and manners'. She was, the magazine ventured to say, 'the best English singer that ever made her appearance in public'.[235]

Fanny Burney went to hear *Alexander's Feast* at Drury Lane that March and sat in the box of Mrs Stanley, wife of the conductor. She

---

* In an undated letter to Tom this year, Nardini thanked him for news of Agus, which Dr Gribble takes as evidence that Tom continued his friendship with Agus once they were both together in London, and that he maintained a correspondence with Nardini. The same letter refers to some oboe reeds which Nardini has sent to Tom for the German oboist and composer Johann Christian Fischer, working in Bath and London (Rebecca Gribble, *Linley*, doctoral thesis, University of Southampton, 2015, p. 31, quoting an autograph letter from Nardini to Thomas Linley, Firenze, 1773, now in the James Marshall and Marie–Louise Osborn Collection, Beinecke Rare Books and Music Library, Yale University).

thought Elizabeth's voice was 'soft, sweet, clear & affecting, and she sings with good Expression, & has great fancy & even taste in her Cadences'. As the box was high and she was very short-sighted, she could only pick out that 'Miss Linley's figure was extremely genteel, & the form of her Face very elegant', but nothing more than that, till she persuaded a friend to admit her to the Green Room, where she saw Linley, Mrs Linley, Tom, and finally the siren herself:

Had I been, for my sins, Born of the male Race, I should certainly have added one more to Miss Linley's Train; she is really beautiful; her Complection [sic], a clear, lovely, Animated Brown, with a blooming colour on her Cheeks; her Nose that most elegant of shapes, Grecian; fine, luxurious, easy setting Hair, a charming Forehead, pretty mouth, & most bewitching Eyes. With all this, her Carriage is modest & unassuming, & her Countenance indicates diffidence, & a strong desire of pleasing; a desire in which she can never be disappointed. I most sincerely & earnestly wish her well, safely, & happily settled.[236]

It cannot have come as any surprise, after all that royal patronage, that the King should have commanded Linley, Elizabeth and Tom (Mary was ill) to give a private concert in the Queen's House (now Buckingham Palace) on 31 March. But it may have surprised all concerned that they were expected to play for five hours, and that no one except Linley at the harpsichord, was allowed to sit down. The King and Queen, accompanied by their children and a lady-in-waiting, are said to have been particularly affable – to the point of suggestiveness on the King's part[237] – and 'His Majesty told Mr Linley that he never in his life heard so fine a voice as his daughter's'. She was a credit to him, and would he please accept this bank note for £100 (about £8,000 today)?[238]

It is ironic that in the very week Linley received this mark of royal generosity he himself should have been caught out in an act of conspicuous ungenerosity. The Foundling Hospital for the Maintenance and Education of Exposed and Deserted Children had turned to him for the assistance of his daughters and son at the annual oratorio performance, and he had agreed to lend their services – for a reduced fee. When it was hinted to him that even this was beyond the Charity's means, he agreed to knock £10 off, but refused to go any lower. The governors of the Hospital were so eager to have the benefit of the Linleys' extraordinary popularity that they agreed, and the oratorio went ahead on that basis. But the *Bath Chronicle*, which knew Linley well, took a dim view: 'how different', it told its readers pointedly, was 'the conduct of some of the other performers, who ... contribute their services gratis'.[239]

Drawn by the Linleys, some eight hundred people packed into the Hospital's Chapel in Bloomsbury for *Messiah*, which, at Handel's own express wish, had long been associated with the Charity. Elizabeth and Mary were among the soloists and Tom led the orchestra. The papers reported that 'the gentlemen governors were extremely civil in conducting in the audience' and during the performance there was 'no clapping or talking, but all was silent', the singing 'heard with pleasing satisfaction'.[240]

Elizabeth by now had given up on Richard, assuming that his long silence meant he had lost interest. But he hadn't, and he was equally in despair, assuming she had given him up. In the spring of 1773 she wrote to tell him that a gentleman from London – 'not a young man, but a worthy one' [a baronet called Sir Thomas Clarges, who was actually only twenty-two] – had proposed marriage, and that though she didn't love him he didn't seem to mind at all, while her father would be delighted. In the light of this, she asked Richard to return all her letters, saying, 'You see how I am situated ... I could never be your wife, therefore ... I conjure you to leave me ...'.[241]

Faced with the prospect of losing her, and sensing that the letter might be a *cri de coeur*, Richard rode straight to the rescue, for the second time. He arrived at the Theatre Royal, Drury Lane, at the height of the oratorio season. Linley at first refused to let him in until he promised not to see Elizabeth alone, but finally he agreed to a meeting, overseen by himself, in a nearby coffee house. Richard pressed his advantage and proposed, Elizabeth accepted, Linley refused to give his consent, Elizabeth threatened suicide, Richard persisted with his usual tenacity, and Linley at last gave in.

The *Bath Chronicle* broke the news on April Fool's Day, revealing not only that she and Richard had been married for some time, but that they were about to wed again in London – and that afterwards the Maid of Bath would never sing again:

> *Miss Linley, the celebrated Syren of the present age, deaf to all mercenary intreaties, and blind to every immediate prospect of ambition, has generously resolved (soon after the Oratorios for the present season are finished) to surrender herself at the sacred altar to her champion Sheridan – determined also never more (after the happy day) publicly to appear in the character of a singer. Mr Sheridan is become a member of the Temple, with a design to prepare and qualify himself for the bar.*[242]

Richard was adamant about banning Elizabeth from singing once they were married. Keenly ambitious, he had hopes of breaking into society at the highest level. Elizabeth's celebrity and famous charms would provide the open sesame, but only if she were free from the social stigma of performing in public. In his view, though he was soon to plunge in himself, the theatre was 'the greatest Nursery of Vice and Misery on the Face of the Earth', full of 'practised Harlots … and profligate Scoundrels', where Elizabeth would be 'haul'd about and kiss'd by beastly pimping Actors!'. To continue performing would demean her and bring shame to him, for 'No Gentleman of Character and Fortune ever yet took a Wife from behind the Scenes of a Theatre'.[243] But actually Elizabeth herself was, by now, heartily sick of the theatre and music profession and the unwelcome attention of celebrity, and not at all averse to a quiet life at home.

For what was supposed to be her swan song, she gave a concert in the King's Theatre, Haymarket, on Easter Monday, 12 April, as a benefit for Tom, before 'a very crowded audience of the first nobility and gentry of this kingdom'.[244] In the first part she and Mary sang a programme of English and Italian airs and duets, and in the second she and Tom and a group of instrumentalists gave the first performance of an extraordinarily imaginative orchestral cantata, *In yonder grove*, for which she herself had written the words and Tom the music.[*]

The work consists of a series of recitatives and arias (together with an instrumental march) scored for oboes, horns and strings, somewhat in the manner of Thomas Arne and J. C. Bach. The Linley scholar the late Dr Gwilym Beechey, and the conductor Peter Holman have described both the composition and the scoring as highly accomplished for a sixteen-year-old composer.[245] The enigmatic words, which the papers printed in full, record the love of 'Emma' for her 'Harold', who seems to be dreadfully dead in his grave at the beginning but gloriously restored to life at the end.

The very next morning, Tuesday 13 April, Elizabeth Ann Linley, still only nineteen, was joined in marriage to Richard Brinsley Sheridan, now twenty-one, by the Rev. Dr Daniel Boote in St Marylebone Parish Church. Decorously and conventionally Elizabeth and Richard were legal at last. After the ceremony they and their two witnesses, with their families and friends set out for Richmond Hill and a celebration dinner at the Star and Garter, followed by a ball. The guests then returned to town, 'and left the young Couple at a Gentleman's House at Mitcham to consummate their Nuptials'.[246]

Sheridan senior attended neither wedding nor party, as he was

---

[*] *In yonder grove* was recorded in 1994 by Paul Nicholson and the Parley of Instruments Baroque Orchestra with the soprano Julia Gooding and is available on Hyperion CDH55256.

still not reconciled to his impetuous son – he received the news of the marriage 'with the most violent anger'.[247] But Mr Linley, earlier so keen to keep the couple apart, had come round to the union to such an extent that he not only gave the bride away, but also gave Richard, as Elizabeth's dowry, £1,500, representing half the £3,000 which old Long had paid up when he was forced to break off his engagement. Today this portion would be worth about £120,000, and, together with a present of £600 (about £48,000), from a 'Great Personage ... out of her privy purse',* it provided a secure foundation on which to build their lives, now that Richard had sealed off the gold-mine of his wife's public singing. The father's gift was criticised by newspapers far and wide. In America, the *Virginia Gazette* wrote that 'This Sort of Liberality may be called Profuseness, but when it is considered that within these few Years Miss Linley has gained her Father near *ten Thousand Pounds*, it will not probably be termed *extravagant* Generosity'.[248]

The young Sheridans started their married life at East Burnham Cottage near Farnham Royal in Buckinghamshire, off the Great West Road to Bath. Richard called it a 'grand little mansion', but a Victorian historian of the village described it as 'a small but genteel cottage'. At all events it was private, with extensive grounds of seven acres, overlooking 'some of the prettiest scenes imaginable', and the young couple were as happy and as settled as either had been for years, perhaps ever – and probably never would be again.[249]

In June Linley and Elizabeth's sister Mary spent an equally happy time with them, getting to know Richard more intimately than had been possible before. Certainly the postscript to Linley's thank-you letter from Bath later shows a new-found confidence in his son-in-law, when he writes, 'Do, my dear Sheridan, give young master [Thomas] a little wholesome advice'.[250] But it shows less confidence in Tom. So what was the problem?

---

* First reported in the *Kentish Gazette*, 21 April 1773, as an annuity, later corrected to a one-off gift (*Hampshire Chronicle*, 26 April 1773).

Clementina Black thinks that 'wholesome advice' conveys 'a hint of idleness' in Tom's character, though she concedes that he had been 'extremely industrious since his return from Italy'.[251] Indeed he had been industrious from the beginning – how else could he possibly have achieved so much in so short a time? And Tom's friend, Matthew Cooke, made a point of noting in his memoir of Tom that his 'Industry, and perseverance made him indefatigable'.[252] If anyone was idle it was turbulent, volatile, pleasure-loving Richard Sheridan, who always left everything to the last minute, delegated to others as much as he could, and always got away with it.

Linley's remark is much more likely to have meant that he hoped his son-in-law might whisper to Tom something of the joys of married life. Tom was now seventeen, and the sap was rising – or should have been – but there was no indication that he was showing any interest in the opposite sex, at a time in his life when his conventional parents might have expected, and hoped for, a wedding and their first Linley grandchild.

Who knows whether Richard ever did give Tom a dose of any such medicine? It seems unlikely. There are only two brief mentions of his brother-in-law in all Richard Sheridan's published correspondence – which suggests that they did not have much to do with one another outside the theatre. Yet they should have got on, given that both were unconventional young artists struggling to free themselves from controlling fathers. Perhaps Richard was himself too controlling for Tom – or Tom too unconventional for Richard. Instead of birds and bees, the boy buried himself in his music. But he must have had his own secret thoughts on the subject – and perhaps they hadn't moved on from Florence and the spring of 1770, for Wolfgang and Tom were still corresponding, even if no letters survive.

As things turned out, Tom's Benefit Concert on Easter Monday 1773 was not the last time his sister sang, however much Richard had insisted it should be. It is true she turned down many lucrative offers at this time – worth, it was said, £3,200 (or a quarter of a million pounds)[253] – but her father had signed two significant singing contracts before her marriage, and he insisted these should be honoured.

The first of these engagements was at Oxford in the summer: a concert celebrating the installation of the Prime Minister, Lord North, as Chancellor. Richard at first refused to give his permission, but when it was suggested that the Prime Minister would regard his acquiescence as a personal favour, he relented, well aware that he might be glad to call in the favour one day. So, with Mrs Sheridan, Miss Linley, Master Linley and their father, he took the coach to Oxford in the first week in July. The Sheldonian Theatre was packed to capacity for a programme of Italian songs in part one, and Handel's *l'Allegro ed il Penseroso* in part two. The band was led not by Tom but by Giardini, and Elizabeth donated her fee to the Radcliffe Infirmary. The Scottish philosopher James Beattie, who was among the one thousand people present, called it 'the finest and most magnificent musical entertainment I have ever seen.'[254]

The other outstanding engagement was for the Three Choirs Festival at Worcester in September. Having given in to Oxford, Richard was even more determined to hold firm on this engagement, arguing that the contract was no longer valid, because it had been signed by Linley when Elizabeth was his property, and now, as his wife, she was his. For a while matters hung in the balance, but two invitations to stay in grand houses nearby during the festival made all the difference, and Richard caved in.[255] As in Oxford, Elizabeth was a dazzling success. The Gloucester paper said she 'showed amazing powers' in four Handel oratorios over three days, and 'took leave of an admiring public, in the full lustre of unrivalled talents, leaving the minds of her enraptured audience impressed with … her sweet and powerful tones … generosity and benevolence.'[256] Again she gave her fee to charity.

What most of the papers failed to mention, in their adoration of the Maid of Bath, was that the Worcester festival had begun with a new choral work by Tom, a large-scale anthem for soloists, chorus and orchestra, setting Psalm 68, *Let God Arise*, and modelled on Handel's Chandos anthems.* According to Matthew Cooke, 'this production confirmed his Talents with the Public'.[257]

Tom returned to Bath and his family – it could not have been otherwise, since, as a minor, he had no place of his own, and no money of his own. At the beginning of the new year of 1774, his father conducted the orchestra in the Linley subscription concerts every Wednesday night in the New Assembly Rooms, Tom was leader and soloist, his beautiful brother Samuel, now fourteen, played the oboe, and Mary, now sixteen, sang the roles that her elder sister used to sing.

Without Elizabeth, the Lent oratorios at the Theatre Royal, Drury Lane, seem to have evaporated this year; instead the Linleys staged their own mini oratorio season in Bath, with *Messiah*, for which the third sister, Maria, eleven, joined in. And the regular concerts in the New Assembly Rooms went on, punctuated with oratorios in Winchester, Bristol and other venues in the south and west.

In Bristol Tom met Sarah Wesley, musical wife of Charles, the Methodist leader, who was away preaching. Their younger son Samuel was a prodigy aged seven, who played the violin, the harpsichord and the organ, and was now composing. Tom was profoundly impressed by the boy and alerted his teacher, Dr Boyce, who subsequently visited the Wesleys at their house in Marylebone. 'Sir,' said Boyce to Charles Wesley, 'I hear you have got an English Mozart in your house: young Linley tells me wonderful things of him.' Samuel was summoned, and when asked what he was writing, he produced the manuscript

---

* Recorded in 1997 by Julia Gooding, Sophie Daneman, Robin Blaze, Andrew King and Andrew Dale Forbes with the Holst Singers and the Parley of Instruments conducted by Peter Holman on Hyperion CDH55302. The art historian Dr Susan Wallington records that Tom's anthem 'is preserved in a beautiful manuscript written for King George III in 1780' (Wallington, 'Thomas Linley', in Waterfield, *A Nest of Nightingales*, p. 83).

of an almost finished oratorio of *Ruth*. Boyce read it carefully, then pronounced his verdict: 'These airs are some of the prettiest I have seen,' adding, to the father, 'this boy writes by nature as true a bass as I can[,] by rule and study'. Afterwards Samuel finished the composition and sent it round to Boyce, who replied by presenting his compliments and thanks 'to his very ingenious brother-composer, Mr S. W.', promising to preserve the score 'with the utmost care, as the most curious product of his musical library'.[258]*

Dr Boyce must have been similarly impressed with Tom himself, the original English Mozart, when he too was seven years old, and perhaps Boyce wrote him a similar letter, but, like every other letter to or from Thomas Linley junior, there is no trace today.

The young Sheridans had left their love nest in Buckinghamshire at the end of 1773, and, missing London, moved in with musical friends in Marylebone – in Orchard Street, off Portman Square – and in February the following year they found a house of their own in the same street, filling it with furniture given by Linley, and a piano. The new house had a large music room, and despite the ban on Elizabeth's singing in public, Richard allowed, even encouraged, her to sing in private, twice a week, to a select group of superior friends, who paid handsomely for the privilege.

Fanny Burney was among these friends – with her father, Tom's companion in Florence – and she noted that 'the highest circles of society' were drawn to Orchard Street by Mrs Sheridan's 'triple bewitchment' of 'talents, beauty and fashion'. Admission 'was sought not only by all the votaries of taste, and admirers of musical excellence, but by the leaders of *ton* [high society], and their numerous followers, or slaves, with an ardour … that was as eager for beholding as for listening …'.[259]

When he wasn't collecting the ticket money and expanding his social network, Richard Sheridan was now writing a play. He had

---

* This autograph score is now in the British Library, Add MS 34997, ff. 89 (8 September – 26 October 1774).

decided to turn the story of his elopement with Elizabeth and the subsequent duels with his rival Mathews into a comedy, which was soon to become a sensational hit at Covent Garden as *The Rivals*. By November the play was in rehearsal, but simultaneously Elizabeth had a miscarriage, and was seriously ill for a while. Linley wrote to Richard to say that he 'must absolutely keep from her, for every time you touch her, you drive a Nail in her Coffin'.[260] He did as he was told – and took it as an opportunity to play the field, for Richard Sheridan was now almost as much in vogue as his wife had been before her singing was silenced, and the 'fine ladies', who meant so much to him now, began to run after him and he didn't discourage them; and when they didn't pursue him he actively pursued them, then and thereafter.

Elizabeth had recovered by Christmas, when the Linleys paid a visit one evening. Richard's friend Henry Angelo – son of his fencing master – was there on this occasion, and observed with surprise the extent of Richard's control over his wife. After supper there was some music making, and Mrs Linley asked Elizabeth if she would sing a certain favourite air. Richard was having none of it, not even at home amongst the family, and he made his feelings clear – as Angelo remembered it, 'a single glance from her juvenile lord and master kept her mute'.[261]

Tom had lost his favourite sister, his childhood confidante, and had little in common with her brash and opportunistic, if brilliant, husband. The time had come to cut away and make a life for himself.

VIII

Sturm und Drang

LONDON 1774

A decade after their appearance in Edinburgh in the 1760s, the epic poems of Ossian, recounting deeds of valour in the Scottish Dark Ages, were still creating ripples and inspiring the music and literature of the early Romantic movement.* Their 'translator', the Scottish poet James Macpherson, then in his twenties, claimed they were old Gaelic ballads written by a blind bard of the third century called Ossian, and that he had re-discovered them in ancient manuscripts in the Highlands. But no such manuscripts were ever found, and it was widely believed that Macpherson himself had invented them. Dr Johnson wasn't alone in denouncing him as 'a mountebank, a liar and a fraud', whose poems were 'a mere unconnected rhapsody, a tiresome repetition of the same images' – *Ossian*, in his opinion, was one of the great forgeries of history.[262]†

But what a grand forgery, if forgery it actually was, and what ripples it generated. Written in a rich but simply-constructed poetic prose, the stories are set in a wild and majestic Roman Scotland, in a melancholy, misty past of glorious heroes and bloody battles, of

---

* Published as *Fingal, An Ancient Epic Poem, in Six Books: Together with several other POEMS, composed by OSSIAN the Son of FINGAL. Translated from the Galic* [*sic*] *Language, By JAMES MACPHERSON* ..., London, 1762.

† But, as Graham Johnson has aptly pointed out, 'Samuel Johnson hated Macpherson as he hated all Scots and things Scotch (until he went there with Boswell, of course).' (GRJ, email, 11 May 2022.)

FINGAL,
AN
ANCIENT EPIC POEM,
IN SIX BOOKS:
Together with several other POEMS, composed by
OSSIAN the Son of FINGAL.
Translated from the GALIC LANGUAGE,
By JAMES MACPHERSON.
Fortis falsa patrem.   VIRGIL.

LONDON:
Printed for T. BECKET and P. A. DE HONDT, in the Strand.
M DCC LXII.

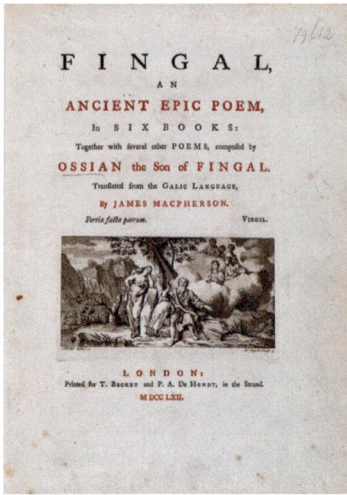

courtly love, duels, chivalry and honour. They had an enormous influence on artistic sensibilities all over the western world, and Thomas Linley junior, still an adolescent, every inch the isolated poet, was one of the first composers to recognise their romantic appeal and to respond to them in music; where he led the way, Beethoven, and later, Schubert, Mendelssohn, Schumann and Brahms followed.

When a new edition of Ossian came out in 1773, Tom decided to set one of the poems to music, and just as he was about to start he heard news of another literary sensation – this time in Germany, where Goethe, then an up-and-coming young law student, had published his revolutionary novel *Der Leiden des jungen Werthers* (The Sorrows of Young Werther). It was not yet available in English,* but everyone was talking about it, and Tom soon learned that it was all about a tragic romance that ends in suicide – furthermore that it appealed so powerfully to confused young people that it had led to a rise in the suicide rate. At the very least, as David Constantine has written, it altered the way its readers viewed their lives.[263] Perhaps it might have affected Tom's life – maybe he and Mozart discussed the new book in their lost correspondence. We do not know what Tom was thinking at the time, but there are indications that he may have seen himself as a romantic outsider, misunderstood and alone, and that he buried his feelings in work.

Like other sensitive young idealists touched by Werther, Tom

* and would not be till 1779.

might have identified with Goethe's hero and his unrequited love, and perhaps even toyed with the idea of suicide. He may not have been as rich and impressively educated as Werther, but he was nothing if not an artistic youth boiling with *Sturm und Drang*. Perhaps falling under the spell of Werther Fever, he would have followed the fashion and adopted Werther's uniform of blue coat, yellow waistcoat and breeches, and leather top-boots.

Werther is cast as a series of letters in which the eponymous hero, a gifted and passionate young artist, tells a friend about his unrequited love for a girl who is engaged to someone else. When the girl marries her fiancé, Werther realises his cause is doomed, and decides that life now holds nothing for him. Losing himself in fantastic dreams, he fires a pistol at his head and slowly dies.

In the first part of the novel, when Werther is full of hope that eventually he will win his beloved, he enjoys reading Homer's *Odyssey*, but in the second part, when all hope has gone, he wallows in the darkness of Ossian, wandering over pathless wilds, blown by impetuous whirlwinds, sighting the spirits of his ancestors by the feeble light of the moon, and hearing the lamentations of a maiden sighing on the mossy tomb of her warrior lover.[264]

The romantic Tom might have felt at home in this Gothic world, with its dramatic griefs and joys, and its elegiac language, and in

1774, under its influence, he wrote a cantata called *Darthula,* based on one of the Ossian poems. It tells the tragic story of Princess Darthula who is captured by her father's sworn enemy, the elderly Cairbar, but rescued by the young noble Nathos. The two fall in love, and make their escape across the seas, till a storm drives them back to the shore where Cairbar is waiting for them. His archers draw a thousand arrows, Nathos is killed, and Darthula is wounded, her 'breast of snow' stained with blood from an arrow lodged in her side. Falling on her lover's body, her hair spread over his face, she dies, in a *Liebestod* owing as much to Shakespeare as to a Wagner as yet unborn.[265]

Thomas probably intended the cantata for Elizabeth,[266] with whom he must have discussed both Ossian and Werther, for she was keenly interested in romantic literature, as her own poems and writings reveal. There is no record of any performance in his lifetime but the score was published later.[*]

No longer singing in public, Elizabeth still loomed large in the public consciousness: in fact her seclusion only stoked the myth – as did a new portrait by Sir Joshua Reynolds, which was unveiled at the Royal Academy exhibition in May. The title in the catalogue identified it only as 'A lady, in the character of St Cecilia', but there was no doubt who the subject was, and crowds were flocking to see it – in the Academy's old home in the north wing of Somerset House. The painting shows Elizabeth as the patron saint of music, sitting on a low stool playing a pipe organ. She is not reading the music in front of her, but gazing up at a vision in rays of light bursting through a cloud which billows above her and two singing cherubs. She is wearing a timeless muslin dress, with

---

[*] The score of *Darthula* was published by Tom's mother in London in about 1800, in a two-volume set, entitled *The Posthumous Vocal Works of Mr Linley & Mr T. Linley.* In 1994 the cantata was recorded by the soprano Julia Gooding with the Parley of Instruments Baroque Orchestra and Choir directed from the harpsichord by Paul Nicholson, on Hyperion CDH55256.

a belt at the waist, and it is not too fanciful to suggest that when Elizabeth took Tom to see the picture in Reynolds's studio, he saw the embodiment of his Princess Darthula, the most famous beauty of antiquity: 'Daughter of Heav'n, fair art thou! The silence of thy face is pleasant'.

The American scholar, James Porter, who studied the score of *Darthula* for his book on Ossian and the musical imagination, describes the music as astonishing for so young a man, 'his handling of the vocal lines and orchestral texture the sign of an assured and sensitive composer'.[267] And Beechey calls the writing 'magnificent and highly dramatic'.[268]

Whatever he may have thought privately about his brother-in-law, Richard Sheridan recognised in Tom's *Darthula* a mastery of word-setting, inventive tune-spinning and a dramatic use of orchestral colour, and he saw that these qualities could be put to more modern use. He had been looking around for a new stage project ever since the success of *The Rivals*, and, once Tom was free of the oratorio seasons at Drury Lane and in Bath, and the concert circuit in Oxford and Cambridge, Richard invited him to move in to Orchard Street so they could work together, with Elizabeth, on a new piece, which was to become the comic opera, *The Duenna*.

The plot re-tells something of the love story of Richard and Elizabeth themselves, shifted to Spain, where a father wants his daughter to marry a rich old man, while the daughter wants to marry a poor young one. A duenna arranges assignations between the young lovers, but is found out and sacked, and the daughter locked up. The daughter then disguises herself as the duenna, escapes and secretly marries her young man, leaving the real duenna to marry her father.

The words were in Richard's hands, with Elizabeth's help, and Tom was supposed to provide the music, with his father's help. But time was short, because the piece was scheduled for production at the Covent Garden Theatre in the winter, and the musical construction was far from plain sailing. Since it was a pastiche opera, the composers were required to arrange existing popular numbers from London's latest operas and traditional Celtic airs, and to add some new and original songs of their own. Mr Linley was never told what the opera was about – presumably because the role modelled on him (the father of the heroine) ends up as the laughing stock of the piece – and anyway he was reluctant to come up to London, with so much work in Bath. So Richard sent the lyrics down to Bath by post, scene by scene, hoping Mr Linley would be able to set them out of context. Linley wasn't having any of this. 'No Musician', he wrote, 'can set a Song properly unless he understands the Character, and knows the Performer who is to exhibit it'.[269]

Linley's heart was never really in the project, because he was afraid that working on a production destined for a rival theatre would upset Garrick, who had earlier offered to employ the whole family at the Theatre Royal, Drury Lane – a plan which Richard Sheridan violently opposed, presumably because he wanted to keep them all for himself and *The Duenna*. In an impassioned rant to Linley, started in early May and finished six weeks later, Richard called Garrick, 'one of the most artful and selfish Men that ever imposed on Merit or Honesty', and condemned his invitation as a plan to entrap the Linley girls into becoming 'the unblushing Objects of a Licentious gaping Croud', servants of the town and licensed marks for Libertinism. And 'poor Tam [Thomas] would be hedg'd in to answer the temporary Purpose of a singing Boy – or Chorus in a Sphere which He would soon grow out of, and be fit for nothing else there, nor anywhere else'.[270]

Reeling from this long tirade, but not deflected from his determination to avoid alienating Garrick, Linley delegated most of the composing to Tom, in a gesture described by Matthew Cooke as 'a discernment, and Generosity unparreled [*sic*]' – designed 'to add a ray of lustre to his Son's fame'.[271] But actually Linley's motives were less benevolent than selfish, and he wasn't that keen on handing it over to Tom anyway, telling Garrick 'my son has not had experience in theatrical compositions though I think well of his invention and musical skill'.[272]

The Duenna; or, The Double Elopement opened on 21 November 1775 (four nights after Elizabeth had given birth to her first child, and named him Tom, after her beloved brother).* The pit and gallery were crowded every night, the boxes booked for weeks in advance, and the production ran for an unprecedented seventy-five performances.[273†] No wonder, said the *Public Advertiser*: 'at a period remarkable for productions of wit and humour none received more general approbation than *The Duenna*', which, the paper said, contained 'no thought or expression of an indelicate or equivocal kind'.[274] In an introduction to an edition of *The Duenna* published nearly fifty years later, the actor William Oxberry described it as the most perfect opera in English: 'the gaiety of the dialogue, the neatness of the plot, the interesting simplicity of the whole, and still more the beauty of the airs', making it a welcome favourite with English audiences.[275] William Hazlitt thought the new airs had 'a joyful spirit of intoxication in them, and a strain of the most melting tenderness'.[276] And Lord Byron judged *The Duenna* to be, simply, the best opera ever written.[277]

Audiences must have recognised the story from the *Maid of Bath*, but they had to guess who wrote the piece, because the names of the composers and librettist were omitted from the programme, and even when the vocal score was published that too was anonymous. There is some evidence that Richard wanted to print Tom's name,

---

* But the chosen name would have been seen by her father and her father-in-law as a tribute to them.

† On one night in a later revival, the audience suddenly burst into 'a Complication of violent Sounds, such as Hissings, Clapping, Hooting, etc', when the towering head-dress of a lady in the gallery caught fire (the *Public Advertiser*, 6 January 1777).

but he was thwarted by Linley.[278] The musicologist Roger Fiske who studied the music that survives in print and manuscript, concluded that Tom's contributions include many of the best items – such as the Overture, a Mozartian rondo song in Act 1 and the finale of the act, a Revenge aria and a Scottish song in Act 3 and its finale. In his view, 'the younger Linley had remarkable talents which would be seen today as genius'.[279] Other modern musicologists have sometimes dismissed the music as too derivative of Handel, but the Cambridge don Richard Luckett believed that the 'songs and their harmonization come nearer to an authentic Mozartian idiom than anything else in the English repertoire'.[280] *
Dr Linda Troost, Professor of English at Washington and Jefferson College, has written that Tom's score saved *The Duenna* from shallowness.[281] Other scholars claim that it was actually the main reason for the opera's success.

The miracle is that Tom was able to find time to write anything at all. He was not only directing rehearsals at Covent Garden, and leading the orchestra there (which upset the resident leader, John Fisher, who walked out in a huff),[282] but he was also leading his father's Drury Lane and Bath orchestras in their regular concert seasons, and playing concertos in the intervals. Later in the year he led the orchestra in a revival of his anthem, *Let God Arise*, given by his younger sisters and the castrato Rauzzini at the Three Choirs Festival at Gloucester, and a few days before Christmas 1775 he was rewarded for all his hard work with his own benefit concert in the New Assembly Rooms in Bath.[283]

---

* A copy of the 1775 edition of the score of *The Duenna*, lacking the Overture, is preserved in the Royal Music Collection at the British Library (R.M. 22. c. 3), and manuscripts of some of the songs are held in 'A collection of dramatic music' in the British Library (Egerton 2493), transcribed by the Drury Lane singer Joseph Gaudry in 1780, and identified as Tom's work by his brother, William, in 1812. *The Duenna* was revived by Opera da Camera for the Camden Festival in 1976, and by English Touring Opera in 2010. The Overture was recorded by the Parley of Instruments Baroque Orchestra conducted by Paul Nicholson on Hyperion CDH55256 in 1995.

Throughout the Lenten season of the new year Tom was busy playing in the Drury Lane oratorios, two of them in the presence of the royal family. Even without his sister, the retired queen of the genre, oratorios were still the most fashionable musical entertainment in Georgian England. The *Bath Chronicle* suggested that 'The *grave* and *sublime* are more agreeable to our national character than the unmeaning jingle of notes and effeminate pathos, which characterize the Italian opera'.[284] But the oratorios also provided one of the very few chances then available for the experience of hearing choral and orchestral music. Apart from music-making at home – if you had a keyboard, violin or recorder – in church (with organ and an occasional rudimentary band) or in the tavern (for those who favoured bawdy ballads), larger-scale music was necessarily confined to cathedrals, concert halls, assembly rooms and pleasure gardens. Tickets were correspondingly expensive – five shillings (or about £20 today) for Linley's concerts in Bath, the same for the London oratorios (and double that for seats in the pit and boxes). But audiences considered the sacrifices were worth it for a ticket to realms beyond everyday life.

Despite the heavy demands of the oratorio season, Tom found time to write a major new choral work for Drury Lane. Responding to the Shakespeare frenzy which had swept the nation after Garrick's triumphant Shakespeare Jubilee of 1769, and filled with the fey Romanticism which had taken hold of him since reading Ossian, he now wrote one of his grandest works, *A Lyric Ode on the Fairies, Aerial Beings, and Witches of Shakespeare*, an eighty-minute piece for sixty performers – three soloists, including his sisters Mary and Maria, chorus and orchestra.

At this time Tom was still only nineteen, but his two collaborators were even younger. The librettist, French Laurence, was seventeen (and had been only fifteen when he actually wrote the words at Winchester College), and Tom's assistant and chief copyist, Matthew Cooke, was just fourteen. Technically all three were

A page of the autograph score of the first violin part of the *Shakespeare Ode* (University of Michigan: US–ELmsu PR 2884.L76.pt.3).

children, but all uniquely talented: as Tom had told the visiting bishop at home in Bath when he really was a child, 'We are all geniuses here, Sir'.

Laurence was a family friend from Bath , where his father was a watchmaker; later he became Regius Professor of Civil Law at Oxford. Cooke had been a treble at the Chapel Royal, St James's Palace, but his voice had just broken and he was now 'retired'. Tom had first met Cooke through Boyce, and later they became friends when the Children of the Chapel were called in to augment the sopranos in the oratorios at the Theatre Royal.*

---

* Matthew Cooke was born at Bosham in Sussex in 1761. After a season or two with Thomas Linley junior at the Theatre Royal he was appointed organist to Elizabeth, Dowager Countess of Essex, at Cassiobury House, Watford, and in 1788 he became organist of St George's, Bloomsbury, where he also taught. As a composer he wrote some harpsichord lessons, songs and hymns, and as an inventor, he created an 'Apparatus for Teaching Blind Persons Music'. He died, possibly at his house in Charles Street, Berkeley Square, in 1829.

Presumably Tom was looking for fresh ideas when he recruited these clever boys, but he may simply have preferred working with young people – and perhaps, at a deeper level, he was seeking to recapture something of the highly-charged musical and emotional climate of his friendship with Mozart in Florence five years earlier.

Laurence's words took the form of a poetical essay in a language that Peter Holman has described as 'more Milton than Shakespeare'. The plot, which isn't entirely clear, is set in the 'sacred land, Where Avon's wood-crown'd waters stray'. In the first part it's all *A Midsummer Night's Dream*, with fairies and elves and 'Oberon's nutshell car'; and in the second, it's all *Macbeth*, with witches, cauldrons and hags. If it has any message, beyond a hazy evocativeness, it's that Shakespeare is sadly missed in the modern world. 'Oh!', it ends, 'give another Shakespear [sic] to our Isle'.[285]

The work received its first performance at the Theatre Royal on 20 March 1776, with the orchestra, chorus and soloists all actually on the stage, visible rather than hidden in the pit, arranged behind a low, curving decorative wall, as the musicians had been for Garrick's own *Shakespeare Ode* seven years before.

Looking back thirty-six years later, Cooke wrote in his own hand-written copies of the vocal and instrumental parts of the

John Lodge, *Mr Garrick delivering his Ode, at Drury Lane Theatre, on dedicating a Building & erecting a Statue, to Shakespeare.* (etching, 22.8 cm × 16.3 cm, British Library).

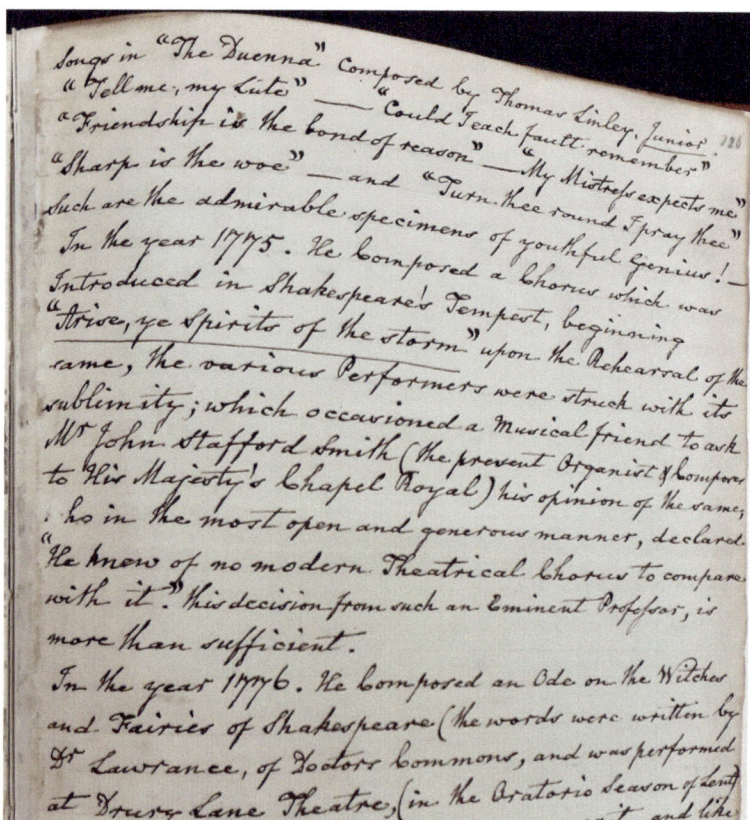

From Matthew Cooke's MS biography of Thomas Linley junior (British Library, Egerton MS 2492 f. 126 r, reproduced by permission of the British Library Board).

Shakespeare Ode,[*] (and in his memoir attached to it), that this 'Sublime Production', possessing 'uncommon merit' was 'most deservedly esteemed & applauded'.[286]

---

* Cooke's manuscript of the *Shakespeare Ode*, which contains violin and tenor parts in the hand of the composer himself, together with the only surviving copy of the printed word-book, are now preserved in the Folger Shakespeare Library, Washington D. C. (W.b.517–525). Another manuscript copy in Cooke's hand is in the British Library (Egerton 2492), with Cooke's 'A Short Account of the late Mr Thomas Linley, Junior', and the Royal Music Collection at the British Library contains another manuscript score – in the hand of Joseph Gaudry (R.M. 21. h.10). In 1812 Cooke adapted some of the Shakespeare music for performance with organ accompaniment (Egerton MS 2512, BL).

Tom may have been surprised that among the first to hail the new work was the *Westminster Magazine*, which, in a moment of rare generosity (or perhaps 'J. H.' was on holiday), called it 'an extraordinary effort of genius in so young a man'. The fugue of the Overture was 'masterly', the magazine wrote, and there was 'a taste' in the airs and accompaniments that 'would not disgrace a Sacchini or Bach'. What deserved the highest praise, though, was the power of the choruses: invention and fine airs were all very well, but the knowledge and command of harmony that were needed to write a good chorus could never be acquired without long and laborious study. The *Westminster Magazine* concluded that, 'If *Mr Linley, jun.* pursues his studies, he will one day stand foremost in the list of modern composers'.[287]

The Whig newspaper *The Morning Post* thought that 'this young composer has the brilliancy and warmth of invention' which so often comes with 'the spring of life'. It was clear that, for all his youth, his talent was 'certainly sufficient to challenge the warmest encouragement from the public, even though', it added provocatively, 'our Amateurs should not yet be brought to overlook the misfortune of his being – an Englishman'.[288]

Of modern critics, Roger Fiske regarded the *Shakespeare Ode* as 'Linley's most remarkable achievement'. Despite traces of French baroque and Handel, it was, he thought, broadly light-hearted and ornamental, but 'One must assume that, like Mozart, Linley set out to strengthen the *galant* style with a stiffening of counterpoint'. And Fiske found the long chorus, 'What howling whirlwinds rend the sky' superb, and 'paralleled only in the slightly later storm chorus from [Mozart's] *Idomeneo*'.[289]* Storms were to become something of a leitmotif in Tom's music – and in his life.

---

* The *Shakespeare Ode* is available on CD in recordings made in 1992 by the Parley of Instruments conducted by Paul Nicholson on Hyperion CDH55253, and in 1998 by Joanne Lunn, William Purefoy and Roderick Williams with the Musicians of the Globe conducted by Philip Pickett on Philips Classics 446-689-2.

IX

Outing Tom

LONDON 1776

A fortnight after the *Shakespeare Ode* opened at Drury Lane, Tom returned home to Bath, and the same old round of leading his father's orchestra in the Wednesday concerts, and playing concertos in the intervals. But perhaps to take on a new role too, for Dr Burney had recommended him as music master to a Norfolk gentleman called Brigg Fountaine, of Narford Hall near Swaffham, who was visiting Bath for the season:

> *If you take a Master for the Violin, during your Residence at Bath* [Burney wrote to Fountaine], *I wd recommend to you Mr Linley Junior, who is a Charming Performer, and of a Good School, having been under Nardini, Tartini's best Scholar, in Italy, for a considerable time.*[290]

Whether or not Brigg Fountaine ever did follow up this recommendation, Tom was soon training singers at Drury Lane, relieving his father, whose own reputation as a voice coach and music teacher was so high, and his services consequently so much in demand, that in that same spring Garrick and the other proprietors of the Theatre Royal engaged him to 'instruct and perfect in the art of singing' all those apprentices hired to sing at the theatre for the next three years. Furthermore his fee was to be a staggering £500 a year (about

Signature of Thomas Linley junior, with the signatures of his father and brother-in-law, 1776 (Add. MS 60391, reproduced by permission, British Library Board).

£39,500 today), over and above the fees he earned as conductor and music director and the father of three highly-paid musical children, Tom, Mary and Maria. Tom remained in London till 8 April to attend the drawing up of the contract, and to sign as chief witness.[291]

Once he was safely back in Bath, at home in The Crescent, Tom must have been glad he was well out of London, and Drury Lane in particular, for in May the theatre world was rocked by a sex scandal which was to reach its tentacles right into the upper reaches of society for the rest of the year. A radical political paper, *The Public Ledger*, published an article alleging that the popular actor and play-wright Samuel Foote, manager of the Haymarket Theatre, and late purveyor of *The Maid of Bath*, was 'addicted to sodomy and pre-ferred love in a stable'.[292] Tom knew some of those directly involved in the affair, and he and his family had good reason for remembering *The Maid of Bath*, which had so dramatically disrupted their lives.

The writer of the *Ledger* piece was its editor, the Rev. William Jackson, a revolutionary Irish clergyman and journalist (aka 'Dr Viper'),* who was in the pay of the bigamous Duchess of Kingston in

---

* After an unscrupulous newspaper editor of that name in Samuel Foote's 1776 satire, *The Capuchin* (Matthew Kinservik, 'The Politics and Poetics of Sodomy in the Age of George III'. *British Journal For Eighteenth Century Studies*, 2006, vol. 29 no. 2, pp. 219–236.

her dispute with Foote over his account of her amorous adventures in another of his plays, *The Trip to Calais*.

Sometimes known as the English Aristophanes, Foote's skills as a wit and conversationalist were acknowledged even by those who feared him.[293] Dr Johnson, who did not like him, admitted, after dining with him one day, 'the dog was so very comical that I was obliged to lay down my knife and fork, throw myself back upon my chair, and fairly laugh it out, No, sir, he was irresistible'.[294] Garrick regarded him as 'a man of wonderful abilities, and the most entertaining companion I have ever known.'[295] By the public he was loved for the very qualities for which he was feared; by the royal family too, for the King and Queen attended his performances five times in the Haymarket season of 1776 alone.

Who knows whether Foote was what *The Ledger* accused him of being? He was briefly married and later had two children by unnamed women, but he often appeared on stage in drag, playing women, fops and effeminate 'mollies', and his impersonations of living people – such as the Linleys and Sheridans – often landed him in trouble.

Such accusations were not unknown at this time. One Samuel Drybutter, jeweller and bookseller and a notorious 'molly', said to be the leader of the Macaroni Club, was arrested for attempted sodomy several times in the 1770s but never actually convicted, though he was beaten up by the mob in 1777. And in July 1772 Lieutenant Robert Jones, an officer in the Royal Artillery, otherwise known as 'Captain Jones', master of fireworks displays, proponent of figure skating, and a well-known dandy, was convicted of sexual assault on a twelve-year-old boy.* At his trial at the Old Bailey he

---

* Mrs Piozzi's diaries claim that 'Captain Jones' was the man who created the spectacular fireworks, simulating the eruption of Mount Etna, at a concert in Marylebone Gardens (when Tom Linley played a violin concerto), but that did not happen till September 1772, by which time Jones had already fled to France. The Etna fireworks at Marylebone were devised by Morel Torré, former pyrotechnician at Versailles.

was found guilty, on the boy's word alone, and sentenced to death, but the King, who was fond of fireworks (it was he who commissioned Handel's *Music for the Royal Fireworks*), granted him a pardon, on condition he left the country. He did, and went to live in France, but the case stirred a wide and heated debate about 'mollies' and 'macaronis'. That same year, 1772, no less a figure than Garrick himself was lampooned as a sodomite in William Kenrick's play, *Love in the Suds*, about an affair he is supposed to have had with the dramatist Isaac Bickerstaffe * 'Go where we will, at every time and place', wrote the poet and satirist Charles Churchill, commenting on morals of the times, 'Sodom confronts, and stares us in the face'.[296]

Things got worse for Foote on 6 May 1776, when his former coachman, John Sangster, appeared before the Bow Street Magistrate and swore that he had been the victim of what the papers coyly called 'an unnatural crime on his person' twice in the week preceding. When the case reached the Middlesex Quarter Sessions a grand jury indicted Foote on two counts of attempted sodomy.[297]

A fortnight later – on Tom's twentieth birthday, as it happened – Foote sued the *Ledger* for libel, and won. But William Jackson wasn't so easily beaten. Sacked from the *Ledger*, he bounced back under the pseudonym of 'Humphrey Nettle', and published a stingingly malicious poem, *Sodom & Onan*, which described itself as 'A Satire inscrib'd to [Samuel Foote, identified by a drawing of a large naked foot] Esq, alias the DEVIL upon two Sticks'. And his fire wasn't confined to Foote. Among others he named among the 'Buggers all' in his twenty-nine pages of libellous rhyming couplets, were Peregrine Bertie, Duke of Ancaster ('View stradling Bertie, that Bedchamber Lord ... ne'er in my house a welcome Guest he'll be, Ent'ring my

---

* Kenrick almost immediately published a renunciation of his charges against Garrick in *The Recantation and Confession of Dr. Kenrick*, 1772. But no one withdrew any charges against Bickerstaffe, 'long a suspected "molly"'. (See Rictor Norton, 'The Macaroni Club – Homosexual Scandals in 1772', in *Homosexuality in Eighteenth-Century England – a Sourcebook*, online at rictornorton.co.uk)

doors, he'll want to enter me'); the Florentine Lords Tylney and Cowper ('Britain's cast outs, revel uncontroul'd, Who for their Beastial lust their Country sold, Who dissipate Estates in Foreign Climes To buy indulgence, for their darling Crimes'); George Germain, Viscount Sackville, Secretary of State for the Colonies ('Coward, and Catamite'); Foote's friend and patron, John Savile, Earl of Mexborough; William Jewell, treasurer of the Haymarket Theatre; Garrick's friend, Bickerstaffe; and Samuel Drybutter.[298]

Now the affair began to lap at Tom's shore, for Ancaster was his long-term patron, who had financed his studies in Italy, and Tylney and Cowper had been his champions in Florence. The Linleys probably knew William Jewell as well, through theatre contacts, for Jewell was Elizabeth's book-keeping counterpart in the rival theatre, and they certainly knew Mrs Jewell, the singer Ann Edwards, once Foote's servant, now a popular performer who had appeared in Thomas Sheridan's *Attic Entertainment* in 1769, and in the *Maid of Bath* in 1771 (playing the heroine).[299] As far as is known not one of William Jackson's named victims ever sued for defamation, which might suggest they all had something to hide. Or perhaps they took the view that the storm was best left to blow itself out – as it soon did, but not without leaving questions hanging in the air.

In July Jackson's backer, the Duchess of Kingston, repeated the accusations against Foote, and he was arrested. After five months the case came before the Court of the King's Bench. Sangster was called to give his evidence again, but William Jewell followed him into the witness box and swore that his master could not have committed the alleged offences because he wasn't in London at the time. The presiding judge, the Lord Chief Justice himself, Lord Mansfield, ruled that the case was nothing but a conspiracy to blacken Foote's name, whereupon 'the special jury … at once cried out together, Not guilty.'[300] Samuel Foote may have been acquitted, with even the King and Queen standing by him, but the trial broke his spirit, and he had a stroke in Dover ten months later, dying as he was preparing to sail to France.*

The Foote case was a symptom of England's obsession with the 'nameless act' in the 1770s. Ever since the Restoration, fops had been more or less acceptable, because they were seen as basically heterosexual, but these new macaronis – 'sweet-scented, simpering He-She things' – were beyond the pale.[301] Public opinion saw them as a threat to the sober manliness of the nation. A Scottish Presbyterian minister summed up the cause in a book in 1777: the ruling character of the times, he wrote, was one of 'selfish and vicious effeminacy'. Corrupted by vanity, narcissism and luxury, the British male had gone soft – and worse.[302] At the bottom of it all was music. Whether you enjoyed music, or made music, moralists saw the practice as thoroughly dangerous, because it encouraged those tender feelings which led to vice and the crime of the blackest hue. Lord Chesterfield, in one of his letters to his son, then in Italy on the Grand Tour, urged him to resist the siren call of music:

If you love music, hear it; go to operas, concerts, and pay fiddlers to play for you; but I insist upon your neither piping nor fiddling. It puts a gentleman in a very frivolous, contemptible light; [and] brings him into a great deal of bad company.[303]

As a professional musician, Tom was doubly damned. In the judgement of Georgian society, music-making was not only unmanly (and, when enjoyed too much, positively effeminate – as the American critics were to say of Rudy Vallée in the 1930s), but it was

---

* Jewell brought his body back to London and is said to have buried him secretly, by torchlight, somewhere in the cloisters of Westminster Abbey, without any memorial. But a marble epitaph in St Mary's Church, Dover, records in Shakespeare's words, 'he had a hand open as day for melting charity' (['Samuel Foote'], in *The London Quarterly Review*, issues 187–90, October 1854, pp. 251–285; and Rictor Norton (Ed.), 'Sodom and Onan 1776', in *Homosexuality in Eighteenth-Century England – A Sourcebook*, online at rictornorton.co.uk)

ungentlemanly too. No amount of posing for a portrait with a cocked hat could win a man a place at a gentleman's table. But Tom had two trump cards – he was a star, and he was the brother of the Maid of Bath. These provided his entrée to society, as he led the Drury Lane orchestra in the oratorio season, and his father's orchestra in Bath, before the Foote scandal broke. With *Judas Maccabaeus* on May 16, the Linley subscription concerts shut down for the summer, and Tom was able to take a rest. But no sooner had he put his violin back in its green baize bag than everything changed.

Garrick had retired from the stage, after giving nineteen farewell performances, and on 24 June, in a move that took everyone by surprise, he sold his interest in the Theatre Royal for £35,000. The buyers were Tom's father, who put up £10,000 (largely from his children's concert earnings), Sheridan, who found another £10,000 (no one knows how), and Dr James Ford, a fashionable man-midwife who was physician extraordinary to Queen Charlotte (and owner of an estate in Jamaica), who contributed the final £15,000.[304]

The Linleys now left their large house in Bath, and moved up to London – to a smaller house in Norfolk Street (long since gone, but it used to run from the shore of the Thames up to what is now Australia House in the Strand). From there it was a six-minute walk west to the Theatre Royal. Richard Sheridan took control of the theatre as general manager; his father, Thomas Sheridan, was appointed artistic director (on condition he agreed never to act, which infuriated him to such an extent that he walked out within a year); Elizabeth left the baby with a nursemaid, and took over the daily administration of the theatre; Mr Linley was resident composer and co-director of oratorios; Mrs Linley became wardrobe mistress, 'which gave her parsimonious character full play';[305] and Tom was leader of the orchestra and solo violinist in the oratorios.[306] According to William Parke, principal oboe in the orchestra for forty years, Tom was 'one of the finest violin players in Europe' and a great favourite with the public'.[307]

The change of proprietors was announced on the opening night of the new season, 21 September 1776, with a production called *New Brooms!* by the comic dramatist George Colman – a 'pleasant trifle ... intended to usher in the new managers, Messrs. Sheridan, Linley, etc., and to compliment the seceding one, Mr Garrick'.[308] Although this was well received by the audience, the new team met a barrage of opposition from a press far from convinced that any of them knew how to run a theatre – its finances, its procedures for selecting new plays, controlling temperamental actresses, and 'all the minutiae so expertly taken care of by their great predecessor'. But it soon appeared that they did, as *The London Stage* records:

> [Richard] *Sheridan was astute enough to produce on ninety different nights* [of the first season in 1776–7] *plays which he had either originally written or had altered. The culmination, not only of the season but also of his career as a dramatist, came in May* [1777], *on the famous opening night of his masterpiece, 'The School for Scandal'.*[309]

Like *The Rivals* and *The Duenna*, *The School for Scandal* drew on the drama of Richard's life, and included some comic duel scenes, with which he was more familiar than most. And like its predecessors, the new comedy was an enormous hit. After the opening night, the *Gazetteer and New Daily Advertiser* reported that 'No modern theatrical piece ever met with a fuller success, nor deserved it more', and Hazlitt said that, 'Besides the wit and ingenuity of this play, there is a genial spirit of frankness and generosity about it, that relieves the heart as well as clears the lungs'.[310]

Another of Richard Sheridan's successes in that first season was an even more contemporary production – a brand new look at *The Tempest*, with incidental music specially composed by Tom, astonishing sets, scenic effects and stage machinery designed by Philip de Loutherbourg, and an off-stage musical instrument, half-piano and half-harpsichord, made by the Belgian inventor John Joseph Merlin.* The production marked the stage debuts of Sheridan's current mistress, the courtesan Margaret Cuyler, who played Miranda,† and of Tom's pupil, a child called Ann Field, who played Ariel. Tom's music involved new choruses and songs, including a colourful setting of Ariel's 'Full Fathom Five' song, with orchestral imitations of barking at 'Hark, hark! ... The watch-dogs' and of a crowing cock at 'The strain of strutting Chanticleer'.[311]

But the music that made the greatest impression was the chorus which Tom wrote for the shipwreck in the first scene. This thrilling piece starts softly with urgently repeated quavers in the strings, then builds to a climax as the storm breaks, with agitated strings accompanying the chorus, before subsiding in slower chords.[312] To portray the drama on stage de Loutherbourg designed a fantastic shipwreck tableau, incorporating thunder and lightning (which went awry on one of the nights of the opening run, sending a 'shower of flammable matter' and smoke into the auditorium, choking the audience for the next two acts.)[313] This Storm Chorus made such an impression on the performers when they first heard it in rehearsal that they 'were struck with its sublimity', which may be a way of

---

* De Loutherbourg had worked with Richard Sheridan and Linley senior on the comic opera *Selima and Azor* (Drury Lane, December 1776), a re-hash of *Beauty and the Beast*, for which he created a spectacular fairy palace, and a flying car drawn by dragons spitting fire and rolling their eyes, but on the opening night the flying equipment broke down, stranding two actors in mid-air (*Morning Post*, December 6, 1776). The same paper (17 February 1776) revealed that de Loutherbourg's technique involved 'a just disposition of light and shade, and critical preservation of perspective' to deceive the eye of the spectator. Merlin's other musical inventions included a piano with a compass of six octaves for Dr Burney, a barrel organ-harpsichord that played nineteen tunes, and a one-man orchestra. He also built a mechanical garden, a Hygeian Air-Pump for expelling foul air, prosthetic legs and the first pair of roller skates, on which he crashed into a large mirror and injured himself badly.

† But Cuyler was soon replaced in his affections by the beautiful young actress Mary Robinson, poet, dramatist, novelist and general celebrity, later known as the *English Sappho*, who played Amanda in his Vanbrugh re-working, *A Trip to Scarborough*, at Drury Lane in February 1777. And her reign ran somewhat concurrently with that of Frances, Lady Crewe, the dedicatee of *The School for Scandal*.

[After Thomas Rowlandson and Augustus Pugin], *Theatre Royal, Drury Lane, c.*1808 (aquatint engraving published as Plate 32 in R. Ackermann, *The Microcosm of London*, 1808–10).

saying they broke off to applaud the composer.[314] It is no surprise that it became the smash hit of the day, and remained one of the most popular theatre choruses of the eighteenth century – and is still drawing admirers today.* The late Roger Fiske called it 'one of the most remarkable achievements in English music'.[315]

Sheridan's *Tempest* had opened at the Theatre Royal on 4 January 1777,† and the *Public Advertiser* reported that the production and

---

* Hyperion recorded the complete *Tempest* music by Thomas Linley junior in 1994, with Julia Gooding and the Parley of Instruments Baroque Orchestra conductor Paul Nicholson (CDH55256). And on YouTube there is an exciting video of the Storm Chorus, 'Arise! ye spirits of the storm', sung by the Russian vocal ensemble *Intrada* with the original instruments of the Russian chamber orchestra *Pratum Integrum*, conducted with great energy and precision by Ekaterina Antonenko. The score is preserved in the British Library (Egerton MS 2493), in a manuscript copied in 1780 by Joseph Gaudry, who sang in the Chorus of Spirits in the opening run.

† A few weeks earlier, in November 1776, the Theatre Royal, Drury Lane, staged a new *Macbeth*, for which Thomas Linley Jr is sometimes said to have written wind parts to

the performance were 'received by a crouded Audience with universal Approbation'.[316] Word soon got around, and the show ran for twenty more performances that season, and remained in the Drury Lane repertoire for a further nine years. With heavy irony, an unsigned review in the *Westminster Magazine* – possibly by 'J. H.' again – congratulated 'the sentimental Sheridan' on his 'thrilling touch' as director, and 'the musical Linley' on his 'surprising talents' as composer and leader of the orchestra. The unnamed reviewer went on to criticize the music as 'too consequential', whatever that meant. All in all, he added sourly, the new *Tempest* was no more than 'an enchantment suited to the childish taste of the present times'.

Tom led the orchestra in every performance, yet still found time for a rash of oratorios throughout January and February, including a command performance of *Alexander's Feast* for the King and Queen on St Valentine's Day. The royal couple evidently enjoyed the concerto which he played in the interval, but the *Westminster Magazine* was, as ever, harder to please:

> *Mr Thomas Linley has merits as a performer on the violin, but the good effects of them are more than counter-acted by a certain settled assurance and conceit in his manner, which he seems to communicate to the very tones of his instrument.* [317]

This spiteful notice was more *ad hominem* than *ad violinem*, and seems to suggest something of a vendetta by the *Westminster Magazine*'s anonymous reviewer, who was to continue to swipe at

supplement the music composed for earlier productions, but there is no clear evidence of this, because the parts were lost in the theatre fire in 1809. But whether written by Tom or his father, the new music 'produced a very fine characteristic effect' ([John S. Sainsbury], *A Dictionary of Musicians* ..., London, 1824, vol. ii, p. 68). And Mrs Melmoth, making her debut, was a 'very wild' Lady Macbeth, improperly dressed in Habits of the Times' (George Winchester Stone Jr. (Ed.), *The London Stage, 1660–1800* ..., Southern Illinois University Press, 1960–1963, part 5, vol. i, p. 39).

Tom for the rest of his life. (If he wasn't 'J. H.', he may have been the satirist, Edward Thomas, a serving captain in the Royal Navy, whose contributions to the *Westminster Magazine* were known for their 'merciless satire utterly free of any anxiety that it might offend'.)[318] So, Tom was pleased with himself, a little arrogant perhaps, like Werther – who wouldn't be, who shouldn't be, after all that he had achieved in just twenty years? But there is more here than meets the eye. The words 'conceit' and 'assurance' are the clues. They fall into the same category as 'luxury', 'languor' and 'frivolity', and translate as 'effeminacy', than which nothing was more abominable.[319]

A century and a half later the romantic crooning tenor Rudy Vallée – the world's first pop idol – ran into the same sort of trouble for the same sort of reason. For all that he was resoundingly heterosexual, his singing style – intimate, soft, high-pitched and vulnerable – was perceived as effeminate, and worse, by conservative pundits in the Depression. But, as with Tom and his violin, women adored him – among them, the maverick war correspondent, Martha Gellhorn. Writing in *The New Republic* in 1929, under the headline, 'God's Gift to Us Girls', she described a Vallée performance in terms that capture something of the effect of Tom's playing on the ladies of Georgian England:

> *The audience goes mad* [as Rudy Vallée joins his band, the Connecticut Yankees, on stage]. *A murmur of delight rises like a tidal wave, becomes an envious moan, pants into a yearning sob … Suddenly Rudy picks up a megaphone, stands quietly at the corner of the stage and begins to sing. The audience holds its breath in joy, in adoration, The words drift from the megaphone like a caress. A billet doux for each gasping female in the vast theatre … The audience is enraptured, fanatical. It has been carried up Parnassus on this insinuating wooing voice. He is their darling, their Song Lover …*[320]

Like Tom's critic on the *Westminster Magazine* in the 1770s, the BBC in the early 1930s declared that musical emotionalism of the crooning variety was 'particularly odious' and 'not fit for men'.[321] And in New England the Cardinal Archbishop of Boston (William Henry O'Connell) warned that crooning was actually eroding sexual mores.[322] Other American church leaders warned that crooners were immoral, pathological, 'not true men', and psychologists put forward Freudian theories to argue that they were narcissistic and therefore sexually deviant – which is essentially what the *Westminster Magazine* was driving at, when it accused Tom of 'settled assurance and conceit'.

If Tom was stung, perhaps he ignored it, but his family will not have liked it. And a month later the same hand struck again, when reviewing his latest work, *The Song of Moses*, a grand oratorio in the manner of Handel, which was given its first performance as an 'afterpiece' with *l'Allegro ed Il Penseroso* at the Theatre Royal, Drury Lane on 12 March.* Refusing to recognize, or even consider, the majesty of the five fugal choruses or the beauty of the four early-classical arias, the *Westminster Magazine* reviewer could only vent his spleen on the composer himself:

> ... *young Linley has mistaken a middling talent for playing on the fiddle, for that of writing Music, and the impulse of Conceit for that of Genius; of which the Composition of this evening discovered not the least share.*[323]

But the Westminster Momus was on his own, for the new oratorio was received warmly by a larger than usual audience for the Lenten Oratorios, and the *Morning Post* expressed itself surprised to find *The Song of Moses* 'executed in so capital a manner by so

---

* Among the soloists were Tom's younger sisters, Mary and Maria, and his older sister Elizabeth's former admirer, the counter-tenor Thomas Norris (the *Morning Post*, 13 March 1771).

young a musician', who showed 'a strength of genius, inferior to but very few musical writers in this stile'.[324] Since these very few included Purcell and Handel, Thomas Linley junior might be thought to have made it. And after a further performance of his *Moses* three nights later, the same paper made an an interesting point about the status of English composers vis-à-vis their Italian and German counterparts. It said that 'the very warm applause he [Tom] received last night proves that an English audience will give proper encouragement to true merit and genius, even though it is the production of their own country'.[325]

The work was set to words by the poet and dramatist Dr John Hoadly, who was also the incumbent of a plurality of parishes in the gift of his father, the Bishop of Winchester. Drawing on the biblical account of the flight of the Children of Israel from their captivity in Egypt, he concentrates on their hymn of thanks to God for parting the Red Sea, so they could escape while Pharaoh and his army were drowned. 'The wave hath closed above each warlike head', run the words of the second chorus, and the Egyptian pursuers are 'sunk like a lifeless stone, vanished, and dead', the music emphasizing the sensation of sinking.[326] Perhaps it was no coincidence that this was the third time that Tom had set a storm in his music.

His young friend Matthew Cooke was no longer working as copyist at the Theatre Royal, Drury Lane, but probably still assisting him,* and in his opinion, recorded thirty-five years later, *The Song of Moses* was a masterpiece:

> *In this Composition He has given us the finest specimen in the Simple, Affecting, Grand, and Sublime styles that was ever produced by the pen of a Musician. In one of the Chorusses beginning 'All Canaan's heathen race', He has imitated the style, and manner of the Immortal Handel so close – that many of the most*

---

* Cooke was now Organist to Lady Essex (see footnote on p. 126), and his place as copyist at the Theatre Royal, Drury Lane, had been taken by the actor and singer Joseph Gaudry.

eminent Musical Professors, have unanimously declared, that the above Chorus might have been safely attributed to Handel himself. Such is the Tribute we must render to <u>a Boy of Twenty-One years of Age</u>.' [Actually he was still only twenty in March 1777.] [327]

Sainsbury's *Dictionary of Musicians* (1824) expressed astonishment that 'this extraordinary production' was not published at the time of its success.[328] But this was put right in 2000 when Professor Peter Overbeck of the University of Music, Karlsruhe, brought out an edition, with an Introduction and Critical Report.[329]*

Work never stopped for Tom. Two days after the premiere of *Moses*, he was leading the orchestra in *Acis and Galatea* on the same stage, then playing in his *Tempest* the following day, with a *Messiah* in Oxford on 17 March, and a dash back to London for two more performances of *Messiah* in Drury Lane. On the 20th he played a concerto at the anniversary concert and ball of the Society of Freemasons (when the Brethren were 'desired to attend cloathed as Masons').[330] Another *Messiah* and a concerto the next night, but he did not take part in a charity performance of Giardini's *Ruth* with his sisters and the castrato Rauzzini in the Chapel of the Lock Hospital (for the treatment of sexual diseases) in Grosvenor Place on the 26th, probably because Giardini would have wanted to lead the orchestra himself, and play the concerto. But his patron, the Duke of Ancaster, was there in his capacity as perpetual president of the Hospital – and smarting, perhaps, because he had just been passed over to succeed Lord Harcourt as Lord Lieutenant of Ireland. (What the duke didn't know was that the Prime Minister, Lord North, had dismissed his candidature with the vivid snub, 'It

---

* In 1997 the Holst Singers (director Stephen Layton) and the Parley of Instruments (conductor Peter Holman) recorded the complete *Tempest* music with sopranos Julia Gooding and Sophie Daneman, tenor Andrew King, bass Andrew Dale Forbes and alto Robin Blaze (Hyperion CDH55302). The score for *The Song of Moses*, beautifully written in the hand of Joseph Gaudry in 1779, is preserved in the British Library (R.M.21.h.9, ff. 1r–131r).

Presented by Mrs Sheridan to the Catch Club. Tho.s Linley Jun.

Madrigal

Hark hark the Birds me_lodious fing and fweet _ _ _

Hark the Birds me_lodious fing hark hark hark hark

Hark Hark the Birds me_lodious fing hark hark hark hark

Hark hark hark hark hark

Hark hark hark hark hark

_ _ ly fweetly ufher in the Spring and fweetly and fweetly and

hark the Birds me _ lo _ _ dious fing and fweetly and fweetly and

hark the Birds me _ lo-dious fing and fweetly and fweetly and fweetly

the Birds me _ lo _ _ dious fing and

the Birds me_lo _ dious fing and

The opening page of the five-part madrigal, 'Hark! Hark! The Birds' by Thomas Linley
Junior (from a printed score presented to the Catch Club by his sister Elizabeth).

is impossible to send into such a responsible station, such a very
egregious blockhead, who is besides both mulish and intractable'.)[331]

And in whatever leisure time he could find, Tom was writing
songs, duets and glees, one of which, the five-part madrigal,
Hark! Hark! the Birds was composed for his sister Elizabeth, who
sang the top part – and after his death (and probably after hers too),
Sheridan gave the manuscript to the Noblemen's and Gentlemen's
Catch Club.[332]

The next we hear of Tom is on 11 April, when he is leading the
orchestra at a Benefit Concert for a triple harpist from Bath called
Evans. Thereafter he seems to have gone to ground – presumably
exhausted after too many months' burning the candle at both ends
as performer and composer. In a letter to Mr Linley, Richard
Sheridan expressed some concern, not on his own behalf but on
Elizabeth's:

Betsey [the family's nickname for Elizabeth] *has been alarmed about Thomas, but without reason. He is in my opinion better than when you left him, at least to appearance, and the cold he caught is gone. We went to see him at Battersea, and would have persuaded him to remove to Orchard-street; but he thinks the air does him good, and he seems with people where he is at home, and may divert himself, which, perhaps, will do him more good than the air, – but he is to be with us soon.*[333]

Perhaps Richard was too wrapped up in himself to sense that Tom's problems, which worried Elizabeth so much, are likely to have been more of the mind than of the body. Perhaps Tom was depressed – over-worked, persecuted by that Westminster reviewer, wondering where he was going as a composer, just who he was. Perhaps he was having a breakdown. But Battersea?

At this time Battersea was a village of barely two hundred houses surrounded by open fields. Two acquaintances of Tom had connections there: the father of the young harpsichordist and violinist Henry Condell lived at Cave House,[334] and the father of one of Mr Linley's pupils, the teenage singer Anna Maria Phillips (later Mrs Crouch), had a summer retreat there.[335] Though she was notably sympathetic, Anna Maria Phillips is unlikely to have been allowed to spirit Tom off to Battersea for a cure, but her father might have done: Peregrine Phillips was a lawyer, poet and pamphleteer whose radical politics might have chimed with Tom, and it could have been he who proposed a little holiday in Battersea for the exhausted musician. There is no evidence that Tom was friends with twenty-year-old Henry Condell, but he would certainly have known him, because he played alongside him in the first violins of the Drury Lane orchestra, so it is possible that he was the companion who was diverting Tom so happily in Battersea.

That spring the Sheridans moved from Orchard Street to a grander house in Great Queen Street, Lincoln's Inn, just five minutes' walk from the Theatre Royal. Neglected by her husband, who was busy with rehearsals and his ladies, Elizabeth was, nevertheless, pregnant again, suffering considerably, and missing her sisters. On the night before the premiere of *The School for Scandal*, which was to bring Richard Sheridan one of the greatest successes of his life, Elizabeth lay critically ill at home, all alone and in labour. The *London Evening Post* reported on the 13th that she had been 'delivered of a fine chopping [strapping] female, likely to live for ever'. But it wasn't to be – the baby girl was stillborn.

On 7 May Tom came of age, but he does not appear in any concert records till August when he joined the Royal Society of Musicians, on the recommendation of John Parke, principal oboe at the Drury Lane Theatre, and a regular at the Lenten oratorios and the Three Choirs Festival. He figures only briefly in records of the Drury Lane theatre season which had started on 20 September, and the Linley subscription concerts in Bath which started on 13 October.

At the end of October 1777 the Sheridans went down to Bath to supervise rehearsals of *The School for Scandal* at the Theatre Royal there, and stayed with other members of the family, including Tom and Maria and the youngest children, at Fountain Buildings, the home of the Linley grandparents, William the builder and Maria his wife. They were joined for a time by an old friend, the artist Ozias Humphry, fresh from Italy where he had been travelling and painting for four years.[336] Like Tom, and like every other Englishman who had ever made the Grand Tour, Humphry had been bowled over by Italy and its 'indescribable delights'. Yet for all that he regarded Italy as 'the most eligible residence under Heaven', he returned home to his native land, as Tom had done a few years earlier, 'with heartfelt joy'.[337]

It was probably in Bath during that autumn of 1777 that Humphry drew two charming miniature portraits of Tom and Maria – Tom in profile, with a powdered wig, a ruffled shirt front and a blue coat – handsome but a little starchy; Maria, in a man's frockcoat standing

Above: Ozias Humphry, *Maria Linley, c.*1777 (watercolour on paper, 15.24 cm × 11.43 cm). Below: Ozias Humphry, *Thomas Linley* [junior], *c.* 1777 (watercolour on paper, 11.43 × 8.9 cm). Both paintings reproduced by kind permission of the Victoria Art Gallery, Bath, and North East Somerset Council.

beside a rock under a tree.* Now that Elizabeth was sequestered by marriage to Sheridan, and the second of the three singing sisters, Mary, was occupied with the welcome attentions of Sheridan's friend, the playwright Richard Tickell (whom she was to marry in 1780), Maria, had become Tom's new best friend. Difficult, eccentric and possibly lesbian,[338] she was almost as good a singer as Elizabeth, not as beautiful but a better actress – and an amusing companion.

The sittings with Humphry must have been fun, as the two young men, garrulous and indiscreet, shared their memories of Italy – of Livorno and Florence, of the Grand Duke Pietro Leopoldo, Lord Cowper (who commissioned from Humphry a miniature to be set in a bracelet),[339] Lord Tylney (who wouldn't buy anything),[340] and the other larger-than-life characters they had both met abroad.

After this domestic interlude, and much-needed rest, Tom returned to London before Christmas to work on an 'operatical farce' due to open at the Theatre Royal, Drury Lane, in January 1778. Called *The Cady of Bagdad*, it set a libretto concocted by Abraham Portal from *The*

* The catalogue of the Dulwich Gallery's Linley exhibition, *A Nest of Nightingales* (pp. 89–90), suggests that the portrait now in the Victoria Art Gallery in Bath may be a copy made after Maria's death in 1784 by Richard Westall, who added, as a commemorative device, a lyre, hanging unplayed from a tree.

148

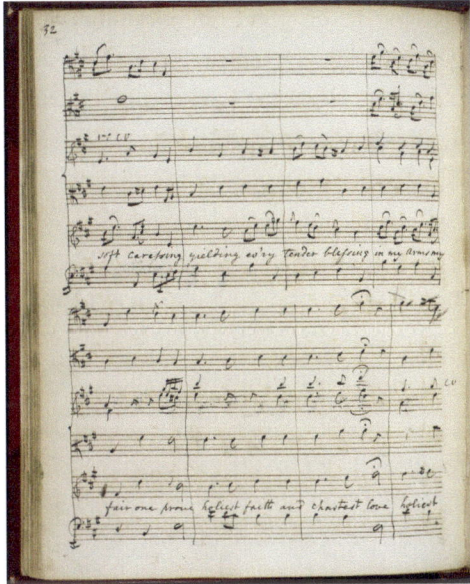

A page of the score of *The Cady of Bagdad* by Thomas Linley junior, in the composer's own hand (British Library, Add. MS 29297, reproduced by permission of the British Library Board).

Arabian Nights, and further tweaked by Richard Sheridan. (Portal was not only a poet and dramatist but a silversmith and bookseller too, and when his businesses failed be became a humble box-keeper at the Drury Lane Theatre.)

The Cady is about a vindictive old judge who tries to humiliate his enemy Abdullah by arranging for Abdullah's daughter, Zemroude, to marry a thief, but the thief turns out to be a king, and Zemroude turns the tables on the Cady by forcing him to marry the ugly daughter of Caca, a drunken dyer. If the best tunes go to Caca, including a vivid drinking song, the star of the show was the beautiful Zemroude, played by the celebrated courtesan, Mrs Baddeley, full-time mistress of Lord Melbourne, and purveyor of part-time pleasures to the Dukes of Bedford, Cumberland, Dorset, Grafton and York – and Tom's patron, the possibly bisexual Peregrine Bertie, Duke of Ancaster.* (Tom and Mrs Baddeley had worked

---

* For further details of the piquant life and loves of Mrs Baddeley see *The memoirs of Mrs. Sophia Baddeley, late of Drury Lane Theatre ... in Six Volumes* (ostensibly by her female companion, Elizabeth Steele, but possibly by Alexander Bicknell), London, 1787 .

together before – on Linley senior's comic opera, *Selima and Azor* (Drury Lane, December 1776) – when the principal oboe in the orchestra, William Parke, reported that Mrs Baddeley's song, 'No flower that blows is like this rose', was rapturously encored, and that Tom's violin obbligato in another of her numbers 'excited the highest admiration and applause'.)[341]

The Cady of Bagdad was considered a bit of a shocker at the time, and nothing if not politically incorrect by today's standards – as the opera critic John Steane wrote in a review of a London revival in 1992: 'It makes light work of Baghdad and its prophet,' he wrote, 'and is hardly in tune with modern sensibilities on the subjects of the deformed and the disabled'. But Steane thought the music was charming, in an elegant and spirited style.[342] Nearly two hundred years earlier *Town and Country Magazine* felt much the same:

> *... there are many absurdities in this opera, which prevented its meeting with the favourable reception [to] which Mr Linley's excellent music justly entitled it ... It is sincerely to be lamented that such good music should be thrown away on such indifferent writing, teeming with indelicacies. It must indeed undergo several alterations before it can be a proper regale for a polite audience ... This opera has since been banished from the stage by the public voice. We hope, however, that the music will be preserved.*[343]*

The *Westminster Magazine* went further – a great deal further. After criticising the librettist for failing 'to give his personages suitable and decent language', with the result that the dialogue was 'rendered too low and offensive, even for the taste of our Galleries ...' the reviewer turned his fire on his favourite target:

---

* Thanks to Tom's youngest brother, William, who inherited the autograph score, the music has been preserved, in a leather-bound volume, at the British Library (Add MS 29297). This provides a fine example of Tom's notation and hand-writing, and, though some pages seem to have been written at breakneck speed, they are never unreadable.

The managers [of Drury Lane] *shew but an indifferent opinion of the talents of Mr Linley, jun., by associating him with so wretched a writer as the author of 'The Cady of Baghdad'. Indeed this young man seems to us in all his performances, to be under the influence of conceit rather than genius, and to have talents formed only for the production of those* prettinesses *in sentiment & manner, which are as offensive as faults.* [344]

And a fortnight later at a Lenten performance of *Acis and Galatea* in the presence of the King and Queen, the prejudices of the *Westminster Magazine* surfaced again:

Mr Linley, jun., led the band; and though we must own that he discovers [i.e. displays] *great knowledge of his business, and great power of execution, yet there is something in his finest tones analogous to the piercing voice of feminine assurance, which always offends us.* [345]

First 'conceit', then 'prettinesses', and now 'piercing voice of feminine assurance' – these were conscious euphemisms for what the *Westminster Magazine* knew its readers would recognize as evidence of 'molliness'. Tom was nice looking, with a winsome manner, he dressed carefully, posed attractively while playing the violin, made the most of sentimental passages in the music, and may have had 'macaroni' friends. Therefore Tom was 'one of them' – a 'fribble' or a 'daffodil', as late eighteenth-century society called a man drawn to his own sex. It was 'hard to treat of a nauseous subject, without some loathsome expressions' (as Daniel Defoe had written on this subject at the beginning of the century), but let's not beat about the bush (the *Public Ledger* didn't): the *Westminster Magazine* was outing Tom. [346]

But the magazine was on its own, no one else saw anything offensive about Tom. And the following month, after he had led the orchestra in five more Handel oratorios, one of them a command performance, the *Morning Post* gave him his due – the band, it said, was led 'with great judgement by young Mr Linley whose excellence also as a solo performer needs not the aid of Panegyric to recommend it'.[347]

As if Tom's own possible sexual confusion, or the *Westminster Magazine*'s perception of it, weren't enough, his friend from Italy, the violinist Joseph Agus, now a soloist at the King's Theatre, Haymarket (who had just published a set of six duets for two violins), appeared in court that same month on a charge of attempting to rape an eleven-year-old girl. The victim was Agus' godchild, Elizabeth Weichsel, daughter of Carl Weichsel, principal oboe at the Haymarket Theatre, and Frederica Weichsel, a popular singer at the Vauxhall Gardens.

The case attracted considerable attention because the little girl was herself a celebrity prodigy, as pianist and composer. At the trial at Kingston Assizes, she told the court that one afternoon the previous summer Agus, who was 'exceedingly intimate in her mother's family' (and may possibly have been her lover), had come to the house for lunch and stayed on, when her parents went off to their respective theatres. At about eight that night the girl told him she needed to go upstairs to curl her hair. Agus offered to do it for her, and in the process he 'used many indecencies both in words and actions'.[348] Without leaving the courtroom to reach their verdict, the jury found him guilty of attempted rape, and, though there is no record of the sentence, it is unlikely that he would have avoided prison, but it is thought he fled to France, where, later in the century, he seems to have found work as *Maître de solfège* at the Paris Conservatoire.[349]

On the night after the trial, the victim, now twelve, performed at Covent Garden, playing a piano concerto (after which her brother, aged nine, played a violin concerto). In an unusually benign review, the *Westminster Magazine* described the girl Weichsel as a chaste fairy and the boy as a cherub, and said 'they held the whole house, even the very orchestra, in the most pleasing astonishment'. If they continued to progress with their studies, they would 'undoubtedly be the first performers in Europe'.[350]

Six weeks later Elizabeth Weichsel shared the platform with Tom at a Benefit Concert for the Viennese baryton player Andreas Lidl in the New Rooms in Tottenham Street. Similar to a viola d'amore, the baryton was little known in London, and Lidl's instrument would have been unique, because he had increased the number of understrings to twenty-seven, to allow a fully chromatic accompaniment, though these modifications made it extremely difficult to play. The concert began with a duet for the baryton and violin by Lidl, then a concerto for violin by Tom, and finally a trio for violin, viola da gamba and cello by Lidl. In the second part, 'Miss Weichsel played a concerto on the pianoforte by particular Desire'.[351*]

James Ward, after Joshua Reynolds, *Elizabeth Billington* (*née* Weichsel, 1803 (engraving, Gerald Coke Handel Collection, Foundling Museum/Bridgeman Images).

Shortly after his twenty-second birthday Tom received an invitation that was especially welcome at a time when he may have been feeling persecuted by his nemesis on the *Westminster Magazine*, harried by his family to find a wife, troubled about who he was, what he really wanted and how to find it, isolated by a sense of 'otherness', identifying more and more with the melancholy Werther, and

---

* Not long after this Elizabeth Weichsel changed tack, and concentrated on developing her voice. In 1783 she married her singing teacher, and, as Mrs Billington, became one of the most famous opera singers of the late eighteenth century – Haydn called her 'a great genius', the Prince of Wales fell in love with her, and Reynolds painted her as (another) Saint Cecilia.

exhausted by overwork. His patron, the Duke of Ancaster, asked if he and one of his sisters would like to spend the summer at Grimsthorpe Castle. Tom accepted with alacrity, and suggested bringing his third sister, the precocious Maria, now making a name for herself as a singing actress. She may have been only fourteen but she had been raised to perform, to charm and to hold her own.

Presumably they were invited more as friends than servants, but they would still have been expected to sing for their supper. The previous summer the tenor Gabriele Piozzi (husband of Dr Johnson's friend, Hester Thrale) had been invited to Grimsthorpe on the same basis, and understood that he was to perform for their Graces in the evening, and to help the elder daughter, Lady Priscilla Bertie, with her harpsichord studies.[352] He wasn't treated as one of the family at all, he complained, but 'as a mere musician', and he hated it, haranguing his friend Dr Burney with letters about the loutish behaviour of the English upper classes at home. At dinner, he said, he was 'sent to the 2nd table and kept at a great distance from the Duke & Duchess'. He was expected to devote all the morning to Lady Priscilla, and at night he was never called to sing till as late as nine or ten. So, in Burney's re-telling of Piozzi's letter, he used to 'lock and barricade his chamber door with trunks, boxes and all the lumber he cd find that he may not be forced to quit his *gite* like a dog … to shew his tricks.' Burney wrote a sympathetic letter back, in Italian, encouraging Piozzi to stick it out, on the English understanding that this too will pass. If Grimsthorpe provided so few pleasures, he wrote, just think of all the advantages that might accrue from such 'Penitenza!'. Besides Piozzi should realise that a regular life wasn't the way of the English aristocracy – on the contrary a universal disorder reigned in their houses:

It is said that at the Duke of Devonshire's, neither the master nor the mistress is ever seen – not at Breakfast, lunch or dinner. The whole Company is at liberty to Eat or to Die of Hunger. I believe that Grimsthorpe will be a beautiful School of Patience and Philosophy – And, what a magnificent Thing it would be to become a true Filosofo di Campagna! [like the hero of the comic opera of that name by Galuppi].[353]

But for all Burney's soothing words Piozzi couldn't take any more of the social divide at Grimsthorpe, and caught the next coach back to London. Perhaps Tom fared better – after all, he had been taken up by the Ancasters when he was a small boy, and anyway he knew how to play the English social game.

Thomas wasn't able to leave London for Lincolnshire till early June because he was working on some music for Charles Dibdin – setting songs for his comic opera, *The Shepherdess of the Alps*,[354] (based on a story by Jean-François Marmontel about a beautiful woman of noble birth who is forced to live as a farm labourer).* And the Ancasters could not leave till mid-June, because they had to attend Their Majesties at a Grand Court at St. James' on 29 May, then there were all the firings of guns and Ceremonies of Compliments for the King's fortieth birthday on 4 June. These included an entertainment at Ancaster House the next night (probably with Tom playing), and, a few days later, a review of the duke's Royal Southern Battalion, Lincolnshire Militia, in Hyde Park (after which 'the King expressed great satisfaction in their appearance and behaviour').[355]

At last the diary was clear, and by July Tom and his sister Maria, and a servant, were on their way up the Great North Road to Grimsthorpe.

---

* Dibdin's three-act opera was eventually staged at Covent Garden on 18 January 1780 (without any acknowledgement of Thomas Linley junior's contribution).

X

Finale

The chief difficulty facing any biographer of Thomas Linley junior is the absence of any of his letters or papers. But, thanks to the foresight and generosity of his younger brothers, Ozias and William, who bequeathed to Dulwich College the music and pictures they inherited, some of his scores survive; one or two of them in his own hand. The richest source of all Linley music manuscripts is now the British Library.

The Library's Additional Manuscripts collection holds eighteen separate musical items under the name of Thomas Linley junior. Descriptions of all of them, and the contents of some of them, were examined many times during the research and writing of this book. But, as so often happens, the one that matters slipped through the net. At number ten in the Linley list is a document that falls under the bibliographic reference, 'Add MS 61691–61710 B: H. Political and Historical Tracts, Catalogues, Etc (1453–1999)':

Add MS 61709: Blenheim Papers. Vol. DCIX (ff. 31). Dialogues between two Gentlemen French and Italian in London; aft. 8 July 1779 ...

At first sight the description didn't look relevant, but nothing is irrelevant till it has been proved to be, and the least likely clue is often the most fruitful. On the last of many return visits to the B. L. website, the date in that entry suddenly jumped off the screen, 8 July 1779. This is given as the earliest date on which it was supposed the document could have been created, but it also happens to be the day on which the Duke of Ancaster's wild young son and heir, Robert Bertie, the new fourth duke, died at Grimsthorpe, a year after Tom's drowning. Suddenly the manuscript took on some significance. A click on 'Details' brought up the completion of the first brief entry – and, with it, an epiphany for anyone who has ever wrestled with the mystery of Tom's death:

> ... Including (ff. 21–22b) an account of the death of the composer, Thomas Linley the younger, 5 Aug. 1778.

In the Manuscripts Reading Room on the second floor of the British Library at St Pancras, the pre-ordered Add MS 61709 was waiting at the enquiry desk. Neatly-packed in a burgundy buckram wrapper inside a matching solander box were three MS objects of different sizes. One was a very small marbled booklet, containing the miscellaneous notes of a bishop of St David's, another was a quarto catalogue of the papers of Sarah, Duchess of Marlborough, and the third was a thin, bound volume with marbled covers, three inches wide by five high. This was the one containing the *Dialogues* – thirty-nine folios handwritten in brown ink, followed by fourteen further folios, written in a different hand. But these pencilled pages are all trimmed down to nothing but stubs in the margin, leaving the reader to deduce their content.*

The text, in English throughout, starts with a chance meeting in

---

* This caused a hiccup when an attendant approached the author's desk while he was photographing the volume (as Reading Room rules allow), and asked him to account for the missing pages. Had he torn them out? Escorted to the Superintendent's booth, carrying the vandalised document, other readers' eyes following with interest, the author was pardoned when the Catalogue revealed that the excised pages had been noted in the original accession from Blenheim.

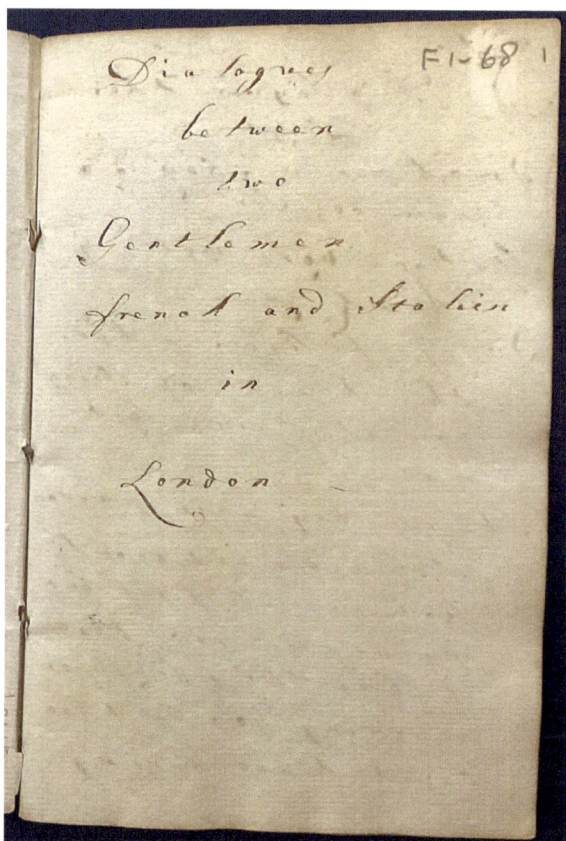

Title page, *Dialogues between two Gentlemen French and Italian* ... (British Library, Add MS 61709: Blenheim Papers. Vol. DCIX ff. 31, reproduced by permission of the British Library Board).

London of the two unidentified gentlemen of the document's title – one Italian, the other French. The Frenchman (*'Fr.'*) says he believes he had the honour of seeing the Italian (*'It.'*) in Paris the previous year. The Italian says he left Paris only last week. The Frenchman invites him to dinner, and the Italian accepts, but first they take a walk in St James's Park, which they both agree is very splendid, though the Frenchman can't help observing that it's not quite as splendid as the Jardin des Tuileries. The Italian responds indignantly that the Tuileries gardens may be gayer but they're certainly not as fine. How long, he asks, is the Frenchman planning to stay in England? Only five weeks, says the Frenchman. No longer, says the

Italian? What's the point, replies the Frenchman, who's been told by a friend there's nothing to see. To scotch his Anglophobia, the Italian says that actually he himself much prefers England to France, and with the Frenchman's permission he should like to persuade his new friend of England's attractions.

Come five o'clock they find a tavern and dine together, the Frenchman regretting it isn't Paris, where they would have been sure of a decent dinner – since it's well known that the English eat nothing but roast beef and plum pudding. *It.* begs to differ, and the tavern fare proves him right: 'the English', he confirms , 'can dress a good dinner'. Whereupon he proposes they drink a glass of wine. 'With all my heart', says the Frenchman – 'and let us drink, if you please, to the King of France.' The Italian is not impressed: 'I beg your pardon, Sir, to the King of England first, we are not in France. Let us be prudent.' It is the duty of any foreign gentleman, *It.* says, always to respect the manners of any country in which he finds himself. *Fr.* accepts this reproof, and thanks *It.* for his kindly advice.

Won over by his companion's gracious manners, *It.* says he judges *Fr.* to be one of the most superior specimens of French gentleman he has ever met, and, since he, the Italian, plans to travel for three or four years, he would find himself very happy in the Frenchman's company. *Fr.* returns the compliment. *It.* drinks his health, and *Fr.* drinks his. They agree to see all Europe together (though it is clear they have already seen quite a lot of it), and, in the interests of toleration and good fellowship, they undertake to abandon their national prejudices. But that doesn't stop *It.* remarking that the French talk a great deal too much, and very often 'without knowing nothing about the matter [*sic*]'. Surprisingly *Fr.* agrees, and asks *It* to give him a description of London. *It.* reels off the names of some of the great squares and bridges. They agree that the Tower is very large but not a fine and strong fortress. They think St. Paul's truly magnificent but second to St. Peter's in Rome for size and richness. *It.* recommends the Royal Exchange, Guildhall and Mansion House.

Of hospitals, *Fr.* thinks nothing can compare with those of Paris. *It.* rates Somerset House one of the finest buildings in Britain, and proceeds to enumerate some of the great streets of London. *Fr.* says Paris is bigger, *It.* contradicts him – London has 1,100,000 inhabitants, and Paris not quite 800,000.* Talking of London's night watchmen, both agree they are the 'greatest black gards in England'. Of the Pleasure Gardens, *It.* recommends 'Vaux-all'; of Concert Rooms, the Hanover Square Rooms and the Pantheon, but there is no mention of the masquerades and routs for which the Pantheon was notorious, and a not a single reference, at any point, to ladies.

And so it goes on, neither man saying anything of material interest, *It.* continuing to challenge *Fr.*'s judgements, with much beggings of pardon, and *Fr.* admitting that he speaks 'without reflexion' and is grateful to *It.* for his 'complaisance'. At length *Fr.* asks *It.* what he thinks of the English themselves. *It.* says they're strong and generous, good soldiers and great suitors, adding, 'the English by their virtue have acquired a great fame all over the world'. *Fr.*: 'But if it is So, how did they lose America?' For once *It.* is nonplussed:

> **It.** *As I don't like to meddle myself in politic affairs, so I hope you will excuse me for the answer.*

> **Fr.** *I see my fault, and I beg your pardon.*

In the second part, which continues without a break, the Italian and the Frenchman have now embarked on their travels, and are on their way to York, en route to Scotland. After breakfast in Barnet ('a pretty village'), then passing through Stevenage and Biggleswade, they find themselves in the neighbourhood of Stamford. *It.* announces that there are two fine country seats nearby – Burghley

---

* As the population of London did not reach one million till 1801, when the population of Paris was 547,000, it looks as though the document was written at about the turn of the century.

House, belonging to the Earl of Exeter, and Grimsthorpe Castle, belonging to the Duke of Ancaster. *Fr.* wonders if *It.* has ever visited either of these places:

> **It.** *Yes Sir, I have been there many times; and in the year 1778 I met with a great misfortune at Grimsthorpe ... In the Summer, I went in to the country with his Grace, where I found one Sgr. Linly [sic], a young man of a great merit in the musical way. In the morning of the 5th of Agust [sic] this young man came in my apartment and invited me to go with him in one of his Grace's pleasure boats. I was not willing to go, as I could not swim; but having excused my Self above half an hour, to no purpose, I went with him and the water man, in to the boat. About a quarter of an hour after, the boat was overturned and we fell off all three in to the pond!*

> **Fr.** *I hope that no body was hurt by this accident.*

> **It.** *I beg your pardon, the poor young man was drowned and we had very nearly borne the same fates!*

> **Fr.** *A great misfortune indeed! Pray, how did you save your Self? ... The waterman saved me: in making me reach the borders of the boat* [the gunwale – the top, flat edge of the hull] *where I stood, till her Grace who saw from the windows of her apartment what appened [sic] sent down all the servants of the house to our assistance.*

> **Fr.** *And could not the poor unfortunate young man be saved?*

> **It.** *No Sir, when they took him up, he was quite dead.*

> **Fr.** *What did his Grace say to this misfortune?*

40.

Dr. Pray, how was it?

A. In the Summer, j went in to the country with his Grace, where j found one Mr. Linly, a young man of a great merit, in the musical way. In the morning of the 5th of Agust, this young man came in my apartment and invited me to go with him in one of his Grace's pleasure boats. j was not willing to go, as j could not swim; but having excused my self above half an hour, to no purpose, j went with him and the water

It. *His Grace was very much hurt by the news of it, as he was extremely ill at that time, and he died eight days after.*

Fr. *Did you return again in that Country Seat after that misfortune?*

It. *Yes Sir, with the young Duke his son.*

Fr. *Is this nobleman alive now?*

It. *No Sir, I had the misfortune to lose him the eight [sic] of July 1779.*

Fr. *I am very sorry for it.*

It. *I thank you kindly. If you chuse we will go to Grimsthorpe.*

Fr. *With great pleasure.'*

And at this critical point, the text written in ink comes to a cliff-hanging end. But the conversation continues over the page, written now in pencil, in a different hand – and hurriedly, even wildly, with the character of the Frenchman subtly changing.

It. *We are at Grimsthorpe.*

Fr. *That I could have told you Sir.*

It. *Pray Sir, what do you mean?*

Fr. *O Sir, nothing at all.*

It. *Very well, Sir. This is a pretty place.*

Fr. *I cannot agree with you Sir.'*

There follow the seven excised pages, with only a sliver of each page remaining at the gutter. So we have no idea why the Frenchman disagreed with the Italian's assertion that Grimsthorpe was a pretty place. From the severed pages it is possible to see that the dialogue continues in the same pencilled hand, but impossible to decipher more than a few letters (though a scientific examination of folio thirty-nine and the recto of the back cover might reveal indentations of the pencilled writing on the second and penultimate folios of the pages which were later cut).

A final sentence survives intact on the recto of the marbled cover, and this suggests that the two men have had a fundamental falling-out during the missing pages. The sentence is only thirteen words long, and in poorer grammar than the inked texts, but it is highly significant:

> [**Fr.**] *Sir, Italians are a coward. and I never will travel with an I-talian again.*

And there, dramatically and enigmatically, the *Dialogues* conclude – with no explanation for the Frenchman's final outburst, or for the excision of the pages containing the details of their visit to Grimsthorpe. But there are some clues.

The Italian's story, insofar as it goes, is broadly in line with the newspaper accounts of August 1778, so the Italian gentleman of the *Dialogues* must be the 'Mr Olivarez, an Italian master' named as Tom's companion in the boat that day. The language and manners of the two gentlemen indicate that both are educated and both conspicuously foreign, but perhaps neither is quite a Gentleman in the eighteenth-century sense. Maybe they are tutors, perhaps cicerones accompanying young noblemen on the Grand Tour, as there is much talk of travel and foreign places. Olivarez may have

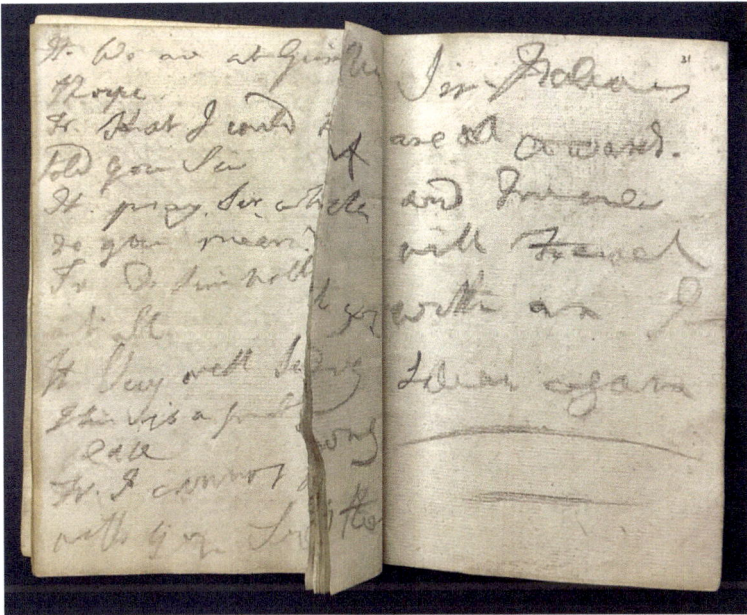

known Tom's patron, Peregrine, 3rd Duke of Ancaster, before 1778, and probably met Tom himself for the first time at Grimsthorpe that summer. But who was the Frenchman, who seems familiar with the castle, has a negative opinion of it, and delivers the *coup de grâce*? Or is he a figment of a fevered imagination – the alter ego, perhaps, of the Italian?

It is likely that Tom's fluent Italian kindled a friendship with Olivarez, with whom he would have been thrown together anyway as a fellow upper servant in a nobleman's house, and it seems that the friendship was sufficiently intimate to allow Tom free access to the Italian's 'apartment' at Grimsthorpe. But he must have had some special hold over the Italian, and remarkable powers of persuasion, to have won the man around to sailing when he was so set against it.

There is indirect evidence in the *Dialogues* that they were written some time between about 1795 and 1805.[*] In recalling the tragedy two decades after it happened, the Italian was probably more profoundly affected by it than he admits to the Frenchman – at least in the surviving pages of the written account, and it may be that the whole purpose of this eccentric document was to provide the Italian with an opportunity to relate a terrible story that had haunted him for so long.

But it is mysterious, and deeply frustrating, that the account should stop with the men's arrival at Grimsthorpe, just when the story is starting, and that the fourteen further folios, which might have explained everything, have been removed. So whose were the scissors, and why the cuts?

It is not known how the *Dialogues* found their way into the col-lection of the state and family papers in the Muniment Room at Blenheim Palace. Perhaps Olivarez joined the staff of the Marlboroughs after leaving the service of the Ancasters when the fourth duke died in 1779. At all events the volume lay at Blenheim till 1978, when the entire collection of Blenheim Papers was allocated to the British Library by the Treasury, in part-payment of death duties on the estate of the late 10th Duke of Marlborough.

Four years earlier, in anticipation of this transfer, the archivist J. P. Hudson had spent some time at Blenheim working through the manuscripts, listing, sorting and valuing them for the Treasury.[356] From his report, it is clear that the collection was substantially re-arranged twice in the nineteenth century: first by the historian Archdeacon William Coxe, perhaps in preparation for his edition of the *Memoirs of John, Duke of Marlborough* (London, 1818–19); and later by the writer and publisher Johnson Stuart Reid, who was commissioned by the 8th Duke of Marlborough to catalogue the MSS for an unpublished report dated 1889–90.[357] Both of these scholars will have examined the *Dialogues*, and either of them might

---

[*] See footnote on p. 160.

have considered the pencilled account so scandalous that he took it upon himself to snip it out, leaving just the final sentence to convey the gist of the excised material (and that could not be obliterated anyway without removing the back cover). Alternatively either Olivarez or the Frenchman (if indeed they were two persons) could have had second thoughts about this potentially revealing section, for the hectic writing of what is left of the pencilled pages suggests an unsettled state of mind.

In the contemporary newspaper accounts of the drowning there is some implication that Olivarez was a musician. If so, it is odd that he himself makes no mention of this when referring to Tom as being 'of merit in the musical way', without expanding on those merits. There is no record of any Olivarez, or anyone of any similar name, musician or otherwise, in other British newspaper reports of the period, and none in the *Dictionary of National Biography, Grove's Dictionary of Music and Musicians, The London Stage Database*, the *Handel Reference Database* or Simon McVeigh's *Calendar of 18th Century Musicians in London*. There was a Venezuelan musician, Juan Manuel Olivares – composer, violinist, harpsichord player and organist – who could have visited England in 1778, when he was eighteen. But there is no evidence that he did, or that he would have been able to spare the time, or find the means, to make the long voyage: he seems to have spent his entire life at home in colonial Caracas. Another candidate could have been the Spanish violin virtuoso and composer, Juan Oliver y Astorga, who was part of the Bach/Abel circle, played regularly at the Hanover Rooms, and was a protégé of the Ancasters' kinsman, the eccentric composer Willoughby Bertie, 3rd Earl of Abingdon. But he would have been forty-five years old in 1778, and all three men in the boat are said to have been young. Besides he wasn't even in England then: he had left two years earlier to take up a post in Madrid.

But were the three men in the boat all young? It is significant that the Italian twice describes Linley as 'a young man', thus implying that, despite the contemporary newspaper accounts, he himself was not. If he was neither a musician nor a young man, who was this 'Italian master'? He could have been a drawing or dancing master, an Italian coach, a history professor – a man whose qualifications might have equipped him to be a 'governor' on the Grand Tour. Given that his *Dialogues* ended up in the Muniment Room at Blenheim, perhaps he was a librarian or an archivist.

The proprietorial tone of his reference in the *Dialogues* to the third Duke of Ancaster's son, Robert, Marquess of Lindsey ('I had the misfortune to lose him the eight [*sic*] of July 1779'), suggests that Olivarez was employed by the son and not the father – presumably from some point in time after Robert had come down from Cambridge, and before he joined the army and went off to fight in the American War of Independence in March 1778. And the *Dialogues* indicate that Olivarez returned to this work when the marquess came back from his American service at the end of 1778, to inherit his father's estates as fourth Duke of Ancaster (for no more than eight months, because he followed his father to the grave the summer following). It seems likely that Olivarez was first taken on by the son in some capacity, then employed by the father as tutor to one or both of the Ancaster daughters while Robert was in America.

Horace Walpole, who knew more than anyone about everyone in society in the late eighteenth century, makes an interesting, and typically lurid, observation about Robert, the young fourth duke, in a letter to a lady friend after Robert's death in July 1779:

> *Are you not sorry, Madam, for the poor Duke of Ancaster, especially since he made so noble and sensible a will ... I hear he has left a legacy to a very small man that was always his companion, and whom, when he was drunk, he used to fling at the heads of the company, as others fling a bottle.*[358]

According to Walpole, Robert was 'of a turbulent nature; and though of a fine figure, his manners were not noble'; he died, he says, 'of a scarlet fever, contracted by drinking and rioting'.[359] Another contemporary described him as 'a young nobleman of extraordinary eccentricity of character, and capable of undertaking any enterprise, however desperate or dangerous'.[360]

It is tempting to speculate that Robert Ancaster's very small man-mis-sile might have been Olivarez himself, but he probably wasn't. In an extensive

Richard Cosway, *Robert Bertie, Marquess of Lindsey* (later 4th Duke of Ancaster) as an officer, *c.*1770 (miniature watercolour on ivory, Nelson-Atkins Museum of Art, Kansas City).

Will (signed 29 May 1779, proved 23 July 1779), the young duke makes generous bequests, ranging up to £600 each, to eleven named male servants, including butler, groom and apothecary. But not one of these beneficiaries has a foreign name, or any name, given or family, resembling 'Olivarez'. Besides even a drunken duke of turbulent nature is unlikely to have abused an educated man in such a humiliating and dangerous way – at any rate, not twice.

Whoever Olivarez was, the disgust which the Frenchman expresses about him on the last folio of the *Dialogues* ('Italians are a coward') suggests that he played a dishonourable part in the drowning. But what could he have done that was so craven, and why had Tom insisted on his joining the boat trip that day, when the poor man couldn't swim and didn't want to come?

The answer to these questions may never be known. There is no mention of the tragedy, even *en passant*, in the published volumes of his brother-in law Richard Sheridan's letters, or in the surviving manuscript letters of his sister Elizabeth or the other sisters or their father, or of Mary, Dowager Duchess of Ancaster. The only known record that might have offered an explanation is Olivarez's *Dialogues*.

Part of the front cover of the *Dialogues*, with two heads in the marbling (British Library, Add MS 61709: Blenheim Papers. Vol. DCIX ff. 31, reproduced by permission of the British Library Board).

A curious piece of evidence came to light after an examination of the contents of the *Dialogues*. Cleverly disguised in the marbled swirls of the front cover – so cleverly that they are barely detectable – are two small heads, the upper one grinning, the lower one a skull. These macabre pictograms have been so skilfully incorporated into the marbled design that they seem part of it, their outlines camouflaged so they are not immediately identifiable, like geckoes resting on a log. Whoever was responsible may have planted them as a warning of darkness within.

But they might also indicate that the author was riddled with guilt. Why otherwise does the volume begin calmly and end in hysteria, the fine inked hand degenerating into a barely coherent pencilled scrawl? What is the point of the conversation about the relative virtues of England and France, and why the ostentatious loyalty to England? The volume must have been written by one man, and that one man must be the Italian. And if he really is Olivarez, perhaps he believed himself to be personally responsible not only for the death of young Tom, which, at the least, he witnessed, but also for deaths of the third and fourth dukes, all in the space of eleven months. He may have felt he jinxed all those around him, which could have brought on 'survivor guilt', which after a number of years of suffering cost him his reason.

If this were the case then the *Dialogues* could be read as the ravings of a lunatic. Using the pretext of a conversation with another foreigner, he sets out first of all to express his allegiance to England and her traditions, and then to unburden himself of an overwhelming sense of shame and remorse for what he believes to be guilt, culminating in an enigmatical rant which he later regrets and removes.

But what if his guilt were to some extent justified? What if he really had played a part in the drowning?

It seems likely that Tom had been troubled for months before he went to Grimsthorpe. Stung by the *Westminster Magazine* vendetta, he may have been worried about where this was going next – for a soft and graceful young man could have been seen as effeminate, an effeminate young man was widely assumed to be a sodomite, and sodomy was punishable by death (even though the charge was rarely brought, because of the difficulty of proof). But the very allegation of attempted sodomy was often enough to send a man so accused into voluntary exile abroad, pursued by a baying mob – as in the cases of Samuel Foote, Lord Tylney and Samuel Drybutter. Perhaps the *Westminster Magazine* had some information that he knew could lead to public exposure, even to a criminal trial, and perhaps Tom couldn't face this. He may also have been uneasy about the continuing musical demands of his domineering father and his manipulative brother-in-law Sheridan. He was twenty-two now – would he never be free to write his own music? Immersed in the dark worlds of *Ossian* and *Werther*, obsessed with storms and drownings and drama, unsure of himself, and fighting his demons alone, he would have been acutely susceptible to the romantic lure of salvation through suicide.

Epilogue

Since the Middle Ages the office of Coroner has existed in England to investigate sudden, violent or unexplained deaths, and, in the case of Tom's death, it would have been the responsibility of his host, the Duke of Ancaster, to see that the accident was reported to the local Court of Quarter Sessions in order to set up an Inquest, and, if necessary, a post mortem examination of the body to establish the exact cause of death. It was not the Coroner's business to determine liability or to apportion blame, but only to examine witnesses to discover 'how the deceased came by his death', and the findings of such an Inquest might have thrown light on the unknowns of Tom's death. But there is no surviving record of any such Inquest in the National or Lincolnshire Archives, or in the *Lincolnshire Inquests Volume 1*, sourced from the Lindsey Quarter Sessions of 1773–1848, and no report of any such Inquest in any contemporary newspaper in London or the provinces.

It is unlikely that there wasn't an Inquest, given all the unanswered questions and the level of public interest, and it is hardly surprising that the relevant record should have gone astray in 250 years. But the public interest might also have been a reason to avoid an Inquest. The duke had many reasons for wishing to hush the matter up. For one thing he was dying, for another it was only two years since he had been publicly named as a sodomite – an accusation he never challenged – and his long-term patronage of pretty

Tom may not have been without its own complications. And for another thing, his wayward son and heir, Robert, was already in the scandal sheets of New York as a Don Juan, and the family may have feared further revelations if the press's appetite were whetted. If these matters weighed with the duke, it would have been easy for him, or the duchess or his Steward acting for him, to persuade the local justices that there was no need for an inquiry since the accident was no more than a tragic accident. The Linley family would probably have supported this account, for they would not have wanted their good name associated with any suggestion of scandal, or of negligence, or, worse, of murder – nor of suicide, which the Church saw as a mortal sin, and the law as a crime (punishable, potentially, by the refusal of a Christian burial, and the forfeiture of a victim's property).

Murder seems unlikely. By all accounts there were only three people present at the death. One of them, the boatman, can have had no reason to wish Tom dead, and if the other, Olivarez, were the culprit why did he try so very hard to avoid being there? Agatha Christie might have lined up the duke as a possible suspect, on the grounds that Tom knew too much, but she would have provided the evidence and laid the clues.

It could all have been a tragic accident, as the press reported (presumably at the instigation of the families). A squall could have blown up without warning, and might have overturned the boat if the sail wasn't competently handled. And Tom might well have struck out for the shore in an impatient bid to seek help for the other two stranded on the gunwales. If he had, his waterlogged greatcoat and riding boots would undoubtedly have dragged him down into the mud as he reached the shallower water, just as the newspapers reported.

But why was he wearing a greatcoat and boots for a summer sail anyway – a curiosity which all the newspapers made a point of noting? And why, as the *Dialogues* insist, was he so eager to have

Olivarez with him. Furthermore why don't the *Dialogues* make any mention of a squall, or even bad weather? (Olivarez records simply that '... the boat was overturned and we fell off ...').

So maybe it was suicide. A footnote published by an unidentified acquaintance of Tom's sister Elizabeth, thirty-eight years after the drowning, claims that when the body was recovered from the lake pebbles were found in the coat pockets, 'from whence it was conjectured to have been a premeditated suicide; and no other reason could be assigned for it than a disappointment in love'.[361] There is no corroboration of this theory in any other source, and if it were suicide, it seems perverse, even counter-productive, for Tom to have chosen to end his life in the company of two able-bodied witnesses who were likely to try to stop him, and would surely have noticed that his pockets were bulging suspiciously before he had even climbed aboard. And if the early nineteenth-century footnote is right about the motivation, then with whom might Tom have been in love?

Perhaps Tom had been having, or wanting to have, a relationship with Olivarez or even the boatman (though there is no evidence for this) and perhaps he was spurned. Perhaps one of them had gossiped about Tom's private life, maybe even accidentally triggered some criminal charge which was pending (but again there is no evidence). In either case Tom might have had some perverse reason for wanting them to witness his death, even (unintentionally) to assist it. And if he had been under the influence of 'the Werther Effect' (which was widely believed at the time to have been responsible for an 'epidemic' of suicides in Germany following publication of the novel),* he may have planned a bravura suicide scene, in the rich tradition of the *Sturm und Drang*.

---

* An investigation by two 21st century Swedish scholars has discounted the epidemic theory (Jan Thorson and Per-Arne Öberg, 'Was There a Suicide Epidemic After Goethe's Werther?', *Archives of Suicide Research*, Volume 7, 2003).

On the morning of 5 August 1778, Tom dressed in his Werther outfit – blue coat, yellow waistcoat and breeches, and leather top-boots, with a greatcoat for his own reasons – and made his way to Olivarez's bed chamber, to persuade him to come sailing. Olivarez couldn't swim, was afraid of the water, and hated sailing. But Tom's forcefulness carried the day, and the two set off across the park to the lake.

Once they reached the jetty, where a sailing dinghy was moored in wait, they climbed aboard, and sat themselves on opposite sides, to keep the boat on an even keel. The boatman pushed them off, then jumped into the stern, by the tiller, and paddled the boat out into clear water.

When they reached the middle of the lake, Tom judged they had picked up enough wind to sail, and made as though to hoist the sail. But the boatman had not yet brought the boat into the wind to make the operation easier and safer. Under orders from the duke not to let Tom take charge, he tried to stop him, but Tom was impetuous and headstrong, and the boatman, a mere garden servant, and possibly still a boy, was powerless to overrule him.

Thomas stood by the mast, hauling on the halyard to raise the sail, which immediately filled with wind before the other two men could redistribute their weight to compensate. Olivarez took fright and leapt up. The boatman shifted to the opposite side, as a counterbalance, but it was too late. The boat continued to list, with the gunwale dipping beneath the surface. As water flooded in, they began to sink. In a panic Olivarez grabbed hold of Tom, and, to steady himself, Tom grabbed hold of the boatman, and, with a lurch, all three fell into the lake as the boat went down.

Thomas would have found it difficult to swim because of his heavy boots and coat, which might for a minute or two have provided some buoyancy, but which would then have filled with water and weighed him down. But perhaps he didn't even try to swim, giving himself instead to the lake without a struggle, as though glad to be free of his earthly troubles. The boatman, probably a swimmer himself, would have tried to save him, as he sank below the surface, but Tom apparently directed *him to help the Italian instead. Olivarez wasn't easy to help. Thrashing about in a frenzy of fear, trying to stay afloat, he probably clung to Tom, and may even have trodden him down below the surface and into the silt below. Only then was Olivarez still enough for a moment so the boatman could hook an arm around his chest, and drag him towards the safety of the mast sticking up from the hull of the sunken boat. Grabbing the mast they could both have found a footing on the submerged gunwale, where, waving and shouting for help, they watched in horror as Tom disappeared.*

From her dressing-room window up in the castle, the duchess saw the accident happening, and sent servants running down to the lake. In the boathouse the rescuers found another boat, and rowed out to the sunken vessel, to rescue Olivarez and the boatman. But of Tom there was no sign. The water had closed over his head, and, in the words of his Song of Moses, *he 'was sunk like a lifeless stone, vanished and dead'.*[362]

Everything else would have followed according to the reports in the newspapers in 1778: the search for the body, the grisly attempts to revive it, the arrival of Mr Linley for the funeral, the death of the duke late that same night, the Linley sisters' heartbroken laments for Tom and his violin, the death of their brother, Samuel, four months later, and the death of the new young Duke of Ancaster the following summer.

The boatman, who saw what really happened, was probably paid to hold his peace, and Olivarez would have had to live with the knowledge that he had not only failed to save Tom, but that in his panic he may actually have hastened his end. Like the Ancient Mariner, his conscience condemned him to repeat the terrible story as a penance, and to draw skulls on the cover of his handwritten confession.

———

Was it an oddly theatrical suicide, or an oddly unlikely accident? No one will ever know. What is known is that Linley senior was permanently affected by the loss of his favourite son – 'the pride of his existence, the partner of his studies'. If he couldn't bring himself to accept it as an accident, he certainly wouldn't have been able to accept it as suicide. Suffering from what was then called a 'brain fever', he seems to have made no attempt to gather together Tom's music and papers for posterity, for publication, for a memoir.* But, mourning Tom till the last hour of his life, and outliving four more of his seven sons and at least three of his five daughters, Mr Linley lingered on till 1795, when he died a sick and broken man.[363]

A quarter of a millenium has passed since the death of Thomas Linley junior, but he is not quite forgotten. Enough of his music survives to remind us what English music lost that summer day in 1778, as his pupil, copyist and friend, Mathew Cooke, recorded thirty-four years later, his grief still fresh:

Thomas Linley, junior ... at once the delight and comfort of his Parents, and beloved by a most numerous host of acquaintance ... on the fatal 12th day of August 1778 was unfortunately drowned by the upsetting of a pleasure Boat at The Duke of Ancaster['s] at Grimsthorpe, in Lincolnshire. Thus perished in the bud and bloom of youth this extraordinary Genius, at the Age of 22 years, and 3 months. Oh! lost too early!!![364]

If only he had lived, even into his early thirties, like Mozart and Schubert, he might have achieved so much more, left so much more – and inherited, perhaps, the mantle passed down from Tallis through Byrd, Purcell and Handel as one of the great composers of England.

---

* In about 1800 Linley's widow, Mary, published a two-volume set of the vocal works of father and son without specifying who had written what (*The Posthumous Vocal Works of Mr. Linley and Mr. T. Linley, Consisting of Songs, Duetts, Cantatas, Madrigals and Glees. In two Volumes* [published for Mrs Thomas Linley by [John or Thomas] Preston, London, *c.*1800). Other manuscripts, lying forgotten in the Theatre Royal, Drury Lane, were lost in the great fire which destroyed the theatre in 1809. Yet others, dispersed among his siblings, have simply not made it down to today.

'Thy name, O LINLEY, never shall decay', his sister Maria wrote defiantly just days after the drowning,[365] and Tom's first, closest and most understanding friend, the soulmate of his youth, and the star he chased for the rest of his life, later put his own unique seal on the legend of Thomas Linley junior. It happened at a musical evening in Vienna about five years after the drowning, and the Irish tenor Michael Kelly never forgot it:

> ... that prodigy of genius – Mozart ... favoured the company by performing fantasias and capriccios on the piano-forte ... After this splendid performance we sat down to supper, and I had the pleasure to be placed between him and his wife ... He conversed with me a good deal about Thomas Linley ... with whom he was intimate at Florence, and spoke of him with great affection. He said that Linley was a true genius; and he felt that, had he lived, he would have been one of the greatest ornaments of the musical world.[366]

Acknowledgements

M y interest in Thomas Linley junior was first stirred while researching an earlier book, *Gimcrack: A Rake's Progress* (Shelf Lives, 2020), which begins with a chapter in which the Mozarts arrive in Naples, just three weeks after meeting the thirteen-year-old Linley in Florence. In a corner of their minds both Leopold and Wolfgang were still thinking about that happy week, as the father's later letter home makes clear, and I was so struck by Leopold's account of the boys' brief but passionate friendship that I wanted to find out more about Tom Linley. It wasn't easy.

His two bachelor younger brothers, the Rev. Ozias Linley, an eccentric canon, and the composer William Linley, were ideally placed to write memoirs but neither ever did, perhaps because of a veil of secrecy that seems to have hung over Tom's life. In the 244 years that have elapsed since the tragic drowning there has been no full-length biography, largely because of the lack of source material – no letters or other writings, and all too little music.

The first biographical notice appeared in 1812, in a manuscript by Tom's friend, former assistant and copyist, the organist Matthew Cooke, together with Cooke's copies of some of Tom's scores, now in the British Library. In the following decade two further biographical articles appeared in musical publications, *Sainsbury's Dictionary of Musicians* (1824) and the journal *The Harmonicon* (1825). Much later in the century the first edition of the *Dictionary of National Biography* (1885–) carried a brief notice by Robert Farquharson Sharp.

But it wasn't till the twentieth century that the musical world first took serious note of Tom Linley, when the scholar, organist, editor and composer, Gwilym Beechey, presented a full account of *Thomas Linley, Junior: His Life, Work and Times*, in a doctoral thesis (Cambridge, 1964). Dr Beechey followed this with more Linley studies in *The Musical Quarterly*, *The Musical Times*, and, with Linda Troost, in the *New Grove Dictionary of Music and Musicians* (Oxford University Press, 2001). The late Roger Fiske also contributed to Linley studies, notably in *English Theatre Music in the Eighteenth Century*, and in 2000 the German musicologist Professor Peter Overbeck wrote a further biographical account in his doctoral thesis, *Die Chorwerke von Thomas Linley dem Jüngeren (1756–1778): Analyse, Vergleich, kompositorisches und biographisches Umfeld*. Professor Paul F. Rice added more information in 'Vocal Music in Eighteenth-century Bath from the Pens of Thomas Linley Senior (1733–95) and Junior (1756–78)', which appeared in *The Phenomenon of Singing* (2003), and the following year Professor Suzanne Aspden wrote a new biographical article for the *Oxford Dictionary of National Biography*. Meanwhile in 1988 the director of the Dulwich Picture Gallery, the art historian Giles Waterfield, had organised a Linley Family exhibition in the Gallery, and published a comprehensive catalogue, *A Nest of Nightingales*, with articles about Tom by Drs Susan Wallington and Gwilym Beechey.

There have been several books about the talented Linley family as a whole, and about Elizabeth in particular. The best of them is Clementina Black's *The Linleys of Bath* (1926), which observes that 'Scarcely a spoken or a written word of Thomas Linley [junior]'s remains, only certain elaborate and beautiful written scores' (and most of these in the hand of Matthew Cooke or the singer and copyist Joseph Gaudry). Other books include *Still the Lark – A Biography of Elizabeth Linley* by Margot Bor and Lamond Clelland (1962), *A Nest of Nightingales – Thomas Gainsborough, 'The Linley Sisters'* (1988), by

Giles Waterfield and others, and Alan Chedzoy's highly readable *Sheridan's Nightingale – The Story of Elizabeth Linley* (1997). But Tom is never much more than a spear-carrier in any of them.

The most informative, up-to-date and well-researched source of information is Dr Rebecca Gribble's excellent thesis, *Musicians within the Social Hierarchies of Eighteenth-Century England: The Case of Tom Linley Junior* (2015). This is a remarkably comprehensive, thorough and well-presented study, with original data, detailed charts, pedigrees and bibliography, but, as its title clearly indicates, it is a sociological investigation of the status of a musician in Georgian England, and not a narrative of Tom Linley's life.

Other useful sources have been the novels, *A Nest of Linnets* (1901), by the Irish writer Frank Frankfort Moore, a fictionalised account of the Linley family, and *Trazom – 'n Mozart-verhaal* by the South African writer and music lover Philip de Vos, about the meeting of Mozart and Linley. And for an understanding of what we would today call the gay sub-culture in Tom's time, Rictor Norton's treasury of diligently-researched essays, *Homosexuality in Eighteenth-Century England: A Sourcebook*, 2017 (online at http://rictornorton.co.uk/) is the *vade mecum* for anyone interested in the subject.

But perhaps the most persuasive insights into the mind and music of Linley junior are the recordings made by the Parley of Instruments (director Paul Nicholson) for Hyperion Records a generation ago (*A Lyric Ode* and *Violin Sonatas*, 1992; *Cantatas and Theatre Music*, 1995; *Violin Concertos*, 1996; and *The Song of Moses*, 1998), together with scholarly and revealing essays by the Parley's co-founder, the conductor and musicologist, Peter Holman, who has done so much to revive old English music from the Stuarts to the Georgians.

Many kind friends have read drafts of *Tommasino*. The J. C. Bach expert, Dr Stephen Roe, generously offered specialist advice, Adam Bager and John Byrne combed the text for errors (though any remaining are mine alone), and Michael Bloch, Sidney Buckland, Hugh Cobbe, Graham Johnson and Alexis Aldridge Rothbart made further helpful suggestions from their own authoritative perspectives. I am deeply grateful to them all – and to friends who lent support in other ways, including Viscountess Bridgeman, Dr Christian Carritt, Ania Czepulkowska-Abse, Susan Daly, Johnny de Falbe, Gill Evansky, Arabella von Friesen, Christopher and Hanne Gray, George Hayburn, Karen Macauslan, Tom Perrin, Christopher Ricardo, David and Annie Scotland, Susannah Townsend, Petroc Trelawny, Lorna Vaughan, and especially the typographer Susan Wightman of Libanus Press, who designed and typeset this and other Shelf Lives titles.

I also want to thank the following for professional help: Lucy West, Assistant Curator, Dulwich Picture Gallery; Jim Riseley, Museum Assistant, Victoria Art Gallery, Bath; Chris Scobie, Curator, Music Manuscripts, and Zoe Stansell, Manuscripts Reference Service, British Library; Sian Phillips, Bridgeman Images; Sarah Machin and Kevin Best, Lincolnshire Archives; Abigail Lamphier and Dr Edward Town, Yale Center for British Art, New Haven, Connecticut; Abbie Weinberg, Folger Shakespeare Library, Washington DC; Juli McLoone, University of Michigan Library, Ann Arbor.

For picture permissions I am most grateful to the Dulwich Picture Gallery, London; the Victoria Art Gallery, Bath, and North East Somerset Council; Baroness Willoughby de Eresby, Grimsthorpe Castle; Bridgeman Images; and the British Library Board. Every reasonable effort has been made to trace other copyright holders, and I regret any inadvertent omissions: these can be put right in future editions.

My greatest debt, as always, is to my partner Julian Berkeley.

TS, Baughurst, September 2022

Bibliography

Anderson, Emily (Trans. and Ed.), *The Letters of Mozart and His Family*, Macmillan, 3 vols, 1938, and 3rd edition, Papermac, 1989.

[Angelo, Henry], *Reminiscences of Henry Angelo with Memoirs of his late Father and Friends ...*, vol i, 1828, vol. ii, 1830.

Aspden, Suzanne, 'Linley, Thomas, Junior; Linley, Thomas, Senior; and Linley, Elizabeth Ann', *Oxford Dictionary of National Biography*, 2004.

Barrett, Charlotte (Ed.), *Diary and Letters of Madame d'Arblay* [Frances (Fanny) Burney], vol. i (1778–1784), 1876.

Beechey, Gwilym, *Thomas Linley, Junior: His Life, Work and Times*, doctoral thesis, Cambridge University, 1964.

_____, 'Thomas Linley, Junior, 1756–1778', *The Musical Quarterly*, vol. liv, issue 1, January 1968, pp. 74–82.

_____, 'Thomas Linley, Junior, 1756–1778, and His Vocal Music', *The Musical Times*, vol. cxix, no. 1626, August 1978.

_____ and Linda Troost, 'Linley, Thomas, Junior', *New Grove Dictionary of Music and Musicians*, Oxford University Press, 2001.

Belsey, Hugh, *Thomas Gainsborough – The Portraits, Fancy Pictures and Copies after Old Masters*, Yale University Press for the Paul Mellon Centre for Studies in British Art, 2019.

Black, Clementina, *The Linleys of Bath*, London, Martin Secker, 1926

Bor, Margot, and Lamond Clelland, *Still the Lark – A Biography of Elizabeth Linley*, London, Merlin Press, 1962.

Brown, Jane, *Lancelot 'Capability' Brown – The Omnipotent Magician 1716–1783*, Pimlico, 2012.

Burkert, Mattie (principal Investigator and Project Director), *The London Stage Database*, (drawn from *The London Stage, 1660–1800: A Calendar of Plays, Entertainments & Afterpieces, together with Casts, Box-Receipts and*

Contemporary Comment, compiled from the Playbills, Newspapers and Theatrical Diaries of the Period, Southern Illinois University Press, 1960–68), online at https://londonstagedatabase.uoregon.edu/

Burney, Charles (Ed. C. H. Glover), *Dr Burney's Continental Travels, 1770–1772*, London, Blackie,1927.

———, (Ed. P. A. Scholes), *Dr Burney's Musical Tours in Europe*, Oxford, 2 vols, 1959.

———, (Ed., from the original manuscript, H. Edmund Poole), *Music, Men, and Manners in France and Italy, 1770*, London, 1969

———, (Ed. Alvaro Ribeiro, SJ), *The Letters of Dr Charles Burney, vol. i: 1751–1784*, Oxford, The Clarendon Press, 1991.

Burrows, Donald, Rosemary Dunhill, James Harris, *Music and Theatre in Handel's World: The Family Papers of James Harris, 1732–1780*, Oxford University Press, 2002.

Chedzoy, Alan, *Sheridan's Nightingale – The Story of Elizabeth Linley*, London, Allison and Busby, 1997.

Chilvers, Allan, *The Berties of Grimsthorpe Park*, Author House, Bloomington, Indiana, 2010.

Clive, Peter, *Mozart and His Circle*, Yale University Press, 1994.

Cooke, Matthew, 'A Short Account of the late Mr Thomas Linley, Junior', an unpublished MS, dated 1812, Egerton MS 2492 ff. 2 and 126, British Library.

Cormack, Malcolm, *The Paintings of Thomas Gainsborough*, Cambridge University Press, 1991.

de Vos, Philip, *Trazom – 'n Mozart-verhaal* [Trazom – A Mozart Story], Queillerie, Cape Town, 1992; re-worked as *Tot siens Tomassino* [Goodbye Tomassino], Human & Rousseau, Cape Town, 2007; re-worked again and translated into English by the author, 2008, unpublished.

Diack Johnstone, H, 'Cooke, Matthew', *New Grove Dictionary of Music and Musicians, Oxford University Press*, 2001.

Eisen, Cliff et al., *In Mozart's Words* <http://letters.mozartways.com>. Version 1.0, published by HRI Online, 2011.

Fiske, Roger, *English Theatre Music in the Eighteenth Century*, Oxford University Press, 1972.

Ford, Brinsley and John Ingamells, *A Dictionary of British and Irish Travellers in Italy, 1701–1800*, Yale University Press, 1997.

Gardner, Matthew, Alison DeSimone, *Music and the Benefit Performance in Eighteenth-Century Britain*, Cambridge University Press, 2019.

Green, Emanuel, *Thomas Linley, Richard Brinsley Sheridan and Thomas Mathews, their Connection with Bath*, three Papers read before the Bath Antiquarian Field Club in December 1902, Bath, 1903.

Gribble, Rebecca Denise, *Musicians within the Social Hierarchies of Eighteenth-Century England: The Case of Thomas Linley Junior*, doctoral thesis, University of Southampton, 2015.

Gutman, Robert, *Mozart – A Cultural Biography*, Pimlico, 2001.

Highfill, Philip H., Kalman A. Burnim and Edward A Langhans, 'Linley, Thomas (1733–1795)', in *A Biographical Dictionary of Actors, Actresses, Musicians, Dancers, Managers & Other Stage Personnel in London, 1660–1800*, vol. ix, Carbondale, Southern Illinois University Press, 1984.

Holman, Peter, *Before the Baton: Musical Direction and Conducting in Stuart and Georgian Britain*, Boydell & Brewer, 2020.

Howard, Jean and David Start, *All Things Lincolnshire*, The Society for Lincolnshire History and Archaeology, 2007.

Jenkins, John, *Mozart and the English Connection*, Cygnus Arts, 1998.

Jones, Robert W., 'Elizabeth Sheridan's Post-Celebrity', in *Journal for Eighteenth-Century Studies*, vol. xliii (I), 2020, pp. 61–78.

[Kelly, Michael], *Reminiscences of Michael Kelly, of the King's Theatre, and Theatre Royal Drury Lane ... with Original Anecdotes of Many Distinguished Persons ...*, London, 1826.

Kinservik, Matthew J., *Sex, Scandal, and Celebrity in Late Eighteenth-century England*, New York, Palgrave Macmillan, 2007.

———, 'The Politics and Poetics of Sodomy in the Age of George III', in *British Journal For Eighteenth Century Studies*, 29 (2), 2006, pp. 219–236.

Küster, Konrad, *Mozart – A Musical Biography*, Oxford, Clarendon Press, 1996.

McVeigh, Simon, *The Violinists in London's Concert Life, 1750–1784: Felice Giardini and His Contemporaries*, New York, Garland, 1989.

———, *Calendar of London Concerts 1750–1800, advertised in the London daily press*, Goldsmiths, University of London, http://research.gold.ac.uk/10342/

——— and Susan Wollenberg (Eds.), *Concert Life in Eighteenth Century Britain*, Aldershot, Ashgate Publishing, 2004.

Monjo, F. N., *Letters to Horseface – being the story of Wolfgang Amadeus Mozart's journey to Italy 1769–70, when he was a boy of fourteen*, New York, Viking Press, 1775.

Moore, Frank Frankfort, *A Nest of Linnets*, New York, 1901.

Moore, Thomas, *Memoirs of the Life of the Right Honourable Richard Brinsley Sheridan*, 1825.

Nettle, Humphrey [i.e. William Jackson], *Sodom and Onan. A Satire Inscrib'd to [Samuel Foote] Esq., alias the DEVIL upon two Sticks*, London, 1776.

Norton, Rictor, *Mother Clap's Molly House – The Gay Subculture in England 1700–1830*, 2nd edition, Chalfont Press, 2006.

_____, 'Sodom and Onan, 1776', and 'The Macaroni Club: Homosexual Scandals in 1772', in *Homosexuality in Eighteenth-Century England: A Sourcebook*, 2017, online at http://rictornorton.co.uk/

Ostler, Catherine, *The Duchess Countess*, Simon and Schuster, 2021.

Overbeck, Peter, *Die Chorwerke von Thomas Linley dem Jüngeren (1756–1778): Analyse, Vergleich, kompositorisches und biographisches Umfeld*, doctoral thesis, Hildesheim, Georg Olms, 2000

Parke, W. T., *Musical Memoirs comprising an Accouut of the General State of Music in England from the first commemoration of Handel in 1784 to 1830 …*, 2 vols., 1830.

Porter, James, *Beyond Fingal's Cave: Ossian in the Musical Imagination*, Woodbridge, Boydell & Brewer, 2019.

Rae, W. Fraser, *Sheridan – A Biography*, New York, 1896.

Rice, John A., 'Grand Duke Pietro Leopoldo's Musical Patronage in Florence, 1765–1790', a paper given at the conference of the Ricasoli Collection, University of Chicago, September 1989.

Rice, Paul F., 'Vocal Music in Eighteenth-century Bath from the Pens of Thomas Linley Senior (1733–95) and Junior (1756–78)' in *The Phenomenon of Singing*, [S.l.], vol. iv, 2003, pp. 130–135.

Robins, Brian, 'Gainsborough and Music', earlymusicworld.com

Sainsbury, John S., 'Linley, (Thomas [Jr.])', *A Dictionary of Musicians from the Earliest Ages to the Present Time …*, 1824.

Sheldon, Esther K., *Thomas Sheridan of Smock Alley*, Princeton University Press, 2015.

Sitwell, Sacheverell, *Mozart*, Thomas Nelson, 1932.

Siu, Eric, *Late Eighteenth-Century English Violin Concertos: A Genre in Transition*; doctoral thesis, Rice University, Houston, Texas, 2012.

Sloman, Susan and Trevor Fawcett, *Pickpocketing the Rich – Portrait Painting in Bath 1720–1800*, Paul Mellon Centre for Studies in British Art and Holburne Museum of Art, Bath, 2002.

Temperley, Nicholas, Stephen Banfield, *Music and the Wesleys*, University of Illinois Press, 2010.

Van Lennep, William and others (Eds.), *The London Stage, 1660–1800: a calendar of plays, entertainments & afterpieces …*, Southern Illinois University Press, 1960–1963.

von Nissen, Georg Nikolaus, *Biographie W. A. Mozarts*, Hildesheim, George Olms, 1984.

Wallington, Susan, 'Thomas Linley (1756–1778)' in Giles Waterfield et al., *A Nest of Nightingales*, Dulwich Picture Gallery, 1988, pp. 82–84.

Waterfield, Giles, et al., *A Nest of Nightingales – Thomas Gainsborough, 'The Linley Sisters'*, Dulwich Picture Gallery, 1988.

Waterhouse, Ellis, *Gainsborough*, Spring Books, 1966.

Watkins, John, *Memoirs of the Public and Private Life of the Right Honourable Richard Brinsley Sheridan ...*, 1817.

Williamson, Geoffrey, *The Ingenious Mr Gainsborough; a biographical study*, London, Hale, 1972.

Williamson, George, *Life & Works of Ozias Humphry, R. A.*, London, 1918.

Woodall, Mary (Ed.), *The Letters of Thomas Gainsborough*, revised edition, Bradford, The Cupid Press, 1963.

Wright, R. W. M., *Index of Bath Artists*, with biographical notes, an unpublished, undated MS at the Victoria Art Gallery, Bath.

Source Notes

CHAPTER I

1   Clementina Black, *The Linleys of Bath*, London, Martin Secker, 1926, p. 18.

2   Susan Wallington, 'Thomas Linley (1756–1778)' in Giles Waterfield et al., *A Nest of Nightingales*, Dulwich Picture Gallery, 1988, p. 82.

3   Charles Burney (Ed. P. A. Scholes), *An Eighteenth-century Musical Tour in France and Italy*, Oxford University Press, 1959, p. 184.

4   *Ibid.*, 14 August 1778.

5   Allan Chilvers, *The Berties of Grimsthorpe Castle*, Bloomington, Ind., Author House, 2010, p. 184, claims it covers thirty-six acres.

6   [Burney, Charles], 'Linley, John' [i.e. Thomas Linley senior], in Abraham Rees (Ed.), *The Cyclopaedia ... of Arts, Sciences & Literature*, vol. xxi, 1819.

7   *General Evening Post & St. James's Chronicle*, 8–11 August 1778.

8   Chilvers, *The Berties*, p. 187.

9   *Lincoln, Rutland and Stamford Mercury*, 6 August 1778.

10   *London Evening Post*, 11–13 August 1778.

11   *The Public Advertiser*, 11 August 1778.

12   Dr William Hawes, *Address for extending the benefits of a practice for recovery from accidental death*, Royal Humane Society, 1775.

13   *London Evening Post*, 11–13 August 1778.

14   *Bath Chronicle*, 13 August 1778.

15   'Tête-à-Tête', *Town and Country Magazine*, May 1779.

16   *The Public Advertiser*, 14 August 1778.

17   *General Evening Post*, 8–11 Aug 1778.

18   *Ibid.*

19   M. J. Young, *Memoirs of Mrs* [Anna Maria] *Crouch*, London, 1806, vol i, p. 79.

20   *Bath Chronicle*, 13 August 1778.

21   *Morning Chronicle and London Advertiser*, 30 July 1778.

22   *General Evening Post*, 8–11 Aug 1778.

23   *The Public Advertiser*, 14 August 1778.

24   *Ibid.*, 11 August 1778.

25   Maria Linley, 'On the Death of Mr Linley, Jun.', the *Morning Chronicle*, 17 August 1778.

26   [Elizabeth Sheridan], *A Monody (after the Manner of Milton's 'Lycidas') on the Death of Mr Linley ...*, Wilkie, 1778. This was criticised in the press as being unworthy of its

aspirations, and the following year Mrs Sheridan revised it, still casting Tom as Lycidas, but using the new title, 'On the Death of my unfortunate Brother', *Gentleman's Magazine*, December 1779.

27 'Mrs Sheridan on her Brother's Violin', *Annual Register*, vol. xxvii, 1784/5, pp. 138–9.
28 [Samuel Leigh], *The Harmonicon, A Journal of Music*, London, 1825, vol. iii, Pt 1, p. 221.
29 John Adolphus, *Memoirs of John Bannister*, London, 1839, p. 202.
30 George Charles Williamson, *Life & Works of Ozias Humphry, R. A.*, 1918, p. 23.
31 Thomas Halliday, Book V, 'Mozart and the Four Graves', in *The Counterfactual Mozart*, published online at https://www.thomasholliday.com/the_counterfactual_mozart_.ht

CHAPTER II
32 Hugh Belsey, *Thomas Gainsborough*, Yale, 2019, p. 552, quoting the *Bath Herald*, 9 June 1798; and George Williamson, *The Life and Works of Ozias Humphry*, London, 1918, p. 22.
33 Carl Ferdinand Pohl, 'Paradies, Pietro Domenico', in George Grove (Ed.), *A Dictionary of Music and Musicians*, 1928, vol. iv, p. 44.
34 George Williamson, *Life & Works of Ozias Humphry, R. A.*, 1918, pp. 22–23.
35 Reginald W. M. Wright (long-serving Director of the Victoria Art Gallery, Bath, in the early 20th century), *Index of Bath Artists*, with biographical notes, an unpublished, undated typescript, Victoria Art Gallery, Bath.
36 Black, *The Linleys*, pp. 46–47.
37 Wright, 'Ozias Humphry …', *Index of Bath Artists*, Victoria Art Gallery, Bath.
38 Belsey, *Thomas Gainsborough*, p. 553.
39 Charles Richardens, 'Old Stories Re-Told: Sheridan's Duels with Captain Mathews', *All the Year Round*, vol. xviii, 3 August 1867, p. 128.
40 Lars E. Troide (Ed.), *The Early Journals and Letters of Fanny Burney, volume 1: 1768–1773*, Kingston and Montreal, McGill-Queen's University Press, 1988, p. 249.
41 Belsey, *Thomas Gainsborough*, p. 552, quoting Anna Maria Phillips (later Mrs Crouch).
42 Matthew Cooke, *A Short Account of the late Mr Thomas Linley, Junior*, MS, *c.* 1812, British Library, Eg. 2492, ff. 2 and 126.
43 William Jackson of Exeter, *The Four Ages*, 1798, pp. 147–154.
44 Suzanne Aspden, quoting Ozias Humphry, in *'Sancta Caecilia Rediviva'. Elizabeth Linley: Repertoire, Reputation and the English Voice*, Cambridge University Press, 2015, p. 270.
45 Williamson, *Ozias Humphry*, p. 23.
46 John Smith, *Nollekens and His Times*, 1828, vol. ii, pp. 291–292.
47 Williamson, *Ozias Humphry*, pp. 22–24.
48 [Anon.], *ABC Dario Musico*, Bath, 1780, p. 41.
49 *Bath Chronicle*, 11 November 1762.
50 *Boddeley's Bath Journal*, 25 July 1763.
51 Cooke, *Thomas Linley, Junior*, MS, c. 1812, BL, Eg. 2492, ff. 2 and 126.
52 According to Boyce's daughter who passed this information on to the composer R. J. S. Stevens (Roger Fiske and Roger Platt, 'Boyce, William', in Sadie, Stanley (Ed.). *The New Grove Dictionary of Music and Musicians*, Macmillan, 1995, vol. iii, pp. 138–143).
53 Marie Pellissier, 'Behind the Scenes in the Chapel Royal …', *Georgian Papers Programme*, at https:/georgianpapers.com, and Chris. V. Bridgman, Letter to the Editor, 'The Chapel Royal Days of Arthur Sullivan', *The Musical Times*, 1 March 1901.

54 Philip H. Highfill, Kalman A. Burnim and Edward A Langhans, *A Biographical Dictionary of Actors, Actresses, Musicians, Dancers, Managers & Other Stage Personnel in London, 1660–1800*, Southern Illinois, Carbondale, 1973 – , vol. x, p. 413.

55 *Public Advertiser*, 26 June, 1764.

56 Letter, Leopold Mozart to Lorenz Hagenauer, 28 June 1764, in Emily Anderson (Ed.), *The Letters of Mozart and his Family*, Macmillan, 1938, vol. i, p. 49 and fn. 64; and W. H. Tusk, 'Ranelagh House and Gardens', in George Grove (Ed.), *A Dictionary of Music and Musicians*, Macmillan, 1928, vol iv, p. 325.

57 Sacheverell Sitwell, *Mozart*, Thomas Nelson, 1932, p. 13.

58 John C, Greene, *Theatre in Dublin, 1745–1820*, Lehigh University Press, 2011; and *Bath Chronicle*, 4 September 1766.

59 Highfill, etc., *A Biographical Dictionary*, vol. vii, p. 142, and vol. viii, p. 37.

60 *Lloyds Evening Post*, 3 and 19 February 1767.

61 George Winchester Stone Jr. (Ed.), *The London Stage, 1660–1800: a calendar of plays, entertainments & afterpieces …*, Southern Illinois University Press, 1960–1963, part 4, vol. ii, p. 1222.

62 *Derby Mercury*, 19 February 1768.

63 Wright, 'Ozias Humphry …', *Index of Bath Artists*, Victoria Art Gallery, Bath.

64 *Bath Chronicle*, 14 May 1767.

65 Lady Llanover (Ed.), *Autobiography and Correspondence of Mary Granville, Mrs Delany*, London 1862, vol. iv, p.133.

66 Gwilym Beechey, *Thomas Linley, Junior: His Life, Work and Times*, thesis, Cambridge University, 1964, p. 55.

67 Cooke, *Thomas Linley, Junior*, MS, c. 1812, BL, Eg. 2492, ff. 2 and 126.

68 Margherita Canale, *La 'Scuola delle Nazioni' di Giuseppe Tartini*, at https://www-discovertartini-eu.

69 Black, *The Linleys*, p. 16.

70 [John S Sainsbury], 'Linley, (Thomas), Eldest Son of the Preceding,' in *A Dictionary of Musicians: From the Earliest Ages to the Present Time …*, London, Sainsbury and Company, 1824, vol. ii, p. 67–69. And the Ancasters' patronage is confirmed by Valerie Purton, 'Thomas Linley: A Lost Lincolnshire Link' in Jean Howard and David Start (Eds.), *All Things Lincolnshire*, Socy for Lincolnshire History and Archaeology, 2007, p. 172.

71 Gribble, Rebecca Denise, *Musicians within the Social Hierarchies of Eighteenth-Century England: The Case of Thomas Linley Junior*, unpublished doctoral thesis, University of Southampton, 2015, p. 260.

72 Letter, Thomas Gainsborough to William Jackson, 11 May 1768, in William Boulton, *Thomas Gainsborough*, London, Methuen, 1905, p. 99, and Mary Woodall (Ed.), *The Letters of Thomas Gainsborough*, Cupid Press, 1963, p. 109

73 They appear in a 'Book of Exercises', dated 1768, belonging in 1812 to Thomas's brother William (Matthew Cooke, *A Short Account of the late Mr Thomas Linley, Junior*, MS, c. 1812, British Library, Egerton MS 2492, f 2.

74 William Patoun, *Advice on Travel in Italy* (addressed to Brownlow Cecil, Lord Burghley, 1725–1793), uncatalogued MS, c. 1766, Exeter Archives at Burghley House, in Ford and Ingamells, A Dictionary of British and Irish Travellers. p. liii.

CHAPTER III

75 See Charles Burney, *Music, Men and Manners in France and Italy 1770*, The Folio Society, 1969.

76 H. Edmund Poole, 'Introduction', Burney, *Music, Men and Manners*, p. xv.

77 Letter, Leopold Mozart to Lorenz Hagenauer, 25 April 1764, in Anderson, *Letters of Mozart*, 1938, vol. i, p. 64.
78 Burney, *Music, Men and Manners*, pp. 37–39.
79 Williamson, *Ozias Humphry*, p. 47.
80 Patoun, *Advice on Travel in Italy*, in Ford and Ingamells, *A Dictionary of British and Irish Travellers in Italy*.
81 *Ibid.*
82 Letter, Leopold Mozart to Anna Maria Mozart, 14 April 1770, in Anderson, *Letters of Mozart*, 1989, p. 126.
83 James Fenimore Cooper, Letter XI, 'Florence–Leghorn …', *Gleanings in Europe. Italy: By an American*, Philadelphia, 2 vols in one, 1838.
84 Letter Joseph Denham, Leghorn, to Sukey Denham, London, 11 July 1768, in 'Business Correspondence of Capt. William Earle and his brother … 1751–1852', The Earle Collection, D/Earle/3/1–6, National Archives; and 'Brimstone and Diphtheria', *The Sacred Heart Review*, vol. xxvii, number 14, 5 April 1902.
85 MS Journal of James Martin, quoted by Brinsley Ford and John Ingamells, *A Dictionary of British and Irish Travellers in Italy, 1701–1800*, Yale University Press, 1997, p. 481.
86 Fenimore Cooper, Letter IV, *Gleanings in Europe. Italy.*
87 Louis Stott, 'Smollett at Livorno', blog at louisstott.wordpress.com
88 Fenimore Cooper, Letter IV, *Gleanings in Europe. Italy.*
89 Thomas Nugent, *The Grand Tour, Or, a journey through the Netherlands, Germany, Italy and France*, London, 1778, p. 375.
90 Hester Lynch Piozzi, (Ed. Herbert Barrows), 'Leghorn', *Observations and Reflections made in the course of a Journey through France, Italy and Germany*, 1789, vol. i, pp. 352–55.
91 Peter Earle, *The Earles of Liverpool, A Georgian Merchant Dynasty*, OUP, 2015, p. 141.
92 Brinsley Ford and John Ingamells, *A Dictionary of British and Irish Travellers in Italy, 1701–1800*, Yale University Press, 1997, p. 481.
93 Burney, *Music, Men and Manners*, p. 116; and Douglas MacMillan, *The Recorder 1800–1905*, unpublished doctoral thesis, 2005, vol. ii, p. 25.
94 Giovanni Baretti, *Gli Italiani o sia Relazione degli usi e costume d'Italia* [The Italians or Report of the uses and customs of Italy], Milan, 1818, pp. 209–14.
95 Patoun, *Advice on Travel in Italy*, in Ford and Ingamells, *A Dictionary of British and Irish Travellers in Italy*.
96 *Ibid.*
97 Piozzi, 'Leghorn', *Observations and Reflections*, vol. i, p. 352; and Sidney Lee, 'Andrew Burnaby', in Leslie Stephen (Ed.), *Dictionary of National Biography*, 1887, p. 379; and Louis Stott, 'Smollett at Livorno', at louisstott.wordpress.com
98 Antonella d'Ovidio, 'Pietro Nardini', *Dizionario Biografico degli Italiani*, vol. lxxvii, 2012, at www.treccani.it
99 George Dubourg, *The Violin: Some Account of that Leading Instrument …*, 1852, pp. 77–78; and Christian Schubart quoted by Paul David, 'Pietro Nardini', in George Grove (Ed.), *A Dictionary of Music and Musicians*, 1927, vol. iii, p. 603.
100 Albert M. Petrack (Ed.), *David Mason Greene's Biographical Encyclopaedia of Composers*, Cleveland, Ohio, The Reproducing Piano Roll Foundation, 1985, vol. i, p. 326; and X, 'From My Study', *The Musical Times*, 1 January 1895, p.12.
101 Wallington, *Linley*, p., 82, quoting a remark of the violinist Mr Shaw, cited in I. Woodfield, *The Celebrated Quarrel between Thomas Linley Senior and William Herschel*, Bath, 1977, p. 8.

102   It appears in a 'Book of Exercises', dated 1768, belonging in 1812 to Tom's brother William (Cooke, *Thomas Linley, Junio*r, MS, c. 1812, BL, Eg. 2492, ff. 2 and 126).

103   Biographical note about Nardini on the *Auser Musici* website, http://www.ausermusici.org/en/author/nardini-pietro

104   Peter Holman, CD booklets, *English Classical Violin Concertos*, Hyperion Records CDH55260, and *English 18th-century Violin Sonatas*, Hyperion Records CDA66865.

105   Letters from Sir Horace Mann to Horace Walpole, on 9 April 1768, 18 and 25 October 1768, *Horace Walpole's Correspondence*, Yale Edition Online, 2011.

106   *Gazzetta toscana*, no. 22, p. 86, 3 June 1769; and letter, Giuseppe Tartini to Father Giambattista Martini, 9 June 1769 (Pierluigi Petrobelli, 'P. N.', in Enciclopedia della Musica, Milano, Ricordi, 1964, vol iii, pp. 257–58.

107   Pierluigi Petrobelli, *Giuseppe Tartini - Le fonti biografiche*, Universal Edition, 1968, pp. 13–14.

108   Francesca Bregoli, 'The *Nazione Ebrea* and the Tuscan State: A Fruitful Symbiosis', in *Mediterranean Enlightenment: Livornese Jews, Tuscan Culture and Eighteenth-Century Reform*, Stanford University Press, 2014, pp. 15–38, quoting the chronicler, Pietro Bernardo Prato, compiler of the *Giornale della Città e Porto di Livorno*, 1764–1813, MSS, 63vv.

CHAPTER IV

109   John A. Rice, 'Grand Duke Pietro Leopoldo's Musical Patronage in Florence, 1765–1790', a paper given at the conference of the Ricasoli Collection, University of Chicago, September 1989; and John A. Rice, 'An Early Handel revival in Florence', in *Early Music*, vol. xviii, February 1990, p. 63.

110   Charles Burney, *The Present State of Music in Germany, the Netherlands, and United Provinces*, 1773, pp. 245–246; and Antonella d'Ovidio, 'Pietro Nardini', in *Dizionario Biografico degli Italiani*, vol. lxxvii, 2012, online at https://www.treccani.it/enciclopedia/pietro-nardini_%28Dizionario-Biografico%29/; and Rice, *Grand Duke Pietro Leopoldo's Musical Patronage*….

111   Rice, *Grand Duke Pietro Leopoldo's Musical Patronage*; Mariateresa Dellaborra, 'Pietro Nardini: l'opera per flauto. Un sorprendente itinerario nel repertorio del violinista dell'amore', in *Nuova Rivista Musicale Italiana*, 2003, pp. 345–379; and Federico Marri, *Pietro Nardini, violinista e compositore …*, Comune di Livorno, 1996, p. 6.

112   John Forbes MSS, 22 April 1771, quoted by Brinsley Ford and John Ingamells, *A Dictionary of British and Irish Travellers in Italy, 1701–1800*, Yale University Press, 1997, p. 481.

113   Letter of William, 4th Earl Fitzwilliam, quoted by E. A. Smith, 'Lord Fitzwilliam's "grand tour"', in *History Today*, xvii, June 1967, p. 398.

114   Alexander Drummond, *Travels through Different Cities of Germany, Italy, Greece, and Several Parts of Asia*, 1754, pp. 40–41, 110.

115   Burney, *Music, Men and Manners*, p. 120.

116   Letter from George Finch, 9th Earl of Winchilsea, 2 January 1773, *Winchilsea Letters MSS*.

117   Letter of William, 4th Earl Fitzwilliam, quoted by E. A. Smith, 'Lord Fitzwilliam's "grand tour"', in *History Today*, xvii, June 1967, pp. 393–410.

118   Clinton Elliot, quoting Jeremy Bentham, in *Hidden: The Intimate Lives of Gay Men Past and Present*, AuthorHouse, 2014. See also Brinsley Ford and John Ingamells, quoting Robert Harvey, in *A Dictionary of British and Irish Travellers in Italy, 1701–1800*, Yale University Press, 1997, p. 959.

119 Robert Harvey, *Journal in Italy 1773-4*, MSS, Norfolk County Record Office, MS 20677, T 140B; and see Ford and Ingamells, *A Dictionary of British and Irish Travellers in Italy*, p. 959.

120 F. J. B. Watson, *Thomas Patch (1725-1782): Notes on his Life, together with a Catalogue of his Known Works*, The Volumes of the Walpole Society, vol. xxviii, 1939, p. 23.

121 Patoun, *Advice on Travel in Italy*, p. liii.

122 Elizabeth Gibson, 'Earl Cowper in Florence and His Correspondence with Italian Opera in London', in *Music and Letters*, vol. lxviii, issue 3, 1987, p. 235; and John A. Rice, 'Grand Duke Pietro Leopoldo's Musical Patronage in Florence, 1765-1790', a paper given at the conference of the Ricasoli Collection, University of Chicago, September 1989.

123 Charles Durnford and Sir Edward Hyde East, *Term Reports in the Court of King's Bench*, 1827, vol. iv, pp. 76-79; Thomas Wright and Robert Harding Evans, *Historical and Descriptive Account of the Caricatures of James Gillray …*, 1851, pp. 25-26; and Theodore Schroeder, *'Obscene' Literature and Constitutional Law: A Forensic Defense of Freedom of the Press*, The Lawbook Exchange, 2002, p. 39.

124 Anon., *Satan's Harvest Home: : or the Present State of Whorecraft, Adultery, Fornication, Procuring, Pimping, Sodomy … And other Satanic Works, daily propagated in this good Protestant Kingdom*, a pamphlet published in London and elsewhere, 1749; David Leavitt, *Florence, A Delicate Case*, Bloomsbury, 2013; and Ian Thomson, *Dante's Divine Comedy – A Journey Without End*, London, Head of Zeus, 2018.

125 Michael Rocke, *Forbidden Friendships: Homosexuality and Male Culture in Renaissance Florence*, Oxford University Press, 1996.

126 Harold Acton, *The Last Medici*, London, Macmillan, 1980, pp. 289–290, and Robert Aldrich and Garry Wotherspoon, *Who's Who in Gay and Lesbian History: From Antiquity to the Mid-Twentieth Century*, Routledge, 2020, p. 362.

127 Alessandro Ademollo, *Corilla Olimpica*, Florence, Carlo Ademollo and C. editori, 1885; and Giovanni La Cecilia, *Storie segrete delle famiglie reali*, vol. iv, Genova, 1859, p. 656.

128 Pietro Vigo, *Livorno nell'Ottocento: prima serie di letture fatte al Circolo Filologico nel mese di marzo MCM*, Livorno, 1923, pp. 200–1.

129 Letter Leopold Mozart to his wife, 3 April 1770, in Anderson, *Letters of Mozart*, 1989, p. 124.

130 Burney, *Music, Men and Manners*, p. 102.

131 *Gazzetta toscana*, number 14, 7 April 1770; and Robert Lamar Weaver and Norma Wright Weaver, *Florentine Theater, 1751-1800 : Operas, Prologues, Farces, Intermezzos, Concerts, and Plays with Incidental Music*, Michigan, Harmonie Park, 1993; Peter Overbeck, *Die Chorwerke von Thomas Linley dem Jüngeren (1756–1778): Kompositorisches und biographisches Umfeld*, Georg Olms, Hildesheim, 2000, p. 44; and Otto Erich Deutsch, *Mozart: A Documentary Biography*, Stanford University Press, 1966, p. 114.

132 *Ibid.*

133 Letter Wolfgang Mozart to his father, 19 October 1782, in Anderson, *Letters of Mozart*, 1989, p. 828.

134 Letter Leopold Mozart to his wife, 3 April 1770, in Anderson, *Letters of Mozart*, 1989, p. 125; and L. Chimirri, P. Gibbin, M. Migliorini (Eds.), *Mozart a Firenze... qui si dovrebbe vivere e morire*, Exhibition Catalogue, Florence, 2006.

135 Rice, 'Grand Duke Pietro Leopoldo's Musical Patronage in Florence, 1765-1790', quoting Otto Erich Deutsch, *Mozart: Die Dokumente seines Lebens*, Kassel, Bärenreiter, 1961.

136 Lucien Karhausen, *The Bleeding of Mozart – a medical glance on his life, illnesses and personality*, Xlibris, 2011, p. 3.
137 Letter Leopold Mozart to his wife, 21 April 1770, in Anderson, *Letters of Mozart*, 1989, pp. 129–30; and Cliff Eisen et al., 'Letter 177', in *In Mozart's Words*, <http://letters.mozartways.com>. Version 1.0, published by HRI Online, 2011.
138 Letter Leopold Mozart to his wife, 3 April 1770, in Anderson, *Letters of Mozart*, 1989, pp. 124–5.
139 Letter Leopold Mozart to his wife, 21 April 1770, in Anderson, *Letters of Mozart*, 1989, pp. 129–30; and Otto Erich Deutsch, *Mozart: A Documentary Biography*, Stanford University Press, 1966, p. 115.
140 *Ibid.*
141 A. Basso, 'A. Gavard des Pivets, Giuseppe Marie', in *I Mozart in Italia. Cronistoria dei viaggi, documenti, lettere. Dizionario dei luoghi e delle persone*, Roma, Accademia nazionale di Santa Cecilia, 2006, pp. 567–568; and Cliff Eisen et al., 'Giuseppe Maria Gavard des Pivets', *In Mozart's Words*, <http://letters.mozartways.com>. Version 1.0, published by HRI Online, 2011.
142 Letter Leopold Mozart to his wife, 21 April 1770, in Anderson, *Letters of Mozart*, 1989, p. 129–30.
143 Letter Leopold Mozart to his wife, 3 April 1770, in Anderson, *Letters of Mozart*, 1989, p. 125.
144 Piozzi, *Observations and reflections*, p. 166.
145 Letters Leopold Mozart to his wife, 3, 14 and 21 April 1770, in Anderson, *Letters of Mozart*, 1989
146 Burney, *Music, Men and Manners*, p. 102.
147 Letter Leopold Mozart to his wife, 21 April 1770, in Anderson, *Letters of Mozart*, 1989
148 Susan Wallington, 'Mozart with his Father and Sister', in Giles Waterfield, and others, *A Nest of Nightingales – Thomas Gainsborough, 'The Linley Sisters'*, Dulwich Picture Gallery, 1988, pp. 86–7.
149 Burney, *Music, Men and Manners*, pp. 102, 121.
150 Letter Leopold Mozart to his wife, 21 April 1770, in Anderson, *Letters of Mozart*, 1989, p. 129–30.
151 Peter J. Davies, *Mozart in Person – His Character and Health*, New York, Greenwood Press, 1989, p. 140.
152 *Gazzetta toscana*, 9 June 1770.
153 *Ibid*, 25 August 1770.
154 *Ibid.*; and Burney (Ed. Poole), *Music, Men and Manners*, pp.113–114.
155 '[Fragment 45], Bath November 1747 – February 1748', in Slava Klima and others (Eds.), *Memoirs of Dr Charles Burney 1726–1769*, Lincoln and London, University of Nebraska Press, 1988, pp. 75–76.
156 Burney (Ed. Scholes), *An Eighteenth-century Musical Tour*, p. 184.
157 Burney (Ed. Poole), *Music, Men and Manners*, p.114.
158 *Ibid*, pp. 115–116; and Burney, *The Present State of Music*, pp. 248–250.
159 Burney (Ed. Poole), *Music, Men and Manners,*, pp. 116–117.
160 *Ibid.*, p.128.
161 Burney, *The Present State of Music*, pp. 250–251; and Burney (Ed., Poole), *Music, Men and Manners*, p.116.
162 Burney (Ed., Poole), *Music, Men and Manners*, p.118.
163 Burney (Ed. Tubini), *Viaggio musicale in Italia*, Turin, 1979, p. 224.
164 Burney (Ed. Poole), *Music, Men and Manners*, p.120.
165 *Ibid.*, pp. 121–123.

CHAPTER V

166   *The Public Advertiser*, 22 March 1770.

167   Letter Edward Poore, Oxford, to James Harris, Salisbury, 15 May 1770, and Elizabeth Harris, Salisbury, to James Harris junior, Madrid, 19 May 1770, in Donald Burrows and Rosemary Dunhill, *Music and theatre in Handel's world : the family papers of James Harris 1732–1780*, Oxford University Press, 2002.

168   Letter Charles Burney to Samuel Wesley, 23 March 1808, in Philip Olleson, *Samuel Wesley – The Man and his Music*, Woodbridge, The Boydell Press, 2003, p.74.

169   *Bath Chronicle*, 12 July 1770.

170   Rev Daniel Lysons, etc., *Origin and Progress of the Meeting of the Three Choirs of Gloucester, Worcester and Hereford, ...*, 1865, p. 47.

171   *The Public Advertiser*, 24 October 1770.

172   *Ibid.*, 22 Nov 1770.

173   Suzanne Aspden, 'Linley, Thomas, Junior; Linley, Thomas, Senior; and Linley, Elizabeth Ann', *Oxford Dictionary of National Biography*, 2004; and (Ed. Cecil Price), *The Letters of Richard Brinsley Sheridan*, Oxford, Clarendon Press, 1966, vol. iii.

174   Madame d'Arblay, *Memoirs of Doctor Burney*, vol i, 1832, p. 213.

175   '[Fragment B6], Miss Linley (Mrs Sheridan)', in Slava Klima and others (Eds.), *Memoirs of Dr Charles Burney 1726–1769*, Lincoln and London, University of Nebraska Press, 1988, pp. 191–2.

176   Joseph Roach, 'Mistaking Earth for Heaven: Eliza Linley's Voice', in (Ed. Elizabeth Eger), *Bluestockings Display'd: Portraiture, Performance and Patronage, 1730–1830*, Cambridge University Press, 2013, pp. 123–40.

177   Charles Richardens, quoting both Dr Burney's *History of Music* and William Earle's *Sheridan and His Times*, (vol. i, 1859, p. 31) in 'Old Stories Re-Told: Sheridan's Duels with Captain Mathews', *All the Year Round*, vol. xviii, 3 August 1867, p. 128, and Abraham Rees, 'Linley, John [sic], *The Cyclopaedia, or Universal Dictionary of Arts*, vol. xxi, 1819.

178   Alan Chedzoy, *Sheridan's Nightingale – The Story of Elizabeth Linley*, Allison and Busby, 1997, p. 32.

179   Margot Bor, and Lamond Clelland, *Still the Lark – A Biography of Elizabeth Linley*, London, Merlin Press, 1962, p. 22.

180   'Anecdotes of the Maid of Bath', *The London Chronicle*, 3–6 October 1772.

181   *Ibid*; and *The London Magazine*, September 1772.

182   Black, *The Linleys of Bath*, p. 57.

CHAPTER VI

183   Adalbert Gyrowetz (Ed. Alfred Einstein), *Biographie*, Leipzig: Siegel, 1915, p. 19.

184   Rice, 'Grand Duke Pietro Leopoldo's Musical Patronage in Florence.

185   Letters Sir Horace Mann to Horace Walpole, 12 August 1742 and 15 May 1762, *Horace Walpole's Correspondence*, Yale Edition Online, 2011.

186   John A. Rice, 'An early Handel revival in Florence', *Early Music*, vol. xviii, February 1990, p. 63.

187   Chedzoy, *Sheridan's Nightingale*, p. 190.

188   *Gazzetta toscana*, 4 September 1771.

189   Rice, 'Grand Duke Pietro Leopoldo's Musical Patronage in Florence.

190   Ian Woodfield, *The celebrated quarrel between Thomas Linley (senior) and William Herschel : an episode in the musical life of 18th century Bath*, University of Bath, 1977, p. 84; and 'Bath Assembly Rooms', National Trust online; and Beechey, *Thomas Linley, Junior*, p. 58; and Chedzoy, *Sheridan's Nightingale*, p. 57.

191 Adam Smith, *An Inquiry Into the Nature and Causes of the Wealth of Nations*, vol. iv, 1843, p. 129.

192 E.J. Clery, *The Feminization Debate in Eighteenth-Century England: Literature, Commerce and Luxury*, Basingstoke, Palgrave Macmillan, 2004, p. 10.

CHAPTER VII

193 According to 'Part of a letter of the late Mrs Sheridan [to an unnamed correspondent, 1772] found as waste paper by accident', Add. MS 75000 G, British Library.

194 *Ibid.*

195 John Latimer, *The Annals of Bristol in the Eighteenth Century*, 1893, p. 397.

196 According to 'Part of a letter of the late Mrs Sheridan [to an unnamed correspondent, 1772] found as waste paper by accident', Add. MS 75000 G, British Library.

197 *Ibid.*

198 Letter Thomas Gainsborough to Constantine Phipps, 1st Baron Mulgrave, 31 March 1772, Dulwich Picture Gallery.

199 W. Fraser Rae, *Sheridan – A Biography*, New York, 1896, vol. i, pp. 167–8.

200 *Jackson's Oxford Journal*, 28 March 1772.

201 *Bath Chronicle*, 9 April 1772.

202 William Van Lennep, and others, *The London Stage, 1660–1800: a calendar of plays, entertainments & afterpieces ...*, Southern Illinois University Press, 1960–1963, part 4, vol. iii, p. 1569.

203 *Bath Chronicle* 19 March 1772.

204 *Bristol Journal*, 23 January 1773.

205 *Bath Chronicle*, 7 May 1772.

206 Anecdotes of The Maid of Bath', *The London Chronicle*, 3–6 October 1772;

207 Chedzoy, *Sheridan's Nightingale*, pp. 78–81.

208 *Chester Courant*, 23 June, 1772.

209 Letter Elizabeth Linley to Richard Sheridan, 29 June 1772, quoted by Clementina Black, *The Linleys of Bath*, pp. 62–3.

210 *The Ipswich Journal*, 4 July 1772.

211 Letter Elizabeth Linley to Richard Sheridan, 29 June 1772, quoted by Clementina Black, *The Linleys of Bath*, pp. 62–3.

212 'Anecdotes of The Maid of Bath', *The London Chronicle*, 3–6 October 1772, Margot Bor, and Lamond Clelland, *Still the Lark – A Biography of Elizabeth Linley*, London, Merlin Press, 1962, p. 58.

213 Black, *The Linleys of Bath*, p. 58.

214 Alicia Le Fanu, *Memoirs of the Life and Writings of Mrs Frances Sheridan*, London, 1824, p. 406.

215 *Bath Chronicle*, 2 and 9 July 1772; 'Anecdotes of The Maid of Bath', *The London Chronicle*, 3–6 October 1772; Alicia Le Fanu, *Memoirs of the Life and Writings of Mrs Frances Sheridan*, London, 1824, p. 406; the *Newcastle Weekly Courant*, 11 July 1772; *Town & Country*, 1 July 1772. But the fullest account of the duel is to be found in Emmanuel Green, *Thomas Linley, Richard Brinsley Sheridan, and Thomas Mathews, their connections with Bath*, Bath, 1903, pp. 50–53.

216 *Oxford Journal*, 4 July 1772.

217 Thomas Grenville, quoted by Alicia Lefanu (née Sheridan) in Fraser Rae, *Sheridan*, vol. i, pp. 200–201.

218 Black, *The Linleys of Bath*, pp. 75–6.

219 *General Evening Post*, 4–6 August 1772; and *New Daily Advertiser* and *Public Advertiser*, 1 September 1772.

220 *Hampshire Chronicle*, 31 August 1772.

221 *Bath Chronicle*, 5 November 1772.

222 *The London Magazine*, September 1772; and *Public Advertiser*, 2 October 1772.

223 Letter Thomas Linley to David Garrick, 12 October 1772, *The Private Correspondence of David Garrick* …, vol. i, p. 488.

224 Letter Richard Brinsley Sheridan to Thomas Linley senior, 3 May – 21 June, 1775 (see (Ed. Cecil Price), *The Letters of Richard Brinsley Sheridan*, Oxford, Clarendon Press, 1966, vol. iii, pp. 303–6.

225 Letter Duchess of Portland to Mrs Port, 25 February 1773, *Handel Reference Database*, Stanford University.

226 Fanny Burney, Journal, 17 March 1773, in Lars E. Troide (Ed.), *The Early Journals and Letters of Fanny Burney, volume 1: 1768-1773*, Kingston and Montreal, McGill-Queen's University Press, 1988, pp. 248–51.

227 *The Morning Chronicle*, 5 March 1773, in *Handel Reference Database*, Stanford University.

228 *Kentish Gazette*, 3 April 1773.

229 'The Taste and Critical Observations of J.H.', *The Westminster Magazine*, January 1773, p. 82.

230 Cooke, *Thomas Linley, Junior*, MS, c. 1812, BL, Eg. 2492, ff. 2 and 126.

231 Joseph Agus, 26 February 1773, University of Oregon's *London Stage Database* online.

232 'State of the Oratorios, March 1773', *Handel Reference Database*, Stanford University; and *The Macaroni and Theatrical Magazine* …, October 1772–September 1773, p. 271.

233 *Westminster Magazine*, March 1773, p. 219.

234 Letter Horace Walpole to Lady Ossory, 16 March 1773, *Horace Walpole's Correspondence*, Yale Edition online, 2011.

235 *The Town and Country magazine, or, Universal Repository of Knowledge, Instruction and Entertainment*, vol. v, 1773, p. 128.

236 Fanny Burney, Journal, 17 March 1773, in Lars E. Troide (Ed.), *The Early Journals and Letters of Fanny Burney, volume 1: 1768–1773*, Kingston and Montreal, McGill-Queen's University Press, 1988, pp. 248–51.

237 Chedzoy, *Sheridan's Nightingale*, p. 130.

238 *Newcastle Courant*, 10 April 1773; Bath Chronicle, 13 April 1773.

239 *Bath Chronicle*, 8 April 1773.

240 *Newcastle Weekly Courant*, 17 April 1773.

241 Fraser Rae, *Sheridan*, vol. i, pp. 256–7.

242 *Kentish Gazette*, 3 April 1773; and *Bath Chronicle* 1 April 1773.

243 A rant from Richard Brinsley Sheridan in a letter to Thomas Linley senior, 3 May–21 June 1775, (Ed. Cecil Price), *The Letters of Richard Brinsley Sheridan*, Oxford, Clarendon Press, 1966, vol. iii, pp. 303–06.

244 *Shrewsbury Chronicle*, 17 April 1773.

245 Beechey, 'Thomas Linley', *The Musical Times*, vol. cxix, no. 1626, August 1978, p. 671; and Peter Holman, CD booklet, *The English Orpheus – Thomas Linley (1756–1778) – Cantatas & Theatre Music*, Hyperion CDH55256.

246 *Rind's Virginia Gazette*, Williamsburg, Virginia, 17 June 1773.

247 Black, *The Linleys of Bath*, p. 104.

248 *Rind's Virginia Gazette*, 17 June 1773.

249 Letter Richard Sheridan to his friend Thomas Grenville, 14 May 1773, quoted by

Clementina Black, *The Linleys of Bath*, p. 104; and [Mrs Harriet Grote], Some Account of the Hamlet of East Burnham ..., 1858, p. 17.

250 Letter Thomas Linley to Richard Sheridan, 26 June 1773, quoted by Clementina Black, *The Linleys of Bath*, p. 106.

251 Black, *The Linleys of Bath*, p. 110.

252 Cooke, *Thomas Linley, Junior*, MS, c. 1812, BL, Eg. 2492, ff. 2 and 126.

253 Walter Sichel, *Sheridan – From New and Original Material ...*, Boston, 1909, vol. i, p. 425.

254 James Beattie (Ed. Ralph S. Walker), *London Diary 1773*, Aberdeen, 1946, pp. 67–9.

255 Chedzoy, *Sheridan's Nightingale*, p. 132.

256 *Gloucester Journal*, September 1773, quoted by Margot Bor, and Lamond Clelland, *Still the Lark – A Biography of Elizabeth Linley*, London, Merlin Press, 1962, p. 73.

257 Cooke, *Thomas Linley, Junior*, MS, c. 1812, BL, Eg. 2492, ff. 2 and 126.

258 Daines Barrington, *Miscellanies*,1781, pp. 295–6.

259 Madame d'Arblay [Fanny Burney] (Ed.), *Memoirs of Doctor Burney*, 1832, vol. ii, p. 68.

260 Letter Thomas Linley senior, to Richard Brinsley Sheridan, 15 November 1774, quoted by Cecil Price, *The Letters of Richard Brinsley Sheridan*, Oxford 1966, vol. i, p. 84.

261 [Henry Angelo], *Reminiscences of Henry Angelo, with Memoirs of His Late Father and Friends ..*, vol. i, 1830, p. 87.

CHAPTER VIII

262 James Boswell (Ed. R.W. Chapman), *Life of Johnson*, Oxford, 1980, p. 443.

263 David Constantine, in an Introduction to his translation of Johann Wolfgang von Goethe, *The Sorrows of Young Werther*, Oxford University Press, 2012.

264 Johann Wolfgang von Goethe (Ed. Nathan Haskell Dole, Trans. R. D. Boylan), Letter Werther to Wilhelm, October 12, *The Sorrows of Young Werther*, Dover Publications, 2002; and H. R. Roomaaker Jr., *Towards a Romantic Conception of Nature: Coleridge's Poetry up to 1803 – A Study in the History of Ideas*, Philadelphia, John Benjamin's Publishing Company, 1984, p. 141.

265 James Macpherson (['Trans.']), 'Dar-thula: A Poem', *The Poems of Ossian, the Son of Fingal*, Glasgow, 1799, pp. 26–38.

266 James Porter, *Beyond Fingal's Cave: Ossian in the Musical Imagination*, University of Rochester Press, 2019, p. 197.

267 *Ibid.*, pp. 197–8.

268 Beechey, 'Thomas Linley, Junior, 1756–1778', *The Musical Times*, August 1978, p. 671.

269 Letter from Thomas Linley senior to David Garrick, 28 September 1775, quoted by Roger Fiske, 'The Duenna,' in *The Musical Times*, vol. cxvii, number 1579, March 1976.

270 Letter Richard Brinsley Sheridan to Thomas Linley senior, 3 May–21 June, 1775, in (Ed. Cecil Price), *The Letters of Richard Brinsley Sheridan*, Oxford, Clarendon Press, 1966, vol. iii, pp. 303-6.

271 Cooke, *Thomas Linley, Junior*, MS, c. 1812, BL, Eg. 2492, ff. 2 and 126.

272 Letter Thomas Linley senior to David Garrick, 28 September 1775, in *The Private Correspondence of David Garrick ...*, 1832, vol. ii, pp. 101–2.

273 On one night in a later revival, the audience suddenly burst into 'a Complication of violent Sounds, such as Hissings, Clapping, Hooting, etc', when the towering head-dress of a lady in the gallery caught fire (the *Public Advertiser*, 6 January 1777).

274 The *Public Advertiser*, 29 November 1775.

275   William Oxberry (Ed.), *The Duenna*, Boston, 1822, pp. 3–4.
276   William Hazlitt, 'Lecture VIII – On the Comic Writers of the Last Century', in (Waller and Glover, Ed.), *The Collected Works of William Hazlitt*, London, 1903, vol. viii, p. 165.
277   Lord Byron, Diary, 18 December 1813, quoted in *The Mirror of Literature, Amusement and Instruction*, 1828, vol. vi, p. 269.
278   Letter Richard Brinsley Sheridan to Thomas Linley senior, 31 December 1775, in Cecil Price (Ed.), *The Letters of Richard Brinsley Sheridan*, Oxford, Clarendon Press, 1966, vol. i, pp. 93–95.
279   Roger Fiske, 'The Duenna', in *The Musical Times*, vol. cxvii, number 1579, March 1976; and Roger Fiske, 'A Score for *The Duenna*', in *Music and Letters*, vol. xlii, number 2, April 1961.
280   Richard Luckett, 'The Duenna', in (Holden, Kenyon and Walsh, eds.), *The Viking Opera Guide*, Viking, 1993, p. 572.
281   Linda V. Troost, 'The Characterizing Power of Song in Sheridan's *The Duenna*', *Eighteenth-Century Studies*, The Johns Hopkins University Press, Vol. 20, No. 2 (Winter, 1986–7), pp. 153–172.
282   Chedzoy, *Sheridan's Nightingale*, p. 169.
283   The *Bath Chronicle*, 14 December 1775.
284   The *Bath Chronicle*, 29 February 1776.
285   Peter Holman, 'Introduction', in the Digital Booklet with *A Lyric Ode on the Fairies, Aerial Beings and Witches of Shakespeare*, Hyperion CDH 55253; and *Poetical Remains of French Laurence ...* Dublin, 1872, p. 36; and R. G. Thorne (Ed.), 'French Laurence (1757–1809), of Doctor' Commons', *The History of Parliament: the House of Commons 1790–1820*, Boydell and Brewer, 2006.
286   Cooke, *Thomas Linley, Junio*r, MS, c. 1812, BL, Eg. 2492, ff. 2 and 126.
287   *Westminster Magazine*, March 1776, pp. 154–6.
288   *The Morning Post*, 21 March 1776.
289   R.F. [Roger Fiske], reviewing Gwilym Beechey's performing edition of Linley's 'Shakespeare Ode', in *Musica Britannica – A National Collection of Music*, XXX, London, Stainer & Bell, 1970, pp. 451–3.

CHAPTER IX
290   Letter Charles Burney to Brigg Fountaine, 5 April 1776, Burney, Charles (Alvaro Ribeiro, SJ, Ed.), *The Letters of Dr Charles Burney, Vol. 1: 1751–1784*, Oxford, The Clarendon Press, 1991, pp. 213–14.
291   Miscellaneous Letters and Papers, British Library, Add. MS 60391.
292   Alan Chilvers, *The Berties of Grimsthorpe Park*, Author House, Bloomington, Ind., 2010, p. 209; and Aaron Garrett, reviewing Richard C. Allen, 'David Hartley on Human Nature', in *Albion: A quarterly journal concerned with British Studies*, vol. xxxii, number 2, University of Chicago Press, summer 2000, pp. 312–14.
293   Matthew J. Kinservik, 'The Censorship of Samuel Foote's *The Minor* (1760) ...', *Studies in the Literary Imagination*, vol. xxxii, issue 2, Georgia State University, 1999.
294   James Boswell (Ed. Birkbeck Hill), *The Life of Samuel Johnson*, Oxford at the Clarendon Press, 1887, vol. iii, pp. 69, 70.
295   [Samuel Foote], in *The London Quarterly Review*, issues 187–90, October 1854, pp. 251–285.
296   Charles Churchill, *The Times A Poem*, 1764.
297   Declan Kavanagh, *Effeminate Years: Literature, Politics and Aesthetics in Mid-Eighteenth-Century Britain*, Bucknell University Press, 2017, p. 196; and Rictor

Norton (Ed.), 'Sodom and Onan 1776', in *Homosexuality in Eighteenth-Century England – A Sourcebook,* online at rictornorton.co.uk

298 Rictor Norton (Ed.), 'Sodom and Onan 1776'.

299 Philip H. Highfill, Kalman A. Burnim and Edward A Langhans, *A Biographical Dictionary of Actors, Actresses, Musicians, Dancers, Managers & Other Stage Personnel in London, 1660–1800,* Southern Illinois, Carbondale, 1973, vol. viii, pp. 161–2. *Public Advertiser,* 26 June, 1764.

300 [Samuel Foote], in *The London Quarterly Review,* issues 187–90, October 1854, pp. 251–285.

301 The expression comes from a reader's letter to the *Public Ledger,* August 5 1772.

302 Dr. James Fordyce, *Addresses to Young Men,* 1777, pp. 349–51.

303 Letter Philip Dormer Stanhope, to his son, Philip Stanhope, April 19, 1749, in (Ed. Eugenia Stanhope), *Letters Written by the Earl of Chesterfield to His Son,* 1827, vol. ii, pp. 3–4.

304 *Morning Chronicle,* 19 January 1776.

305 Reginald W. M. Wright (long-serving Director of the Victoria Art Gallery, Bath, in the early 20th century), *Index of Bath Artists,* with biographical notes, an unpublished, undated MS, Victoria Art Gallery, Bath.

306 Charles Beecher Hogan (Ed.), 'Drury Lane 1776–7', *The London Stage, 1660–1800: a calendar of plays, entertainments & afterpieces …,* Southern Illinois University Press, 1960–1963, part 5, vol. i, pp. 8–10.

307 W. T. Parke, *Musical Memoirs comprising an Account of the General State of Music in England from the first commemoration of Handel in 1784 to 1830 …,* 1830, vol. i, pp. 8 and 204.

308 Highfill, et al, *A Biographical Dictionary of Actors,* vol. iii, p. 415.

309 Charles Beecher Hogan (Ed.), 'Drury Lane 1776–7', *The London Stage, 1660–1800: a calendar of plays, entertainments & afterpieces …,* Southern Illinois University Press, 1960–1963, part 5, vol. i, pp. 5 and 6.

310 William Hazlitt, *Lectures on the English Poets and the English Comic Writers,* London, 1876, p. 227.

311 Peter Holman, CD booklet., *Thomas Linley: Music for the Tempest …,* Hyperion Records CDA66767 (1996).

312 Irena Bozena Cholij, *Music in Eighteenth-Century London Shakespeare Productions,* doctoral thesis, King's College, London, 1995, pp. 85–88. See also William Linley, 'Shakespeare's Dramatic Songs', in *The Quarterly Musical Magazine and Review,* 1827, vol. ix, pp. 371–381, and 'Songs and Chorusses in *The Tempest,* as it is Performed at the Theatre Royal in Drury-lane, London', 1777 (copies in the Folger Shakespeare and Huntington Libraries, U.S.A.).

313 *Public Advertiser,* 6 January 1777; the *Morning Chronicle,* 6 January 1777; and Cholij, p. 88.

314 Cooke, *Thomas Linley, Junior,* MS, c. 1812, BL, Eg. 2492, ff. 2 and 126.

315 Roger Fiske, *English Theatre Music in the Eighteenth Century,* Oxford University Press, 1986, p. 420.

316 [Anon.], *Westminster Magazine,* January 1777, p. 43, and *Public Advertiser,* 7 January 1777.

317 [Anon.], 'Oratorios', *Westminster Magazine,* February 1777, p. 86.

318 Edward W. Pitcher, 'Edward Thomas (1738?–86): The Contributions of a Satirist to the *London Magazine* and the *Westminster Magazine*', in *The Papers of the Bibliographical Society of America,* vol. xcii, number 2, June 1998).

319 Lidia Aurora Chang, *Leisure with Decorum: Gentlemen Making Music in the Georgian Era,* doctoral thesis, City University of New York, 2021, p. 65.

320 Martha Gellhorn, 'Rudy Vallee: God's Gift to Us Girls', *The New Republic*, 5 August 1929.

321 David Hendy, *The BBC: A Century on Air*, New York, Public Affairs, 2022, quoting, on pp. 155–6, both *Radio Times* (5 February 1932), and the BBC Controller of Programmes, Cecil Graves.

322 Alison McCracken, *Real Men Don't Sing: Crooning in American Culture*, Durham, North Carolina, Duke University Press, 2015.

323 [Anon.], 'Oratorios', *Westminster Magazine*, March 1777.

324 *Morning Post*, 13 March 1777.

325 *Ibid.*, 16 March 1778.

326 Scott M. Langston, *Exodus Through the Centuries*, Hoboken, New Jersey, John Wiley and Sons, 2013.

327 Cooke, *Thomas Linley, Junior*, MS, c. 1812, BL, Eg. 2492, ff. 2 and 126.

328 John S. Sainsbury, 'Linley, (Thomas [Jr.])', *A Dictionary of Musicians from the Earliest Ages to the Present Time ...*, Sainsbury & Co., 1824.

329 Peter Overbeck (Ed.), *Thomas Linley, Jr, 'The Song of Moses'*, Madison, Wisconsin, A-R Editions, Inc., 2000.

330 *Public Advertiser*, 18 March 1777.

331 Sir John de Blaquiere, 18 Nov 1776, 'Harcourt Papers', vol. x, p. 206, cited in a footnote by Vicary Gibbs in his edition of *The Complete Peerage*, 1910, vol. i, p. 128.

332 Cooke, *Thomas Linley, Junior*, MS, c. 1812, BL, Eg. 2492, ff. 2 and 126; Gwilym Beechey (Ed.), 'Two Madrigals', *Musical Times Supplement*, September 1978; and Thomas Warren (Ed.), *A Twenty fifth Collection of Catches, Canons and Glees ...* Longman & Broderip, n.d.

333 Letter Richard Brinsley Sheridan to Thomas Linley senior, Spring 1777, in Thomas Moore, *Memoirs of the Life of the Right Honourable Richard Brinsley Sheridan*, 1825, vol. i, p. 197.

334 Philip H. Highfill, Kalman A. Burnim and Edward A Langhans, *A Biographical Dictionary of Actors, Actresses, Musicians, Dancers, Managers & Other Stage Personnel in London, 1660–1800*, Southern Illinois, Carbondale, 1973, vols. iii and iv, p. 436.

335 *Ibid.*, p. 86.

336 Wright, *Bath Artists*.

337 Williamson, *Humphry*, p. 85.

338 Chedzoy, *Sheridan's Nightingale*, p. 229.

339 Williamson, *Humphry*, p. 57.

340 *Ibid.*, p. 209.

341 Parke, *Musical Memoirs*, vol. i, p. 204.

342 John Steane, 'An operatical farce', *The Musical Times*, vol. cxxxiii, number 1787 (January 1992), p. 35.

343 *Town and Country Magazine*, January 1778, p. 100.

344 [Anon.,] 'The English Theatre', *Westminster Magazine*, February 1778, pp. 63–4.

345 *Ibid.*

346 Lidia Aurora Chang, *Leisure with Decorum: Gentlemen Making Music in the Georgian Era*, doctoral thesis, City University of New York, 2021, p. 68; and Daniel Defoe, 'On the Public Prosecution and Punishment of Sodomites', in *A Review of the State of the British Nation*, 27 November, 1707, quoted by Rictor Norton, 'Homosexuality in Eighteenth-Century England: A Sourcebook', online at rictornorton.co.uk/

347 *Morning Post*, 26 March 1777, quoted by Gwilym Beechey, 'Thomas Linley, Junior. 1756–1778', *The Musical Quarterly*, vol. liv, number 1, January 1968, p. 78.

348 *The Gazetteer and New Daily Advertiser*, 21 March 1778.

349 John A. Parkinson, 'Who was Agus?', *The Musical Times*, vol. cxiv, number 1565, July 1973.
350 'The English Theatre', *Westminster Magazine*, March 1778, p.120.
351 *Morning Post*, 2 May 1778; and R. D. Gribble, *Musicians within the Social Hierarchies of Eighteenth-Century England: The Case of Thomas Linley Junior*, doctoral thesis, University of Southampton, 2015, p. 196.
352 Fiske, *English Theatre Music*, p. 420.
353 Translation of a letter from Charles Burney to Gabriele Piozzi, 5 August 1777, in Alvaro Ribeiro, SJ (Ed.), *The Letters of Dr Charles Burney. Volume 1. 1751–1784*, Oxford, Clarendon Press, 1991, pp. 228–9.
354 Fiske, *English Theatre Music*, p. 420.
355 *Derby Mercury*, 10 June 1778.

CHAPTER X
356 J. P. Hudson, 'Cataloguing the Blenheim Archive', *Archives*, xiv (Autumn 1979), pp. 88–91.
357 Obituary, 'Stuart Johnson Reid', *The Times*, 30 August 1927.
358 Letter Horace Walpole to the Countess of Upper Ossory, 14 July 1779, *Horace Walpole's Correspondence*, Yale Edition online, 2011.
359 Letter Horace Walpole to Sir Horace Mann, 7 July 1779, in *Horace Walpole's Correspondence*, Yale Edition online, 2011.
360 Henry B. Wheatley (Ed.), *The Historical and the Posthumous Memoirs of Sir Nathaniel William Wraxall ...* 1884, vol. iv, p. 1790.

EPILOGUE
361 Footnote to a piece about Thomas Linley's sister, the singer Elizabeth Linley, Mrs Richard Sheridan, signed 'A.P.', *The Ladies' Monthly Museum, or Polite Repository of Amusement and Instruction ...* London, vol. iv, 1816, pp. 123–4.
362 From the second chorus of *The Song of Moses* (words John Hoadly, music Thomas Linley junior).
363 [Samuel Leigh], *The Harmonicon, A Journal of Music*, London, 1825, vol. iii, part 1, p. 221.
364 Cooke, *Thomas Linley, Junior*, MS, c. 1812, BL, Eg. 2492, ff. 2 and 126.
365 Maria Linley, 'On the Death of Mr Linley, Jun.', *Morning Chronicle*, 17 August 1778.
366 *Reminiscences of Michael Kelly ...*, London, 1826, vol. i, pp. 222–23.

Index

Grand Tour, 13, 45, 47, 49–51, 53, 56,
58–59, 73, 90, 135, 164
Grassi, Cecilia, 95
Great Queen Street, London, 146–47
Gribble, Dr Rebecca, 44, 104 fn,
106 fn, 181
Grimsthorpe Castle, 16–19, 23–25, 29,
154–55, 157, 161, 163–66, 171, 177.
Illustrations: Castle 10, Great
Water 15, both 16
Guarducci, Tommaso, 62

Handel, George Frideric, 34, 37, 42, 50, 53,
58, 79, 81, 87–88, 93, 95, 103–04, 113,
132, 142. Works: *Acis and Galatea* 42,
88, 96, 98, 104, 144, 151; *Alexander's
Feast* 53, 88, 104, 106, 140; *l'Allegro, il
Penseroso ed il Moderato* 81, 113, 142;
Esther 103; *Judas Maccabaeus* 80, 88,
93, 96, 104, 136; *Messiah* 79, 81, 88, 96,
102, 106, 108, 114, 144; *Music for the
Royal Fireworks* 133; *Samson*, 100,
104, 105
Hawes, Dr William, 19. Illustration, 20
Hazlitt, William, 123, 137
Hempson, William, 47–48, 51, 56, 67,
74, 75, 89
Hoadly, Dr John, 143
Holman, Peter, 52, 110, 114 fn, 144 fn, 181
homosexuality, 58–60, 131–35, 142, 171–72.
See also 'macaronis' and 'mollies'
hornpipe, 21, 40, 41
Hull, Thomas, *The Fairy Favour* 40
Humphry, Ozias, 29, 31 fn, 32, 33 fn, 35–6,
46, 147, 148. Portrait (Stuart) 35

Jackson, William, 'Jackson of Exeter', 34
Jackson, the Rev. William, 131, *Sodom &
Onan* 133–34
Jewell, William, 134–35
Johnson, Graham, 117 fn
Johnson, Samuel, 49, 117, 132
Jones, Lieutenant Robert, 132

Kelly, Michael, 178
Kenrick, William, 133
King Street Theatre, Bristol, 93, 95
King's Theatre, Haymarket, 39, 43, 110,
132, 152
Kingston, Elizabeth Pierrepont,
Duchess of, 131, 134

Laurence, French, 125–27
Leghorn, see Livorno
Lidl, Andreas, 153
Lindsey, Robert Bertie, Marquess of (later
4th Duke of Ancaster), 21, 24, 157,
168–69. Portrait (Cosway) 169
Linley, Elizabeth Anne (1754–92), (eldest
sister of Thomas junior, later Mrs
Richard Sheridan), 14 fn, 16; Thomas's
death, 22–23, 27; 29, 33, 35, 39; *The
Fairy Favour* 40–41; 42, 44–45, 79–82;
admirers 83–84; 'The Maid of Bath'
85–86; 91, 102; elopement 92–97;
duels 97–101; 102–03, 106–09;
marriage 110–11; 112–16, 120, 123,
145–47. Portraits: with brother
Thomas (Gainsborough) front
cover; with sister Mary
(Gainsborough)13; as Mrs Sheridan
(Gainsborough) 93
Linley, George ((1753–?), elder brother
of Thomas junior), 27
Linley, Maria (1763–84), 3rd sister of
Thomas junior, 12, 14–15, 22, 27, 93,
94, 114, 125, 131, 148, 155, 178. Portrait
(Humphry) 148
Linley, Mary (1729–1820), mother of
Thomas junior), 18, 23, 28, 32, 35, 39,
136, 177 fn. Portrait (Lonsdale) 33
Linley, Mary (1758–87), 2nd sister of
Thomas junior, later Mrs Richard
Tickell, 12, 14 fn, 27, 32, 41–42, 45, 100,
102–03, 110, 113, 125, 131. Portrait with
sister Elizabeth (Gainsborough) 13
Linley, Rev. Ozias (1765–1831), 5th brother
of Thomas junior, 78, 156